MW01026710

Popular Egyptian Cinema

Popular Egyptian Cinema

Gender, Class, and Nation

Viola Shafik

The American University in Cairo Press
Cairo • New York

First published in 2007 by
The American University in Cairo Press
113 Sharia Kasr el Aini, Cairo, Egypt
420 Fifth Avenue, New York, NY 10018
www.aucpress.com

Segments of different chapters have been published earlier under the titles mentioned below. They have been entirely updated and reedited for the purpose of this book:

"Variety or Unity: Minorities in Egyptian Cinema." In Orient 39 (4) (December 1998), 627–48 (republished as: "Pluralità o unità? Le minoranze del cinema egiziano." In Onde del desideria. *Il cinema egiziano dalle origini agli anni settanta*, eds. Silvia Bazzoli and Giuseppe Gariazzo, 19th Torino Film Filmfestival, 2001, Torino, 272–91).

"Der Zweck heiligt die Mittel: Stars, Genre und Publikum in Ägypten." In *Erlebnisort Kino*, ed. Irmbert Schenk (Marburg, 2000), 200–13.

"Prostitute for a Good Reason. Stars and Morality in Egyptian Cinema." In *Women's Studies International Forum* 24 (6): 711–25.

"El momento de crisis. Estudio del charisma cinematográfico de Nasser." In *Archivos de la Filmoteca* 46:151–71.

"Cinema without Horror." In *Fear without Frontiers*, ed. Steven Schneider, 273–89.

"Negotiations de classes dans le cinéma égyptien." Forthcoming. In *L'Égypte contemporaine*, ed. Vincent Battesti et al.

Dar el Kutub No. 15635/06
ISBN 978 977 416 053 0

1 2 3 4 5 6   12 11 10 09 08 07

Designed by Sally Boylan/AUC Press Design Center
Printed in Egypt

Contents

Acknowledgments

This research received funds from two sources: a Rockefeller Humanities fellowship granted by the Center for Media, Culture, and History at New York University for the part on minorities, and the Middle East Research Competition (MERC, housed until 2002 by the Lebanese Center for Policy Studies [LCPS]) for the part on gender. I would like to thank Faye Ginsburg and Barbara Abrash (Center for Media, Culture, and History) for their hospitality; the Wissenschaftskolleg zu Berlin for hosting me during the editing of this book; editors Lesley Tweddle and Nadia Naqib for their patience and thoroughness, from which this book has profited immensely; as well as all who were willing to share their time and knowledge with me through interviews, to name only Daoud 'Abd El-Sayed, Mustafa Darwish, Ahmad al-Hadari, Khairy Beshara, the late Miriam Donato (including her family and lawyer, as well as Erwin Northoff who helped me to meet her), Samir Saif, and Magid Taufiq; as well as my colleagues and friends, Ateyyat El Abnoudy, Magdi 'Abd al-Rahman, Nabil 'Abd al-Fattah, Lila Abu-Lughod, 'Ala' al-Hamarneh, Dina Craissati, Vivian Fouad, Hanna Grace, Karima Kamal, Garay Menicucci, and Marlyn Tadros for their friendly support, many discussions and the supply of materials. Also

I would like to thank Steven Schneider who inspired me to examine Egyptian horror films and Alberto Elena and the editors of Archivos de la Filmoteca for asking me to consider Nasser's cinematic representation. Thanks go also to Ella Shohat and Robert Stam, who I am very glad to have met so many years ago, enjoying their illuminating and inspiring ideas which are certainly reflected in this book. Last but not least, I am immensely grateful to my son Ani and my husband Onsi Abou Seif (whose own long experience in Egyptian cinema represented a constant source of inspiration and feedback) for their tremendous love, patience, and flexibility.

Note on transcription: In general, when names have already been canonized in a particular form of transcription, that transcription has been used. Also the Egyptian colloquial 'g' has been used instead of the classical Arabic 'j' for the fifth letter of the Arabic alphabet to facilitate their pronounciaton and avoid confusion.

Introduction

Why Popular Cinema?

The last two decades have witnessed a rising interest in issues of popular culture, and in particular popular film. Increasing numbers of publications have been eager to fill a gap that preceding studies have left unexamined. My own interest was certainly inspired by this general trend, yet it was likewise guided by the experiences of my earlier work as film curator in Europe where I encountered strong reservations (including my own) in the face of Egyptian mainstream productions (and the products of other, non-Western industries, such as Turkish, Indian, and early Hong Kongese) in contrast to a clear preference for art and festival films that emphasize the exotic, premodern, or simply 'other' aspects of non-Western culture. Some of the causes of this phenomenon I have discussed elsewhere as being partly rooted in European funding and distribution policies that helped to cement the fact that international 'art film' audiences and distribution circuits apprehend and prefer works financed by European channels and institutions and adhere moreover to a 'highbrow' concept of art (Shafik 2006). The current discovery by Western film aficionados of 'popular' non-Western forms, such as Chinese martial art and Bollywood films is a more recent trend and still has to be assessed.

One of the basic problems of Egyptian mainstream film that has prevented it from enjoying any considerable appreciation abroad was its
technical standard which had deteriorated markedly since the 1970s, and
improved only at the turn of the millennium (al-Naggar 2002, 319). Yet,
despite its often regrettable technical deficiencies, Egyptian cinema has
always remained popular in the region with sufficiently large numbers of
Egyptian and Arab audiences, much to the annoyance of local and international critics, who have often blamed it for its amateurishness, triviality, and
lack of authenticity. This discrepancy, however, was exactly what inspired
my interest. What is it that local audiences see and critics cannot appreciate?
What is it that 'speaks' to some in contrast to others?

Searching for an answer I found film scholar Bill Nichols offering a handy
explanation of why popular cinema as such could be worth investigating. Dis-
tinguishing between documentary and fiction, Nichols described the second as
"documentaries of wish-fulfillment" in contrast to "real" documentaries being
"documentaries of social representation." To him fiction films "give tangible
expression to our wishes and dreams, our nightmares and dreads. They give a
sense of what we wish, or fear, reality itself might be or become" (Nichols
2001, 1). No wonder popular cinema, contrary to the individualist and sophisticated art house film, is characterized by its strong appeal to the masses, due
to (among other elements) its recurrent dramatic patterns, ritualized performances and some almost archetypical, yet partly contradictory stereotypes.
Being the product of its producers' and consumers' inner reality, following at
times some of the most commonly performed strategies of distinction and
exclusion, it offers seemingly trivial, but also blatant and dismissive representations that seem constantly to oscillate between realist referentiality and
symbolical, metaphorical, and allegorical codings. So-called political correctness is therefore often only superficially applied and likely to be contradicted
from within a work. It is this capacity to produce cultural and sociopolitical
meaning that renders popular cinema a thrilling field of examination.

As I dug deeper into the theory of popular cinema two basic complementary theoretical approaches imposed themselves, represented by Laura

Mulvey's work on film and Stuart Hall's considerations on popular culture. Mulvey's examination of female spectatorship and genre still plays a pivotal role for feminist film studies despite the fact that some of it dates back to the mid-1970s and is strongly rooted in Freudian theory. Yet it has not lost its impact because it combines a critical feminist and historical analysis with a strong personal fascination for what seemed, at that time, utterly trivial and politically incorrect cinematic expressions.

In contrast, I started appreciating Stuart Hall's theories because of his pivotal contribution to perception theory, insisting on the active role the spectator plays in receiving mass-mediated messages ranging from refusal, through selection to acceptance (Hall 1980, 135). Hall's other achievement was to shed light on the problematic of the popular in culture and some of the misunderstandings linked to it. He identified several major limited trends of comprehending the popular in combination with his constant insistence on the notion of change as structuring analytical moments as well as on cultural diversity without bowing to the politics of difference (Hall 1981, 227–39). These trends are summarized in the idea of the popular that is based on Horkheimer and Adorno's critique of mass culture as being imposed, inescapable, and inauthentic, and, secondly much in contrast to the first, the idea of the popular as a sign of authenticity, representing a true culture of the people for the people, mostly equaled with folk culture.

The understanding of the popular that Hall proposed in response was poignantly sketched out by Joanne Hollows: "[P]opular culture should not be seen simply as either the means by which dominant groups impose their ideas on subordinate groups, or the way in which subordinate groups resist domination. Instead, Hall defines popular culture as a site of struggle, a place where conflicts between dominant and subordinate groups are played out, and distinctions between the cultures of these groups are continually constructed and reconstructed" (Hollows 2000, 27).

In re-reading Hall, Hollows has also underscored the shaky nature and meaning of 'the popular.' It "is simply part of the process by which texts are classified and, as a result, no text or practice is inherently popular or elite in character, but may well move between the two as historical conditions change" (Hollows 2000, 27). This perspective of struggle (or to put it in a less materialist formulation 'negotiation'), in combination with constant change and alteration, seemed to me worth taking as guidance in 'reading' some of the features and meanings produced and disseminated by Egyptian film.

With the ideas of negotiation and conflict in mind I decided to look first for certain pivotal and pressing social issues in approaching this cinema, not least because it has witnessed a number of radical historical changes on the national level: colonial domination, several wars, and involvement in one major, still-ongoing regional conflict. For the Egyptian film industry developed alongside and in correlation with the nation's endeavors to achieve independence, and was involved in crucial social, political, and economic changes and challenges to the position of 'minorities' and to gender relations.

Why Popular Egyptian Cinema?

Despite increasing competition in the Arab market and an evident diversification of products and services in the Arab media industry—Syria excelling in high-quality television serials and Lebanon in producing music clips and advertisments, and Dubai running an up-to-date, efficient, and unbureaucratic media city—Egypt still hosts the major entertainment industry in the Middle East. With its talk shows, quiz, variety, and television serials (*musalsalat*) Egypt feeds the numerous channels of other Arab broadcasting stations, in particular those of the Arabian Peninsula. Even more importantly, Egyptian movies with their popular film stars are, notwithstanding the temporary sharp drop in production in the mid-1990s, still screened and aired all over the Arab world. Designed for large audiences, they get much more widely circulated than the marginal and sporadic *cinéma d'auteur* or the 'art house movies' of the Maghreb and the Fertile Crescent, and have therefore not ceased to signify both mass appeal and lowbrow art affiliation for the regional elites.

In fact Egypt's predominance in the audiovisual field is based on a long tradition. It is rooted in a vivid theater life that flourished since the late nineteenth century as well as a music industry that was facilitated by the spread of the first musical recordings in the first half of the twentieth century. Confined by a poor domestic distribution network, which excluded the countryside almost entirely, the Egyptian film industry was forced since 1933 to market its products in neighboring countries, thus hampering other regional non-Egyptian efforts to start alternative large scale productions. In exchange, foreign distribution has left its mark, in a varied degree, on film form and content.

While Egypt's oldest film market, the Fertile Crescent, has remained more or less stable, exports to the Maghreb states, that is, North Africa are rather marginal, accounting for some 6–8 percent of Egypt's total film exports in 1991 compared to 60–70 percent for Saudi Arabia and the rest of the Gulf States (Thabet 2001, 51). The reason for this imbalance was due to the fact that with the outbreak of Lebanese civil war in 1975—until which Lebanese distributors had monopolized exports—and the introduction of the video to the Gulf States, Egypt's market had shifted Eastward while Kuwaiti foreign distributors in part took over the earlier role of the Lebanese. After the first Gulf War in 1990, satellite television opened up new (yet initially unlucrative) distribution venues for Egyptian cinema. These affected production quite negatively at the beginning, as the boom in the media industry drained out industrial film facilities as well as technicians. Along with the fact that major producers lacked long-term investment policies, this caused the most serious production drop in Egyptian film history (from a peak of seventy fiction films in 1992 to sixteen in 1997, the lowest output since the 1930s) from which industry started to recover gradually only in the late 1990s, due to its adoption of improved film technology among other things (al-Naggar 2002, 320).

Gender, Class, and Nation

In raising the above-mentioned questions, this book aims to be historically inclusive, its coverage ranging from the emergence of the Egyptian cinema in the 1920s until the present, although it is not meant to be comprehensive

in the quantitative sense, rather discussing works that proved to be of outstanding importance due to their box-office success or originality, or that are
still widely known and popular today, or, in exceptional cases, because they
show a typical approach to the themes raised.

Generally these themes have become the subject of a variety of intellectual and public discourses in and on Egypt, but are also central to numerous
postcolonial studies, that developed a major interest in understanding colonial and postcolonial culture(s) at the intersection of East and West. To repeat
Homi Bhabha's words "gender, race or class" (and religion we should add in
the case of the Middle East) are pivotal to any "articulation of cultural differences and identifications" (Bhabha 1990, 292). As a result it is the
following queries that will be pursued: the status of ethnic and religious
minorities (in particular Nubians, Coptic Christians, and Jews), the formation
of national identity from pre-colonial via postcolonial until neo-colonial
times as well as its crystallization on the global-local ('glocal') nexus, the
role of women in society, the development of feminism, concepts of masculinity and femininity, and last but not least, the wheel of social change that
has driven the reconstruction of social classes and their distinction.

Also, the special preconditions created by the fact that Islam is the dominant religion in the country and has to some extent informed its source of
legislation and national identification will be considered, even though it has to
be underlined very clearly that Islam is by no means a sufficient analytical
device or an exclusive or even dominant factor in any explanation of the
specific nature of contemporary Egyptian culture. Thus, recourses to local history and culture will be used instead to offer qualifications to the universal
methodologies adapted from social sciences, cultural studies, and film studies.

Ways of Reading

One of the problems I encountered during the phase of preparation was the
deficient state of research and publications in the field, despite the fact that
an immense number of publications exist, particularly in Arabic, on the history of Egyptian cinema and also on a variety of topics including some of

those dealt with in this book. In fact Egyptian films have been extensively reviewed and discussed by Arab critics and researchers in respect to the representation of women and other social, political, and religious questions, but with very limited results, because their approaches have been either strongly historiographic, descriptive, or solely concerned with the problem of social representation without looking at other factors that are involved in the production of meaning. Apart from a few more recent exceptions, the majority is preoccupied with judging films either morally or ideologically, comprehending the medium simply as producer of the 'image' of someone or something. Methodologically however, this approach often comes down to mere content analysis disregarding formal, structural, and more general theoretical aspects.

Yet it has to be admitted that not only in Egypt but elsewhere, national film historiography until the 1980s "would construct its chosen films as aesthetically great works (usually seen as made by great directors)" (Croft 2000, 2), or vice versa, as bad films by bad directors, but neglecting the surrounding factors that enabled films to be produced. Quite similarly, 'representation' oriented analysis as it still dominates Egyptian film writing was likewise common in Western film studies until the late 1970s, among authors of second wave feminism for instance (Hollows 2000, 21). Meanwhile Western (and increasingly international) film studies have set out to offer a much more complex understanding of the correlation between reality and representation, underlining the importance of an analysis that focuses on elements as different as production, audiences, discourses, textuality, national-cultural specificity, the role of the state and the global range of nation-state cinemas (Croft 2000, 2). This implies also perceiving the cinematic work rather as a complicated polysemic text, shaped by not only the quasi-industrial production framework and political processes but also by the often contradictory and competing fingerprints of producer, scriptwriter, director, film star, censor, film critic, and audience. The fluidity and negotiability of the medium's meaning moreover may be understood as a result of the gap between the process of "writing" and "reading," to borrow Roland

Barthes' terminology (Barthes 1974, 8), or in other words, it is the product of the dynamics that occur between the film authors' attempt to formulate a message and the active appropriation of the work by spectators.

My own analysis will certainly additionally engage in a textual subject-oriented reading of films. But it goes without saying that content analysis has to exceed the description of character traits, social affiliation, and the retelling of story lines. It must be combined with a contextual and inter-textual reading in order to situate the cinematic work in the larger context of film production, authorship, perception, interaction with other mass mediated messages and, last but not least, the whole sociopolitical framework. The analysis of star personae who also contribute to the writing of the popular cinematic text and the development and conventions of different genres helps for example to enrich the comprehension of any interaction between cinematic work and audiences and the messages circulated. An additional way to achieve this is to supplement the discussion of individual works with other sources, such as press reviews and more general social and political analyses that may offer indications regarding relevant public discourses and ideological negotiations and, moreover, to position the processes and structures that govern film production and distribution in relation to social hegemonies.

The book is divided into three parts, corresponding to the overall order 'nation, gender, and class.' However, since the three aspects are strongly interconnected they cannot be separated in a neat way, and there are frequent crossovers between the different parts. Roughly speaking the first part deals with the attempt to create gendered allegories of the nation, oscillating between a formerly colonized 'raped' female nation that has eventually come to find its male rescuer in the anticolonial national hero Gamal Abdel Nasser, which is preceded by the analysis of the parallel ongoing representation of the three most important Egyptian minorities, Nubians, Jews, and Copts. The on-screen production of meaning is examined historically along with real-life structural movements of either inclusion or exclusion in the film industry itself. The process of Othering through positive and negative

stereotyping is placed in relation to preceding relevant historical phenom-
ena, such as African slavery, the Palestine conflict, and Islamization.

This will lead directly into the second part, the section on gender, organized around two major subjects: 'femininity and feminism,' and 'female
stardom, myth-production, and morality,' crosscutting with generic characteristics and the star system on the one hand and with political and social
processes on the other. The development of off-screen morality, with a special focus on the 1990s, gets investigated in this part through the star system
in general and distinguished star personae in particular. On screen it will be
traced through different motifs, narratives, and structuring elements, most
importantly the virgin–whore dichotomy and gender-specific gazing. Christian as well as Muslim concepts of femininity are weighed out against
attempts to mainstream modernist feminist ideals, either explicitly through
misery feminism or on the structural level through the use of spatiality and
other specific generic vocabularies of action film, thriller, and melodrama, in
combination with certain schematized dramatic figures, such as the female
avenger. Cinematic negotiations of motherhood, the ideals of the bourgeois
family, and female labor are made visible through some of the most pivotal
works in this regard, herewith addressing the question of what role women
played on the representational level during nation formation in addition to
what kind of feminism was propelled and advocated in these works.

The third and last part reviews the impact of class on film, first on the
infrastructural level as regards audience organization, modes of reception,
and more importantly through the strategies of distinction played out by
socially privileged cultural critiques in response to 'cinematic triviality' and
'lower-class' taste. Strategies of distinction are also made visible in film narratives, in the constantly shifting alliances between different social groups
and seemingly distinct classes, but also where attempts of misrepresentation
and exclusion can be observed on the historical axis ever since the advent of
Egyptian cinema. They have reflected indirectly also on the public esteem
and popularity enjoyed by three pivotal film genres, melodrama, realism,
and action film, and their respective star personae, which have often been

pitted against each other on ideological grounds. Gender roles and strategies of distinction and exclusion regarding internal and external Others will furthermore be discussed, in conjunction with the most recent action films that suggest an increased global interaction and exchange on the technological level, along with the assertion of a specific impermeable monolithic male lower-middle class type of national identity.

In sum, the tracing of the above-described constant cultural and political reproduction of 'difference' can be detected as the real common denominator between all three parts of this book. It is a rather essentialist principle of difference—sexual, political, and social—that cuts through its pivotal themes. It is this difference that propels binarist dramatic conflicts, gendered spatial configurations, character traits, and moral dichotomies, and that also governs the process of Othering. True, if we believe Stuart Hall, identity formation itself seems to be based on "difference": it "is a structured representation which only achieves its positive through the narrow eye of the negative. It has to go through the eye of the needle of the other before it can construct itself" (Hall 1991, 21). Yet deconstructing the production of difference can in turn only be achieved through an analysis that follows "a theory of otherness which is not essentialist, a theory of positivity based on notions of . . . 'the changing same'" (Grossberg 1996, 97).

PART I

Nation

CHAPTER I

The Other

The most horrible grievances of the twentieth century, such as social unrest, ethnic cleansing, and forced migration have been commonly linked to the process of modern nation formation that was combined in the so-called Third World with the movement of colonization and decolonization, something that has doubtless left its traces on the art and culture of the affected peoples and made Homi Bhabha state that "The nation fills the void left in the uprooting of communities and kin, and turns that loss into the language of metaphor" (Bhabha 1990, 291). This certainly holds true for people under foreign occupation like the Palestinians, but is it also the case for a country like Egypt, based on an ancient and relatively stable territorial entity? Moreover as Eric Hobsbawm, who investigated the development of nationalism on the international arena since 1789, insisted, "Frictions between ethnic groups and conflicts, often bloody ones, between them, are older than the political programme of nationalism, and will survive it" (Hobsbawm 1992, 164).

Unlike what Anderson claims for quite a number of formerly colonized peoples, it cannot be established that it was colonial census-taking and mapping alone that engendered disparate 'identities' (cf. Anderson 1991, 164) in the Middle East in general and in Egypt in particular. Religious affiliation was a means by which the *millet* system of the Ottoman Empire—intact until 1914—differentiated juridically between Muslims and non-Muslim religious communities protected by the state. This resulted in communitarist identities within the borders of a multi-ethnic and multi-confessional empire. One of its features was a "high level of toleration, communal autonomy, and cultural symbiosis among Muslims, Christians, and Jews" (Beinin 1998, 36).

Yet colonialism and the spread of modern nationalism in the territories of the Ottoman Empire were accompanied by often futile or incomplete attempts to create secular non-religious citizenship on the one hand, while old forms of ethnic and religious schisms and differentiations resulted in hitherto unprecedented sorts of injustice and oppression on the other. Turkish and Iraqi Assyrians suffered displacement. Most of the Arab Jews left, willingly or by force, their countries of origin; many Christian and Muslim Palestinians still live in refugee camps or under occupation, suffering daily humiliation and deadly assaults. The Egyptian and Sudanese Nubians were forced to migrate while the waters of Lake Nasser drowned most of their original homeland.

As states and nationalities do not necessarily coincide (Hobsbawm 1992, 134), nationalism(s) exit in various interrelated or conflicting versions, economic, territorial, and linguistic. In the case of the Arab world it was particularly the language factor that had a strong interregional impact. Even though Arab nationalism at first developed two seemingly competing trends—one of them had a pan-Islamic orientation first expressed by Muslim scholars, while the second tended to be more secular, dissociating nationalism from religion—they were united in their reliance on the Arabic language and later reconciled by state practice. Thus, after an initial liberal phase and in spite of their seemingly secular orientation, the region's most dominant nationalisms, be they in Algeria, Egypt, Syria, or Iraq, chose primarily Islam as the state religion and the Arabic language and Arab culture as unifying factors at the expense of all other religions and languages, marginalizing minorities in the official and to a large extent in the unofficial media.

With independence, regimes like that of Egypt inherited colonial bureaucracy and its ethnic–religious spatial and racial categorizations (mappings), and developed structures close to what Anderson has described for nineteenth-century official nationalism in Europe. The latter's "policy levers" were "compulsory state-controlled primary education, state-organized propaganda, official re-writing of history, militarism . . . and endless affirmations of the identity of dynasty and nation" (Anderson 1991, 101). But immense differences in practice and theory remain between what people can identify with and what leaderships and spokesmen propose, for unlike what official or dominant unitary ideologies aim at, "collective identity is a set of interlocking elements in strife and tension, a set periodically scrambled, reorganized, blocked, and gridlocked by contingencies from within and without" (Connolly 2002, 204). In other words, the process of imagining one's own community was not as coherent and unequivocal as official or dominant rhetoric and discourses suggested, for it may be suspected that what Eric Hobsbawm stated for the colonial period became true also of present-day situations, namely that "pro-national identifications, ethnic, religious or otherwise, among the common people, they were, as yet, obstacles rather than contributions to national consciousness" (Hobsbawm 1992, 137).

This means that any metaphor of the nation will always find itself contested, first because it is the project of constant negotiation between those who are (or are not) admitted to it and second, because of the "Janus-faced discourse of the nation. This turns the familiar two-faced god into a figure of prodigious doubling that investigates the nation-space in the *process* of articulation of elements: where meanings may be partial because they are *in medias res*; and history may be half-made because it is in the process of being made" (Bhabha 1990, 3). This is also what inspired Homi Bhabha to go further and ask, "If the ambivalent figure of the nation is a problem of its transitional history, its conceptual indeterminacy, its wavering between vocabularies, then what effect does this have on narratives and discourses that signify a sense of 'nationness': the *heimlich* pleasures of the hearth, the *unheimlich* terror of the space or race of the Other; the comfort of social belonging, the hidden injuries of class; the customs of taste, the powers of political affiliation; the sense of social order, the sensibility of sexuality" (Bhabha 1990, 2). This question is indeed a thread that leads through this and following chapters.

(En-)Countering the Other

Black-British scholar Stuart Hall clarified that the notions of difference and the 'Other' are widely considered constitutive on the linguistic, social, cultural, and the psychic level, something that renders the term 'difference' highly ambivalent. "It can be both positive and negative. It is necessary for the production of meaning, the formation of language and culture, for social identities and a subjective sense of the self as a sexed subject—and at the same time, it is threatening, a site of danger, of negative feelings, of splitting, hostility and aggression toward the 'Other'" (Hall 1997, 238).

As difference is constitutive to meaning, the process of 'Othering' can hardly be contested, unless a conscious decoding, a 'contest from within' that does not avoid the stereotype but acknowledges that meaning can never be finally fixed, gets applied. Or to take up Jackie Stacey's interpretation of Roland Barthes' ideas, "It might be better, as Barthes suggests, neither to destroy difference, nor to valorize it, but to multiply and disperse differences, to move towards a world where differences would not be synonymous with exclusion" (Stacey 1992, 248).

Hall's view implies also that difference does not simply exist by nature but is also a cultural product. Therefore it is constantly regenerated and reflected in different media formats and is coded often in a very subtle way, even in its positive approach, as has been demonstrated by U.S. cinema. Even though the sympathetic well-cultured African-American cop for instance has conquered the screen, the reversing of stereotype for the sake of political correctness is not enough to recode his binary racialized representation (Hall 1997, 271). Drawing on Edward Said's groundbreaking study *Orientalism*, Hall has therefore occupied himself with unpacking stereotyping as representational practice particularly regarding race and sexuality. In analyzing the most recurrent mechanisms that govern the process of 'Othering' at work in the mass-mediated spectacles of the 'Other,' he has shown to what extent they are caught up in the social and political power structures. Essentialism, reductionism, naturalization, and the creation of binary oppositions are in his view the more conscious strategies of 'Othering,' while the more subtle, subconscious ones crystallize in fantasy, fetishism, and disavowal.

In Hall's eyes "[s]tereotyped" means "reduced to a few essentials, fixed in Nature by a few, simplified characteristics" (Hall 1997, 249). Those few outstanding traits are then declared part of the Other's unchanging natural essence. This may not only be achieved by overtly negative demonizing but also through glorification and/or fetishizing, as can be seen among others in the sexualized representation of black Africans starting with Leni Riefenstahl's Nubians and ending with modern sports photography, a strategy that appears to be positive only at first sight (Hall 1997, 264).

The problem with cinematic representation is its potentially naturalizing or '*real*-ization' effect, which helps viewers to mistake cinematic *discourses* on reality for real-life itself, and that works even better in the absence of alternative representations and balanced information. Local and concrete circumstances are likely to be obliterated. In this respect stereotypes may play an important role in shaping or confirming certain perceptions. Yet Robert Stam and Ella Shohat have warned against isolating stereotypes without looking at the overall cinematic context, for not every stereotype is damaging. Instead they have asked for a "comprehensive analysis of the institutions that generate and distribute mass-mediated texts as well as of the audience that receives them in order to understand the dynamics of stereotyping" (Shohat and Stam 1994, 184). Furthermore, it goes without saying that the Othering effect cannot be generalized, as it depends, as does the perception of realism, on the standpoint of the reader, his/her state of knowledge and experience regarding what is represented.

Toward a 'National' Film Industry

In Egypt the process of nationalist unification and purification has been reflected in film stories and film plots but also became evident in the changing composition of the country's early film industry. Post-independence film historiography in the years following independence underscored national achievements at the expense of cineastes who were later not considered native Egyptians. In fact, this was a more complex issue than it seems to be at first sight (and also torments some European nations today who have a large immigrant population). For what is it that defines nationality: blood, birth, language, or culture, or all of them?

In Egypt, where the population was not only composed of a majority of Arabic speaking Muslims and Copts, but also of other tiny Christian Arab communities, Middle Eastern Jews, Sephardim, Ashkenazim, non-Arabic speaking Muslim Nubians, Arab–Muslim Bedouin tribes, Turks and Circassians, Armenians, and a range of Levantine communities such as Greeks and Italians who were partially Egyptianized *(mutamassirun)*, the issue gained more importance in 1929 with the introduction of the nationality law and subsequent attempts to Egyptianize the economy. It seems that not all who were entitled to hold Egyptian nationality were indeed able to acquire it. It is reported that many members of the *mutamassirun*, but also of the poorer Arabized Jewish communities, were confronted with bureaucratic obstacles when applying for Egyptian nationality (Beinin 1998, 38). On the other hand, some 'native' minorities such as Syrian Christians and Jews had acquired earlier foreign nationalities profiting from the Capitulations, that is, the special legal rights for Europeans. This placed them under the protection of European powers who in turn considered them useful local helpmeets.

With national sentiments on the rise, the identification of the first really native 'Egyptian' films gained increasing importance for Egyptian post-independence film historiographers. Local critics, and accordingly many Western writers, mostly named *Layla/Layla*, which was produced and codirected by the actress 'Aziza Amir in 1927, as the first Egyptian full-length feature film. Ironically, *Layla* may not be regarded as a purely national production as well, for it was the Turkish director Wedad Orfi who persuaded 'Aziza Amir to produce the film. Later, after Orfi and Amir disagreed, Stéphane Rosti, an Italian-Austrian born in Egypt, was in charge of codirection. Subsequently he became a popular actor.

However, as Ahmad al-Hadari unearthed in 1989, the first full-length film produced in Egypt was *In Tut Ankh Amon's Country/Fi bilad Tut 'Ankh Amun* by Victor Rositto, shot in 1923. Its existence was at first obliterated, probably because of insufficient promotion and its focus on ancient Egypt, or because its director was not considered an ethnic Egyptian. The same applies to the full-length feature film *A Kiss in the Desert/Qubla fi-l-sahra'*, directed by the Chilean-Lebanese (or Palestinian) (cf. Bahgat 2005, 118) Ibrahim Lama, whose film appeared almost at the same time as *Layla*.

Ibrahim Lama and his brother Badr (their real names were Pietro and Abraham Lamas), who arrived in Alexandria in 1926, produced, directed, and acted in several full-length feature films. The Christian Lebanese actress Assia Daghir also settled in Egypt in 1922. Her first production *The Young Lady from the Desert/Ghadat al-sahra'* was screened in 1929 and starred herself and her niece Mary Queeny. Several other 'foreigners' were involved in directing too, most notably Togo Mizrahi, a Jew who was born in Egypt but carried Italian nationality, and the German Fritz Kramp.

This is not to say that so-called native Egyptians did not contribute to the creation of a local film industry. Actors and actresses including Yusuf Wahbi, 'Aziza Amir, Amin 'Atallah, and Fatima Rushdi soon discovered the media and joined in to shape it. They did not only act, but directed, produced, and even constructed studios as early as the late 1920s. Others, for example Muhammad Bayumi, who started shooting short films in the early 1920s and worked then as a professional director and cameraman (el-Kalioubi 1995, 44) and Muhammad Karim, who became one of the most distinguished directors during the 1930s and had started working in 1918 as an actor for an Italian production company, had no prior relation to the theater.

The majority of screen performers during this period were 'native' Egyptians from different religious backgrounds: Christians such as popular comedian Nagib al-Rihani, but also Bishara Wakim, who often embodied the character of a funny Lebanese and appeared first in 1923 in Bayumi's short fiction *Master Barsum is Looking for a Job/al-Mu'allim Barsum yabhath 'an wazifa* and Mary Munib, who started her career in cinema during the late 1920s and became a very popular comedian. The most famous Jewish artist was Layla Murad, who remained one of the most acclaimed singers of Egyptian cinema. She made her first appearance in 1938 in Muhammad Karim's *Long Live Love/Yahya al-hubb*, converted to Islam in 1946, and remained in Egypt until her death in 1995. Others who became involved from the 1940s onward—to name just a few—were the Jewish actresses Raqya Ibrahim, Camelia, and most importantly Nigma Ibrahim, who often embodied a gangster woman (*Raya and Sakina/Raya wa Sakina*, 1953), Greek actor Jorgos (Georges) Jordanidis, and Greek dancer Kitty.

Greek businessmen played a decisive role too. Two Greeks, Evangelos Avramusis and Paris Plenes,[1] founded in 1944 the Studio al-Ahram that presented ten films until 1948 (Khiryanudi 2003, 10). Several Egyptian directors, most notably Togo Mizrahi, directed films meant to be distributed exclusively in Greece or made two versions, in Arabic and Greek, of one and the same film. During the 1950s and until the nationalization of the Egyptian film industry in 1963, 80 percent of all movie theaters were Greek-owned, something that changed of course with the subsequent disintegration of the Greek community (Khiryanudi 2003, 11). Kitty, who starred in, among others, *Isma'il Yasin's Ghost/'Afritat Isma'il Yasin* (1954) is said to have left Egypt in the 1960s (Khiryanudi 2003, 13).

Although early Egyptian cineastes came from such diverse ethnic and religious backgrounds, they were unified, first, by the cosmopolitan and francophone elitist culture of the two Egyptian metropolises Alexandria and Cairo and, second, by the needs and rules of the local market, or in other words, by the preferences of the Egyptian audience. Thus, the subjects of Egyptian cinema were not as international or alienated as the origins of their producers may suggest. The love stories, for example, that were presented at that time were not always set in the surroundings of the Europeanized elite but also included local lower-class characters or were projected back into a glorious Arab Muslim past. The majority of comedies starring popular comedians, such as Nagib al-Rihani and 'Ali al-Kassar, had a strong popular orientation. In particular during the 1930s, these comedians presented rather stereotypical roles that they had previously played in theater, such as Nagib al-Rihani's Kish Kish Bek and Kassar's Nubian 'Uthman

'Abd al-Basit. Similar to the lesser known Jew, Shalom, these characters represented poor natives living in traditional surroundings who often landed in trouble, mainly because of their bad economic situation.

It is unclear to what extent Studio Misr was founded (in 1934) with the intention of creating a genuine national film industry and if it was meant to contribute to the Egyptianization of the economy, for it also employed a number of foreign professionals and specialists. At all events, it was subsequently considered to be a profoundly national enterprise because it was financed by Misr Bank, an institution which, in turn, was initiated by a group of Egyptian businessmen under the direction of Tal'at Harb, while Jewish Yusuf 'Aslan Qattawi became vice-president of the board (Beinin 1998, 45). Harb was subsequently sculptured into the direct ancestor of Nasserist etatism, with his statue decorating one of the most central squares in downtown Cairo today.

According to Robert Vitalis it would seem that Harb's 'patriotic intentions' were later over-interpreted, as the prevalent post-1952 discourse attributed the lack of proper capitalist development in Egypt to feudal structure and foreign imperialism, disregarding other factors (Vitalis 1995, 230). "Perhaps the most remarkable and therefore enduring myth of the Revolution is that in 1956 foreigners rather than Egyptians controlled the country's economy, or that after the 'Suez invasion' the regime reversed its policies toward foreign capital generally. The reality is that in sector after sector of the economy, power had shifted steadily in past decades from shareholders in Paris, Brussels and London to owners and managers in Cairo and Alexandria—that is to local capital" (Vitalis 1995, 216).[2] This 'myth' certainly got prolonged and remains in circulation until today. One author even claims that the Egyptian economy between the two world wars was not monopolized just by foreigners, but first and foremost by Jews (!) (Bahgat 2005, 12).

In contrast, in his economic study Vitalis argues that minority investors or 'foreigners' did not necessarily have a 'separatist' agenda but acted as national capitalists (Vitalis 1995, 9) in addition to the fact that they had been already marginalized in that period: "the 1919 generation of Egyptian investors such as 'Abbud, Yahya, 'Afifi, Farghali, Andraos, the Abu Faths . . .

came to displace the positions once occupied by minority resident owners and managers" (Vitalis 1995, 216). In general, the tendency to do without 'foreigners' and to reduce European intervention began to rise from the 1920s. In 1937 the Egyptian government abolished the Capitulations, that is, the special legal rights for Europeans. In 1942–43 Arabic was declared obligatory for the written communications of companies. One year later, a law was promulgated determining the ratio of employed Egyptians as 75 percent of all employees and 90 percent of all workers, and the share of Egyptian capital as 51 percent of all capital (Krämer 1982, 402). Moreover the 1956 Suez war was followed by the sequestration of French-, British-, and Jewish-owned firms, together with a departure from the government's earlier propensity for encouraging the private sector.

This did leave its traces on the film industry too. Togo Mizrahi, who was born into an affluent Jewish family in Alexandria and carried Italian nationality, shot his first film *Cocaine/Kokayin* in 1930 under a Muslim name (Ahmad al-Mashriqi) and eventually became one of the most productive Egyptian directors and film producers of his time. Between 1939 and 1944 his company was second as regards rate of production, with an output of sixteen films, two less than Studio Misr (al-Sharqawi 1979, 73). In 1929 he founded a provisory studio in Alexandria for shooting his first film and later ran another one in Cairo. By 1945 he had completed almost forty films, primarily popular comedies and musicals. He created, among others, a farce film cycle with one of the most successful comedians, 'Ali al-Kassar, in the role of the *barbari* or Nubian 'Uthman. He also directed musicals starring Umm Kulthum, as well as singer Layla Murad, thus contributing decisively to the development of the Egyptian musical. In 1952, the year of the coup, he left Egypt to settle in Rome until his death in 1986. The reasons for his retreat remained unfathomable, as he was only in his forties when he stopped directing in 1946, and any explanations for this—including my own—seem highly contradictory.

Egyptian film critic Ahmad Ra'fat Bahgat—who stated in the introduction to his book that "Egypt turned between 1917 and 1948 into one of the most dangerous centers of Zionism" (Bahgat 2005, 3)—claims first of all that Mizrahi was a very clever businessman who was not willing to lose any money in the immediate postwar period, citing a statement by Mizrahi himself. This seems a strange argument indeed for a time in which production rates in Egypt were booming in an unprecedented way. Second, and more speculative is Bahgat's argument that after the proclamation of the state of Israel Mizrahi had fulfilled his Zionist task in Egypt, namely assisting the production and distribution of Zionist propaganda films in the country. The same applies to the evidence that Bahgat offers from the contemporary press as a sign of Mizrahi's transition to obscurity, namely news of prolonged journeys to Europe and several hospitalizations, one of them presumably in a psychiatric clinic, which he considers were supposed to hide the director's clandestine activities (Bahgat 2005, 60). This version again was contested by Mizrahi's nephew, who denied any hospitalization at that time.[3]

I am not in a position to verify Mizrahi's suspected Zionist activities, but when he left for Italy he is said to have dedicated himself to his hobbies, spending his time traveling around Europe, painting, and building a house for himself in the countryside, an astonishing change for a formerly highly active and successful man. On the other hand economic reasons are somewhat more convincing, because as an entrepreneur and a royalist Mizrahi certainly had good reasons not to feel comfortable any more after 1948–49, given the occasional sequestration of Jewish property during that period, and even more after the deposition of the king in 1952. And indeed his company and private property were nationalized under Nasser, and his brothers and sisters also left to settle in Paris. Allegations of his being ill-treated or pressured by authorities cannot be verified though. This has been confirmed by his wife who claimed that he left for personal reasons only and stopped directing because he "had so many other interests."[4]

The Jewish Exodus

If we agree that referentiality on screen is often metaphoric, a direct reflexive connection can only in rare circumstances be established between the cinematic representation of social reality and that reality itself. This would apply even more to what the screen presents regarding minorities or marginalized groups. Negative or positive depictions cannot necessarily be regarded as an indicator of the degree of integration or equality that the group in question enjoys, and also they do not mean that audiences engage unequivocally with these representations and embrace them unquestioningly. Yet films may contribute to either the assertion or the questioning of certain discourses and political messages, depending on the production and distribution context, ideological positioning of producers and spectators, and film form.

It must be emphasized that in particular the early schematized characterizations of local and indigenous minorities and social groups, such as peasants, Jews, Copts, and Nubians were undertaken according to genre rules, particularly film farce, which shared some of its roots with popular theater, and were used to present ethnic, religious, and linguistic differences for the sake of comic catharsis. In the case of the Europeans, for example, these traditions partly disguised this group's powerful and exceptional position. Thus the objects of laughter were likely to be non-Muslims and non-Arabs (and to a certain extent Egyptians of rural background), but the incidence of these foreigners or minority characters was not a realistic reflection of the status of these groups in Egyptian society. Their function in comedy was to introduce a deviant accent or behavior, which clearly sets them apart from native Egyptians but without resort to any demagogic or xenophobic undertones. In other more earnest genres, such as film melodrama, they provided the relief comic element. The clumsy European *khawaga*, the good-hearted black Nubian servant, or the stupid peasant *(fallah)*, all served the same end in entertainment.

The use of minorities or strangers as an element in comedy is based on a long popular tradition. In Egyptian shadow plays, which have been reported since the fourteenth century, the Copt and the Moroccan were standard figures of fun (cf. Shafik 1998, 69). In Egyptian cinema, however, the depiction and roles of some of the country's most pivotal minorities, such as Jews, Copts, and Nubians changed from this traditional mode of representation to become more politicized and rhetorical over the years. The representation of each of them has taken a different course—and this is my main hypothesis—on the one hand according to genre rules and on the other depending on their position within the evolving national narrative, which draws in turn from different factors, such as skin color, language, religious affiliation, territorial unity, and national loyalty.

Thus, some of the exclusions that took place in reality have been simultaneously rehearsed in the media, that is, in fiction local Jews were first stigmatized as foreigners and then transformed into spies or members of the enemy Israeli army, thus keeping pace with or even exaggerating realities on the ground and disregarding a centuries-old history of coexistence. In fact Egyptian movies (and official discourse) showed great difficulty in comprehending or accommodating the complex and multiple identities of the country's absented Jewish population so meticulously described by Joel Beinin in his book (1998). Half a century ago, at the Lavon Affair or Operation Susannah trial in 1954, the Egyptian prosecutor stated: "Egypt makes no difference between its sons whether Muslims, Christians, or Jews. These defendants happen to be Jews who reside in Egypt, but we are trying them because they committed crimes against Egypt, although they are Egypt's sons" (Beinin 1998, 32). Several young Egyptian Jews, ten men and one woman, were accused of acts of sabotage—or 'terrorism' to use the contemporary term—because they had placed explosives in a movie theater in Alexandria and were evidently planning further acts.

Despite the appeasing statement of the Egyptian prosecutor, Beinin suggests that the actions of this group were responsible for connecting the fate of Egypt's Jews one step further to the Arab–Israeli conflict (Beinin 1998, 20), even though opinions are divided as to whether that conflict had a direct effect on the disintegration of Egyptian-Jewish communities. True, by 1967 only 7,000 Jews (Beinin 1998, 88) remained in Egypt, 10 percent of the seventy-five to eighty thousand resident in 1948 (Beinin 1998, 2). However, contrary to the preferred Zionist narrative, Beinin insists that Egypt's Jewry was not sitting on its suitcases waiting for an opportunity to head for Israel because they were suffering under Muslim rule (Beinin 1998, 72, 15).

Beinin nonetheless admits that the change in the status of Egyptian Jews began with the revolution in 1919 despite the postrevolutionary government's attempt to lay the foundation of a liberal concept of citizenship and equality, a principle that remains highly contested until today. Social critic Samir Murqus divides the congested development of modern citizenship in Egypt into five phases: its emergence with Muhammad 'Ali in the nineteenth century, its crystallization with the 1919 revolution, its premature phase with and after 1952, its absence during the 1970s under Sadat, and the current attempt to regain it (Murqus 2004, 118). The evident difficulties in instilling equality in civic rights and responsibilities during those periods in Egypt is certainly due to the persistence of what Beinin calls a neo-*dhimma* concept crystallized in the discourses shared by Egyptian authorities and minority communities. It is reflected in the fact that despite the introduction of the nationality law in 1929 and the presence of minority representatives in parliament, government, and political parties between 1919 and 1957, Egypt still is a self-declared Muslim state; the *shari'a* (Muslim religious law) has remained vital for its legislation; and the religious affiliation of every citizen is inscribed on his or her identity card.

The *dhimma* concept in its origins is a legal system developed in the Muslim world in the aftermath of early Muslim conquests for the protection of *ahl al-kitab* ('the people of the book'), that is, Christians and Jews who, unlike pagans, are considered by Muslims to belong to heavenly religions. It was further elaborated by the Ottoman *millet* system, which granted religious minorities sovereignty in their personal affairs but also in other communal matters. In Egypt the *millet* system was abolished in 1914 with the breakdown of the Ottoman Empire, but *millet* jurisdiction was abandoned only forty-one years later, in 1955 (Grace 2003, 87). The old multi-community state that characterized so-called traditional Islamic society has consequently never been completely replaced, as evidenced by the fact that the restructured Egyptian state underlined its Muslim identity after 1952 and later during the reign of Sadat even insisted on a legal system based upon the *shari'a*. This contradicted very overtly the fact that the

former *dhimma*-people had been granted equal rights by the national constitution, and forced the largest minority, the Copts, for instance, to retreat
to the confines of their church, which started to assume the role of a political representative particularly after Sadat's temporary backing of the
Islamists in the 1970s (Grace 2003, 90). Similarly, in the case of the Jewish community, Beinin has pointed out that the persistence of the
neo-*dhimma* concept resulted in the political leadership addressing Jews as
a community and not as individual citizens, particularly after the coup in
1952 (Beinin 1998, 73).

This paradox is reflected also on the structural level, as we saw earlier.
Before 1952 the cinematic representation of Jews in Egyptian cinema was
either indifferent or more or less governed by positive stereotypes. Only a
few Jewish characters appeared, and mainly in the role of 'foreign' affluent
store owners. In *The Lady's Game/Lu'bat al-sitt* (1946) by Wali al-Din
Samih, for instance, a rich merchant called Isaac 'Ambar was introduced as
the hero's employer. His character is not caricatured, but depicted in a realist manner, as a positive model, who is willing, despite an over-crowded
labor market, to offer desperate Hassan (Nagib al-Rihani) a job without any
references, and later to entrust him with his whole business. Hassan, in one
of the few farce scenes of the film, proves to be a smart native lower-class
fellow who is more capable of dealing with the Egyptian environment than
his 'Westernized' Jewish employer. When a deaf customer enters the store
and tries to explain by gesticulation what he needs, Nagib al-Rihani manages to give—of course—a funny but accurate translation of these signs to
his helpless boss.

The portrayal of the Jew as a store owner does not lack referentiality
due to the fact that the biggest Egyptian department stores, such as
Chemla and Cicurel, were at that time run by influential Jewish families.
Yet Jews were not necessarily doomed to be categorized as foreigners or
as opposed to the national interest; on the contrary, as Beinin writes, in the
years 1921–22 the Wafd party when calling for a boycott of foreign busi-
nesses had classified the fashionable Cicurel department store as a national

enterprise, and still in 1948 it was described as "one of the pillars of our [Egyptian national] economic independence" (though that did not prevent supporters of the Muslim Brotherhood from firebombing it in the same year because of the Palestine War) (Beinin 1998, 21).

In reality, Egypt's Jewish population was socioculturally very heterogeneous. Half of it could be considered autochthonous (Beinin 1998, 38) being composed of various communities, including Sephardim (Spanish Jews who had arrived in Egypt in as early as 1165), Ashkenazim (Eastern European Jews), and most importantly Karaites *(al-qara'in)*, a special religious community distinguished from Rabbanite Jews and whose presence in Egypt dates back to the eleventh century, if not earlier. In general, Sephardim were the most prominent elements of the Jewish social and business elite (Beinin 1998, 4). Many were able to acquire European nationalities from the nineteenth century, at a time when the Capitulations reserved extra rights for European citizens. As a result, in the early twentieth century many Jews were multilingual and (particularly in Alexandria) even underprivileged Jews tended to be quite cosmopolitan, but nonetheless with a strong Egyptian rooting, if we believe late Jacques Hassoun, a radical Marxist[5] who was expelled from Egypt in 1954 because of his political convictions (Beinin 1998, 269).

Hassoun poignantly described his community's diversity by comparing Egyptian Jewry to the metaphorical exclamations of 'Abdallah al-Yahudi, the beggar of Tatwig Street in Alexandria: "See my galabia, I am Egyptian! See my jacket, I am European!" (Hassoun 1987, 169). According to him, the community was divided between "the world of the Jewish *khawagat*, oriented to Paris and London and crowned by the glittering circles of Jewish beys, pashas, and barons—and the world of the galabia and kaftan, of ful, *mulukhiya*, and *qulqas* . . ."[6] (Hassoun 1987, 172). This division was also expressed linguistically: lower-class Jews used to speak the Egyptian vernacular, whereas the upper and middle class adopted European languages, primarily French, and were thus much easier to classify as foreign *khawagat* (Laskier 1992, 6).

It is precisely the first group to whom some of Togo Mizrahi's early films have been dedicated. In five of his productions, all shot in Alexandria between 1933 and 1937, he presented a farce cycle with Jewish actor Shalom, who always carried his proper name in these films, playing a poor, naive, but nonetheless lucky native. It is not clear how popular the comedian Shalom was—certainly not as successful as Nagib al-Rihani or 'Ali al-Kassar. He was neglected by all current film critics until very recently and has even remained unknown to the *al-Ahram* archive that has kept files on all popular Egyptian personalities. He disappeared abruptly from the screen in 1937, probably because his Jewish name was no longer good for promotion.

In Shalom's two films, which are available today on video, *Mistreated by Affluence/al-'Izz bahdala* (1937) and *Shalom, the Sportsman/Shalum al-riyadi* (1937) both directed by Mizrahi, he represents a naive but lucky *ibn al-balad* (literally 'son of the country'). In general *awlad al-balad* "are highly knowledgeable about everyday life" (van Nieuwkerk 1995, 111); they are seen as hospitable, generous, helpful, and responsible as well as noble and audacious, something that to a large extent applies to Shalom's persona. His affiliation is expressed in his clothes—*gallabiya* and jacket—and in his loyal and generous behavior, but also in his profession: in *Shalom, the Sportsman* he sells the indispensable Egyptian national dish, *ful*, and is, moreover, a fanatical supporter of the Alexandria soccer team.

Shalom's Egyptian identity is made even more obvious in *Mistreated by Affluence*, whose narrative has a stronger coherence and places its Jewish protagonist right in the heart of Egyptian lower-class culture. Shalom and his Muslim roommate 'Abdu live in a poor neighborhood, in a tiny room on top of a building. They are engaged to the girls of two neighboring families, one of them Jewish, the other Muslim. First 'Abdu takes over a butcher's shop, sharing his luck with his friend, while by chance, Shalom makes a big fortune, which allows him and his friend, together with their relatives, to move into a huge villa. Being rich, however, is not easy, so that the two families prefer at the end of the film to go back to their original surroundings, with their poor but friendly people and fine traditional food.

Shalom and 'Abdu Yusuf in *Mistreated by Affluence*, 1937

In his analysis of the film Bahgat considered it clearly biased toward the Jewish element, with Esther's family, Shalom's in-laws, behaving more modestly, and refraining from cursing, in contrast to their Muslim counterparts. The Jewish hero, Shalom, is portrayed as honest and civilized, even exposing the misbehavior of others, such as 'Abdu's self-contradiction in complaining repeatedly when his boss, the butcher, beats him, only to beat his assistants later when he becomes boss (Bahgat 2005, 193). "Mizrahi's view of the Jews in Egypt through Shalom's character is that of an Ashkenazi Jew of Western origin towards oriental Sephardim Jews who had settled in Egypt since centuries and responded to its way of life. Thus, his message was to dismiss this kind of response and to emphasis its futility in view of the faults that have eaten their way into their Muslim neighbors' behavior and in view of Zionist conviction that these poor Jews constitute the stratum that is needed for the construction of the promised land" (Bahgat 2005, 199).

Mizrahi was certainly not of Ashkenazi origin, contrary to Bahgat's evidently uninformed claim. He was a Sephardic Jew who had probably acquired Italian citizenship through his wife, if not earlier, and whose family enjoyed a considerable fortune and cosmopolitanism. Looking at his

Shalom-cycle in the context of overall Egyptian productions, it is evident that some of his Muslim characters' negative sides are linked to the specific farce canon, just as Shalom's sympathetic image mirrors another popular minority farce persona that Mizrahi brought to the screen in the same years: the Nubian 'Uthman. Referentiality cannot be completely excluded even in farce, but it has to be qualified due to the genre's strongly schematized canon and its preference for the carnivalesque and socially liminal. In addition to that, these 'lower-class' personae were most probably designed for, or at least took into account, the tastes of visitors of local third-class movie theaters dubbed the *terzo (tirsu)*.

Apart from the need to qualify the accusation of specific bias or arrogance in those films toward lower-class Egyptians, be they Jews or Muslims, it is certainly telling to see how Mizrahi places the Jewish community within Egyptian society, as that placement was certainly informed by the national unity concept: in a highly symbolic scene, all the protagonists are invited by a Christian neighbor to go to the seaside and have a picnic with smoked and salted fish—a strongly local tradition celebrating the spring festival of *Shamm al-Nisim*. Everybody joins them, including Shalom's and his roommate's future in-laws. Throughout the whole film they remain attached to each other as one big family. In particular their first common meal thus conveys an expressive image of coexistence—disturbed only by Shalom's mother-in-law nagging and quarrelling with him as usual.

Idyllic scenes of this sort still occur, from time to time, in Egyptian cinema. They usually include Copts and Muslims, whereas the Jews have been banned from the common table. Contrary to expectation, it seems that the conjuring up of the idyll of everybody sitting at the same table—as recent developments in the cinematic depictions of Copts also show—indicate early signs of unrest that seem to require the reassuring image of peaceful coexistence. This becomes clear when interpreting the Shalom-cycle against the backdrop of the slightly changing political status of the Jewish community in Egypt during the late 1930s, expressed in a few, still minor, hostilities that foreboded the first confessional fissures in the country's social fabric.

In 1938, one year after the release of Shalom's two films, the first anti-Zionist demonstrations took place. They were partly connected to anti-Jewish sentiment aroused by the Muslim Brothers and the fascist-oriented Young Egypt *(Misr al-Fatat)*, but were also the direct result of the deteriorating situation in Palestine that erupted in armed confrontations between Palestinians and Zionist settlers. At the end of the Second World War, in 1945, anti-British demonstrations brought about attacks on Jewish stores, assaults on the Jewish quarter (Harat al-Yahud), and the burning of the Ashkenazi synagogue at al-Muski (Laskier 1992, 186). In 1948, and particularly after the declaration of the state of Israel in 1949, the situation of the Jewish community became even more precarious, not only because of the Palestine conflict but also because of Zionist and Israeli interference.

In that year bombs exploded, first in the Karaite quarter. On July 15, 1948, during *iftar* (the evening meal that breaks the fast in Ramadan) Israeli planes bombed a civilian neighborhood in Cairo leaving numerous casualties. On July 19, explosives were placed in the Cicurel department store in retaliation (Beinin 1998, 68). Some Jewish firms whose proprietors were suspected of being Zionists were temporarily sequestered (Krämer 1982, 133). Moreover, a few Jews with foreign nationalities were expelled (Krämer 1982, 127). At the same time, Zionist organizations intensified their activities in Egypt, not only trying to mobilize supporters among the local Jewish youth, but also organizing clandestine emigration to Palestine. The Mossad and the Hagana sent emissaries from Palestine to Egypt (Krämer 1982, 98) and organized paramilitary courses. Weapons were smuggled from Egypt to Jewish settlers in Palestine. Jewish organizations started recruiting spies in Egypt from as early as 1940 (Krämer 1982, 102).

As a result of this tense situation, in only one year, between 1949 and 1950 around twelve to thirteen thousand Jews left the country, many of them emigrating to Israel (Beinin 1998, 70). During that period the most profound changes in the cinematic depiction of Jews became visible. At first they turned into rather unpleasant, mostly greedy and cunning foreigners and then, in a second stage, after the Camp David Agreement in 1977 and the formal recognition of the State of Israel, mutated into external enemies, represented either by the Israeli soldier or the mean and false Israeli spy, who is able to speak Arabic fluently because he was born or raised decades ago in Egypt. Hilmi Rafla's film *Fatima, Marika, and Rachèle/Fatima, Marika wa Rashil* (1949), the earliest in this group, dealt with a young Muslim who dates girls after promising them marriage without ever fulfilling his promise. This charming swindler is soon outwitted by the Jewish dancer Rachèle, who is no less a professional than he is at cheating. Backed and advised by her parents she tries to get the maximum of money and gifts out of her supposedly rich admirer. Clearly, the juxtaposition of Jews with greed and money shows similarities to the concepts of Western anti-Semitism that had been disseminated in Egypt by Nazi organizations before the Second World War (Krämer 1982, 128).

Tensions between Egypt and Israel, but also continued Zionist activities in Egypt, contributed to the weakening of the Jewish community's position in Egypt. In 1954, the Cairo trial of the Jewish network responsible for Operation Susannah added, as mentioned earlier, to further antagonization. In the same year the film *Hassan, Murqus, and Cohen/Hassan, Murqus wa Kuhin* by Fu'ad al-Gazayirli appeared, based on an earlier play by Nagib al-Rihani, portraying a rather unpleasant Jewish character, the greedy and cunning Cohen, owner of a big pharmacy. He is supported by his two no less dubious partners, the Upper Egyptian Coptic bookkeeper Murqus—another stereotype—identified by his accent, and the Muslim Hassan. Together they exploit their kind-hearted Muslim employee 'Abbas.

It is suggested that this greedy triad was intended to represent an allegorical affirmation of national unity (cf. Qasim 1997, 244) or to underline the universality of greed, yet what matters in our context is that its positive hero and victim is a kind-hearted Muslim. Moreover, contrary to his two associates, Cohen is explicitly addressed as *khawaga*, although he wears a jacket and *gallabiya* (like the earlier Shalom) and is later depicted in his private, rather shabby surroundings in a traditional alley, most probably referring to the Jewish quarter in Old Cairo. This may have been meant to

Stéphane Rosti (second left) and 'Abd al-Fattah al-Qussari (right) in *Hassan, Murqus, and Cohen*, 1954

underline his greediness, but more likely it indicates the subconscious difficulties of the film's text in coming to terms with its Jewish character's complex identity.

By linking Cohen to Harat al-Yahud but still insisting on his foreigner status, the film combines two in fact largely contradictory states. As we mentioned earlier, the poor, often uneducated, traditional Jewry, represented in old local Arabic-speaking communities such as the Karaites, could not be equated with the affluent and powerful Levantine Sephardim and other more recently immigrated, originally Yiddish-speaking Eastern Europeans. Thus Cohen's cinematic status seems to reflect a growing public readiness to consider Jews as not only non-Muslim but also non-Arab. And it is of course the latter that has the more crucial implications for detaching them from the newly configured Egyptian nation.

In terms of representation, the year immediately folllowing independence may be considered a time of transition. The military coup in 1952 did not result in any drastic changes or draconic measures against Jews. The situation worsened, however, in 1956 because of the Suez Crisis and the subsequent Sinai War. A few hundred detentions, expulsions, and sequestrations led to further Jewish unemployment. Some Jews are said to have been dismissed from work and denied work permits and licenses. Hence, poor Jews in particular were forced to leave to Israel in this first wave of immigration. The Red Cross evacuated six thousand individuals in an operation initiated and funded by the United Jewish Appeal (Krämer 1982, 255–57). Later and in a longer perspective the more affluent followed, but seeking—most tellingly—destinations other than Israel (Beinin 1998, 88).

It is in this period, too, that the first Israeli soldiers appeared on screen, in, among others, *Land of Peace/Ard al-salam* (1957), which dealt with the occupation of Palestine, and *Road of the Heroes/Tariq al-abtal* (1961) where a young woman joins the army as a nurse after her beloved has been hit by an Israeli bullet. Jewish emigration to the 'promised land' was depicted through a Jewish belly dancer who chooses emigration rather than the man she loves in *Battle of Giants/Sira' al-gababra* (1962). In addition secret service activities surfaced in 1967, the year of the Six Day War, with Husam al-Din Mustafa's thriller *A Crime in the Calm Neighborhood/Garima fi-l-hayy al-hadi* (1967). This film was certainly informed by the details of Operation Susannah even though it focused on the assassination of the British minister resident in the Middle East, Lord Moyne, by the radical-Zionist Stern Gang in Cairo in 1944. At the same time, its referentiality to actual historical events remained relatively minimal, as its plot preferred to add a number of fictional elements, such as a belly dancer, for the sake of spectacle.

The portrayal of the film's Jewish protagonists was of course negative. Although the two Zionist activists depicted in the film manage to carry out their task, they are characterized as anxious and insecure. After their arrival in Egypt, they are assisted by two women. One of them is portrayed as older, with a harsh, strong personality (reminiscent in her appearance of Golda Meir), who dictates the group's decisions. The other one is a beautiful young blonde (Nadia Lutfi) who works as a belly dancer in a nightclub and unintentionally serves the police as the key to finding the fugitive murderers. Her morals offer an additional opportunity to denounce the Jewish gang. In one scene she makes love to both activists at once. The members of the gang are thus explicitly portrayed as strangers, both in terms of physical appearance and behavior.

After the Six Day War, the final Jewish exodus took place. By 1968 only a thousand Jews remained in Egypt, diminished again by 1970 to 550 individuals (Krämer 1982, 290). Many at that time preferred to go to Europe, Canada, Australia, and the United States. Their emigration had been less the result of pressures exerted by the Egyptian authorities and more due to a number of different reasons. Even Zionist sources agree that, apart from a few incidents, Muslim Egyptians have not shown any specific cruelty in their treatment of Jews (Krämer 1982, 302). In reality, the Jewish exodus was fueled not only by the foundation of the state of Israel but also by a variety of sociopolitical factors. Conservative authors, such as Michael Laskier, agree with fierce critics of Zionism, such as Ilan Halevi, that the Jewish community would have resorted to communal self-liquidation even without the existence of the Arab–Israeli conflict. In Egypt, the population of the Greek community, for example, was also heavily reduced by the mid-1960s. It dropped from one hundred and forty thousand to thirty thousand persons. Economic pressures and the nationalist politics of Egyptianization were, just as in the Jewish case, the main causes for their departure (Krämer 1982, 301). Another important reason was the socialist-oriented nationalization policy, which affected *mutamassirun* and Egyptians likewise. An additional factor facilitating the Jewish exodus was the Westernization of the community's elites that linked, to quote Halevi, "the Jewry of the Mediterranean Islamic countries to the movement of European expansion, and detached it from the fate of the Arab peoples" (Halevi 1987, 201–202).

The disintegration of the Jewish community left its marks on Egyptian cinema production not only on the fictional, but also on the social level, to name just the case of the singer Layla Murad and her family. Layla Murad was born around 1918 in Alexandria to a Sephardic middle-class family originating from Syria and Morocco. Her father, Zaki Murad, was a musician himself. One of his famous Jewish (turned Muslim) colleagues, Dawud Husni, acted as Layla's mentor and musical coach (Danielson 1996, 144). After appearances on stage and the singing of playbacks, the singer and composer Muhammad 'Abd al-Wahab discovered Layla, asking her to perform as his partner in *Long Live Love* directed by Muhammad Karim in 1938. Two of her brothers also became involved in cinema, Munir Murad as a composer, singer, and actor, and Ibrahim Murad as an author and producer.

Between 1938 and 1955 Layla Murad starred in twenty-eight films, mostly light comedies and a few melodramas, often produced and directed by her husband Anwar Wagdi (separated for the second time in 1952). Gifted with a wonderful voice and (unlike Umm Kulthum, who also tried her luck in cinema) a charming appearance, she was able to become one of Egypt's top film stars. With her delicate stature she seemed destined to represent sensitive aristocratic girls, and was soon nicknamed 'the Cinderella of the Egyptian screen.' However, a few months after the coup in 1952 the singer was accused of having visited Israel and donated LE50,000 to the state. In a humiliating procedure she had to prove her innocence and her former husband Wagdi ventured to testify that their earlier divorce was not the result of religious, national, or political differences. Rumor had it that in an act of revenge Wagdi had himself circulated those accusations, to the very concrete and immediate effect that Syria banned Layla Murad's works for years to come (Magdi 1997, 50). It is not clear to what extent this affair encouraged Layla to stop acting, but the fact is that she withdrew from the cinema only three years later, in 1955. On the other hand she has remained a popular singer, therefore other reasons for her retreat seem plausible. After her marriage to film director Fatin 'Abd al-Wahab in 1954 and the birth of her first child she was allegedly struck by depression and struggled to control her weight; her attempted comeback in 1955 with *Unknown Lover/al-Habib al-majhul* was a box-office flop. Then with increasing age she withdrew from public life in the course of the 1960s, rarely giving any interviews or posing for photographs.

Layla Murad and Anwar Wagdi in *Layla, Daughter of the Poor*, 1945

Yet in 1995, immediately after her death, the singer's Jewish origin was exploited by sensationalist writings. The political magazine *Ruz al-Yusuf*, for example, printed headlines proclaiming "Layla Murad Returns to Jewry in Israel" (Magdi 1997) and "Layla Murad, Israel's Ambassador" (*Ruz al-Yusuf*, July 21, 1997), only to be invalidated by the subsequent text. But the verbal juxtaposition of Layla's Jewishness with Israel, and indirectly Zionism, remained, despite her own and her family's strong roots in Arab culture. The events around this particular case show that Arab Jews soon started to be associated and identified completely with the Israeli enemy, while in reality things were much more complex, as were Jewish loyalties.

Layla Murad's brother Ibrahim Murad for example did not convert to Islam like Layla and Munir Murad; he even left for France in 1956 after the Suez crisis. However he returned a few years later with the idea for a highly spiritual film that he also produced. *Letter to God/Risala ila Allah* (1961) was scripted by 'Abd al-Hamid Guda al-Sahhar and directed by Kamal 'Attiya. It deals with relations between humans and the divine, in telling the story of a father and his little daughter. While he, an engine-driver, experiences inner turmoil because his train has hit a young man, she keeps asking him compelling questions about God's nature and whereabouts. One day she climbs the minaret of the neighborhood mosque to ask God to bring her beloved doll to life. It slips from her hands and smashes on the ground, and although she narrowly escapes falling with it and a new doll is provided, she becomes severely traumatized after the new doll is run over by a truck. Munir Murad's work, with its idea of reaching beyond scriptural doctrine toward a more universal religiosity was also, much later, praised for being unique in uniting a Jewish producer, a Muslim writer, and a Christian director in a single production (Qasim 1997, 254). However, the film was not sufficiently appreciated at the box office, and Murad had to withdraw entirely from producing films (Bahgat 2005, 82).

In general, attempts to look for communalities were rare and not necessarily welcomed. No wonder Youssef Chahine's sympathetic representation of a Jewish family in his film *Alexandria—Why?/Iskindiriyya lih?* was heavily attacked in 1978, the year the film was released. Chahine's sensitive

Letter to God, 1961

depiction, which draws from his childhood memories in cosmopolitan Alexandria, was perceived as political opportunism by those opposed to Egypt's unilateral peace agreement with Israel. For them the Palestine question could not be dissociated from the question of Western imperialism (a view which has certainly some justification although it also indicates an inability to distinguish between Arab Jews, Zionists, and the state of Israel).

During the late 1980s and early 1990s, a whole series of espionage films began to indulge in the representation of Zionists and Israelis. *The Spy Hikmat Fahmi/al-Jasusa Hikmat Fahmi* (1994), by Husam al-Din Mustafa starring Nadia al-Gindi, is set in the Second World War and presents a couple of Egyptian-Jewish spies who continually switch their loyalties. They do not even hesitate to cooperate with German Nazis in order to achieve their main goal: to contribute to the establishment of the Jewish state. In *Execution of a Corpse/I'dam mayyit* (1985) by 'Ali 'Abd al-Khaliq and *Mission in Tel Aviv/Muhimma fi Tall Abib* (1992) by Nadir Galal, both set on the eve of the October 6 or Yom Kippur War, the representation of Israelis is, ironically enough, partly positive. The members of the Israeli intelligence service are portrayed as violent, cunning, clever, and at times even humorous, represented in the case of *Execution of a Corpse* by the corpulent, friendly-looking Yahia al-Fakharani. At the end, however, they are always outwitted by their Egyptian counterparts.

It is noteworthy that *Mission in Tel Aviv* depicts a cordial Muslim-Christian alliance that is reinforced in the face of the Jewish enemy. The heroine played by Nadia al-Gindi, chased in Jerusalem by Israeli secret service agents, disguises herself as a nun; she is then hidden and assisted in her flight by a Christian priest, who was introduced earlier as a political activist and Arab patriot. Thus the film indicates clearly who is and who is not admitted to the body of the Egyptian nation. It may also be no accident that *Mission in Tel Aviv*, shot at a time when several bloody Islamist attacks had been launched against Copts, used such an appeasing, yet strongly rhetorical metaphor for Muslim-Christian coexistence, an 'idyllic' imagery that was to survive and recur to this day.

The Copts: Agents or Victims of National Unity?

It has to be suspected that these kind of metaphorical images of alliance, similar to what was presented earlier in *Mistreated by Affluence*, may be interpreted as a sign of disturbance rather than of real appeasement. Very overtly in many cases recent film plots have, as we will see later, responded to a sense of peril expressed through an assumed foreign/Jewish conspiracy or to Islamist violence by conjuring up a seemingly unchallenged Muslim-Coptic national unity. That phenomenon has — and this is crucial — started to increase unprecedentedly since the 1990s, along with the new morality and Islamization, contrary to the dawn of Egyptian cinema where Copts appeared either as marginal comic figures or not at all. However, Coptic representation did take a different course from Jewish, as this large minority could not as easily be extracted from the nation's body and its territory.

As a matter of fact, only a very limited number of the approximately 3,100 fiction films released by the Egyptian film industry up to the year 2005 deal seriously with the Coptic religious environment. Mosques are often depicted but rarely churches. Religious celebrations, feasts, marriages, funerals, as well as expressions and vows with a religious connotation usually bear an exclusively Muslim mark. Christian ethics, religious culture, and matters of personal status have not been represented (with very few exceptions so far), nor have Coptic history, which shaped the country for several centuries, ever been made the subject of a commercial feature film, despite the fact that Christians form the most visible minority in Egypt.

Their real numbers, however, have always been the subject of controversy ranging of late between 2.5–3 percent of the total population according to official (unpublished) statistics and 12 percent according to Coptic statements.[7] Most Copts belong to the Coptic-Orthodox church, one of the oldest in the world. It dates itself back to the first century AD, long before the Arab-Muslim conquest. Copts represent therefore, along with Nubians, the closest descendants of the country's indigenous ancient Egyptian population, which means that (contrary to the Jewish case) hardly any claims of foreign affiliation could be made.

The limitations facing the integration of the Coptic element into the 'national' Egyptian narrative were nonetheless visible in cinema. From the mid-1920s until the 1950s Copts appeared, if at all, as stereotyped figures of fun, just like other minority characters. In Niazi Mustafa's *Salama is Doing Fine/Salama fi khayr* (1937) realistic characterizations were combined with comic stylizations. Salama, performed by Nagib al-Rihani, who works as a courier in the big department store of a supposedly Jewish *khawaga,* is confronted with different kinds of 'foreigners'. While his boss, a wealthy merchant, is not mocked, the film's Coptic bookkeeper is pictured as an odd-looking, obviously cranky individual, quite short and thin, with big eyeglasses, sitting at his desk counting. When asked a question by Salama he intones his answer in a chant reminiscent of Coptic liturgical songs. The greedy bookkeeper Murqus in *Hassan, Murqus, and Cohen* reflects a similar type. He even combines two negative stereotypes, the Upper Egyptian or *Sa'idi* and the traditional Coptic *sarraf* (treasurer), who was hated by the poor peasantry because of his close relations with big landowners and state authorities.

After national independence in 1952, the depiction of Copts was largely avoided, or in cases where they were represented, it was deprived of any particularity, as can be seen in the melodrama *Shafiqa the Copt/Shafiqa al-qibtiya* (1963) by Hasan al-Imam. Set in the nineteenth century and portraying an unhappy belly dancer (who was actually a historical figure), this film carries a title that may have been intentionally sensational in order to make the commercial exploitation of the film easier, but it sheds no light on the Coptic-Egyptian milieu or on the real history of the woman in question. According to Mahmud Qasim the film was loosely based on a presumably highly fictionalized account of Shafiqa's life published in 1961 by Galil al-Bandari without following the novel closely through (Qasim 1997, 226).

The same strategy of obliterating specifically Coptic characteristics was followed by other, less spectacular films such as *The Postman/al-Bustagi* (1968) by Hussein Kamal, set in the prerevolutionary past and based on Yahya Hakki's story *Dima' wa tin* ('Blood and Mud'). The protagonists of the film, an Upper Egyptian family, are Copts in the original story. The cinematic adaptation, however, does not underline this fact. Its basic plot is of two young lovers who consummate their love before marriage but cannot be wedded due to the tragic involvement of the village postman, who reads and keeps their correspondence for himself, with the result that the girl is killed by her father. This plot is clearly embedded in a realist description of Upper Egyptian traditions, irrespective of religious affiliation. With that the film clearly confirms the idea of a lack of differentiation between Copts and Muslims.

The most pivotal film of the 1960s in this respect, however, was again the historical spectacle *Saladin Victorious/al-Nasir Salah al-Din* (1963) by Youssef Chahine. Here the notion of an (Arab) national identity is worked out cinematically, not only through polarizing Europeans and Arabs, Christians and Muslims, but also Arab and European Christians. The character of 'Issa al-'Awam, a Christian who is depicted as Saladin's right arm, is of major importance to formulating a secular notion of Arabism in the film. At the same time the film clearly underlines Arab moderation as opposed to European bloodthirstiness. Keeping to historical facts, it narrates that the Arab troops and their leader accept and tolerate the presence of Christians in Jerusalem and all the other contested cities, while the crusaders commit bloody massacres among Muslim civilians. 'Issa serves Saladin and his cause with his whole heart but is also seen to have the best knowledge of the camp and crusaders because of his hidden love for female crusader Louisa (Nadia Lutfi). She dares not admit her attraction to 'Issa because of her loyalty to her countrymen, that is, her *national* affiliation. Yet she relinquishes active fighting to nurse the wounded after she understands that 'Issa's support for Saladin despite the fact that 'Issa is a Christian derives from his asserted Arab identity—and also after she witnesses several acts of treason among her fellow crusaders. However, in the end Richard Lionheart, upon his departure from the Holy Land, liberates Louisa from her moral constraints by advising her to follow her heart.

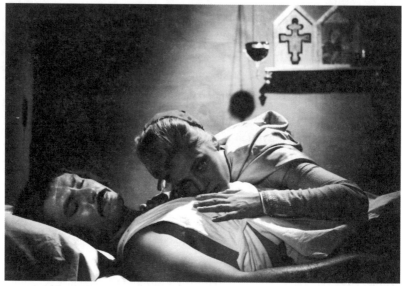

Nadia Lutfi and Salah zu-l-Fiqar in *Saladin Victorious,* 1963

The film unequivocally places Arab identity above religious affiliation, or to be more precise it asserts the conviction that 'religion is for God and the homeland is for all.' Drawing on the spirit of French Revolution, this assertion of national unity disregarding religion dates back to the 1919 unrest that saw a strong mobilization of hitherto politically marginalized segments of society, such as women and Copts, who joined forces to protest British occupation. In cinema this trope was first visualized in Muhammad Bayumi's short comic silent movie *Master Barsum is Looking for a Job* (1923). Barsum's religious affiliation is identified by a picture of the Virgin Mary hanging on the wall of his poor lodgings—alongside, and this is notable, a flag with the ultimate sign of national unity used during the uprising: a crescent enclosing a cross. This image was doubtless meant to emphasize the protagonist's hope of improved social conditions. Hence in the film the two characters, Christian and Muslim, unite to find a job and escape their deprivation, but are also ridiculed. Barsum, the poor Copt, has no bed, just a heap of straw, and gets up to dress himself in Fez and European suit but without any shirt underneath, while his friend, dressed as a *shaykh*, is introduced as a crook who steals someone else's bread to satisfy his hunger.

Due to the ideas that became set at that time, the rhetoric of national unity has preferred to perceive Copts as one element in a coherent national block rather than a minority. It has denied any cultural differences between Muslims and Christians, considering as general the behavior and customs common to all Egyptians, and claiming that Copts cannot be distinguished from their Muslim compatriots whether on the ethnic, geographic, or linguistic level. And indeed during the long decades of colonial domination, beginning with 1882, only a few political crises occurred between the two communities in Egypt. The difference of opinion created by the Coptic conference in 1911, which demanded more religious rights such as official Christian holidays, soon retreated into the background after the revolt in 1919. In the years following and until the 1950s, Coptic political mobilization (like the Jewish) took place within the framework of the political party system.

Muhammad Hasanain Haikal, a major opinion maker during Nasser's time (and still very vocal with his own weekly program on Al-Jazeera) stated that a distinction between Muslims and Copts can only be made regarding their places of worship (Haikal 1994, 2). In this he cited, ironically enough, the colonialist Lord Cromer, British consul-general to Egypt and de facto ruler from 1883 to 1907. Others, like researcher Abu Saif Yusuf, put forward the idea that Copts, although socially entirely integrated, hold a "side-culture that is, in its different material and intellectual manifestations, basically centered in everything that is linked to their religious faith and the values of their worship" (Yusuf 1987, 8). And indeed, cinematic representation of Copts has usually lingered on this last insight, either descending into caricature or ascending into glorification, but only exceptionally proposing something like the 'changing same' or the infinite differentiation of difference.

Not all the films of that period denied difference by insisting on the rhetoric of national unity, but tried instead to underline and keep up the status quo of religious difference. Hence, the 1950s and 1970s saw the production of two different films picturing cross-religious love stories, *Shaykh Hassan/al-Shaykh Hassan* (1954) by Husain Sidqi and *An Encounter There/Liqa' hunak* (1976) by Ahmad Diya' al-Din, which both present rather unhappy love stories between a Muslim man and a Christian girl, touching upon the social taboo of interreligious marriage. They were translated into a more or less melodramatic film form based on the motif of sacrificial love and aborted desire, with the Christian women in both cases paying a high price for their deviation.

Indeed interreligious marriage is a highly sensitive issue, which, particularly on the Coptic side, all too easily ignites fears of that community becoming diluted or even extinguished by the Muslim majority. Stories of seduced or abducted Christian girls forced to marry Muslim men and change their faith do circulate within the community on a regular basis (cf. Gibra'il 2005). In addition, the two above-mentioned films highlighted a decisive structural and legal imbalance between the two communities, inasmuch as *shari'a*-based personal status law allows Muslim men to marry Christian women, but bans Muslim women from doing the same. The only way for a Christian to marry a Muslim woman is to convert to Islam. Such a conversion, even less acceptable to Copts, has never been discussed in any cinematic or televised fiction. Instead, the acceptable and affirmative version—in Muslim eyes—of a Christian woman falling in love or getting married to a Muslim was chosen for the narratives in question.

As Mahmud Qasim reports, *Shaykh Hassan* in particular created strong controversy when it first appeared. Produced in 1951, it aroused threats to burn the movie theater that had shown it. Its screening was delayed until 1954, when it was released upon Nasser's personal order (Qasim 1997, 212). Featuring Huda Sultan as Louisa, who falls in love with al-Azhar student Hassan (Ahmad Sidqi) from the same neighborhood, the narrative has the couple marry and bear a child before bowing to her family's pressure to divorce, after which Louisa dies, grief-stricken. At this point, her corpse and her child have to be handed over to her husband (to give her a Muslim funeral and to raise the child in his religion).

In contrast *An Encounter There,* produced twenty-five years later, was less radical in its portrayal of the conflict and seemingly less biased in its resolution, but with the same effect on the female protagonist. Its main character is 'Abbas (Nur al-Sharif), a student highly skeptical of any form of religious conviction, who loves his Christian childhood friend and wishes to marry her. Nevertheless, at the end he gives in to family pressure and marries his cousin, while his former love decides to refrain entirely from worldly desires and to retreat to a convent. The Christian girl's reabsorption into her own faith is mirrored in 'Abbas's sudden change of attitude in the film's dramatic ending. When his cousin's life is endangered giving birth to their child, he eventually joins his family in reciting the Qur'an, asking God to save her.

With this the narrative clearly depicts each religion recovering its ground after the threat of 'miscegenation,' and marks out the social borders between the two communities that should be upheld under any circumstances. This message was certainly also acceptable to a Coptic audience, to whom the earlier *Shaykh Hassan* not only presented the danger of religious assimilation, but was also a reminder of the above-mentioned legal inequality. This inequality continued despite the simultaneous rhetoric of national unity, and was reflected in political representation during the post-1952 era. Because of the increasing dominance of military in the post-coup power structure and the fact that only Muslims held top positions in the army in 1956, not a single Copt was elected to parliament, to the effect that the government resorted to nominating a few Coptic representatives (Grace 2003, 86). At the same time the 1960s were characterized by cordial relations between state and church, facilitated by the spirituality and traditionalism of Pope Kirollos VI. However, the destruction of the multiparty system during the same period drove Coptic social and political activists into the arms of the Church, something that reflected badly on the country's overall political climate.

The deconstruction of socialist and secular nationalist ideals after the military defeat in 1967, the mismanaged economy, and Sadat's flirtations with the Islamist movement throughout the 1970s, led to a further alienation of the Coptic community to which the accession of the modernizing Pope Shenute in 1971 one year after Nasser's demise certainly contributed. The new pope's personality was characterized by political and social activism that mobilized the community, in particular the youth. At the same time he was able to transform the church into the sole representative of the community before the state, thus developing a somewhat similar concept to the Islamists' *din wa dawla* ('religion and state') (Talhami 1996, 94).

This tendency to polarization was aggravated by Sadat's attempts to domesticate the Islamist viewpoint by declaring his intention to turn the Islamic *shari'a* into the main source of legislation. The increasing instability of the sensitive Egyptian equilibrium was likewise expressed in a confrontation between the religious Coptic leadership and the political power that started in 1972 with the 'al-Khanka incident,' one of the first in a long string of Muslim-Christian clashes. What with this, and Pope Shenute's subsequent refusal to agree to the normalization process with Israel following the Camp David Accords, Sadat resorted to the unprecedented move of annulling the republic's decree by which the Pope had been confirmed in office, and exiled him to a remote monastery. This led to increasing insecurity in Coptic–Muslim relations that included Islamist assaults on Coptic students in Upper Egyptian campuses.

After Sadat's assassination in 1982 and throughout the 1980s and 1990s the social representation of Copts continued to be governed with very few exceptions by the affirmation of unity and a denial of difference, at least at the official level; to speak of ethnic and religious differences was still widely seen as being opposed to national unity. Nonetheless, a growing demand to include images of Copts could be sensed, coupled though with constant attempts of on-screen muting either through the rhetoric of unity or even by means of censorship. Literally, censorship regulations state only that it is not allowed 'to cause a stir or to split confessions, classes, or the national unity' (Shafik 1998, 75). In practice, this means that references to other religions have been avoided so as not to incur the public's displeasure, as was the case with a project that was submitted during the mid-1990s to the censor. The script, entitled *An Indian Film/Film hindi* (the title is a metaphor for triviality), was meant to reflect the youthful experiences of its Protestant author Hani Fawzi. Dealing in a comic way with a sexually frustrated Protestant and his friendship with a Muslim full of the joys of life, it would at that time have been the first Egyptian feature to look in more depth at Christian psychology and upbringing. However, obtaining the approval of the state censors turned out to be complicated. Some of the censors expressed the opinion that no church should be seen and no prayers heard; others wanted the hero, Samuel, to carry a more neutral name. After several rejections, Fawzi and Daoud 'Abd El-Sayed, who was originally intended to direct the film, appealed to the last possible resort, a special independent committee *(lajnat al-tazalumat)*, which finally approved it in 1995. But censorship was not the only obstacle: the search for a production company was difficult, too. Producers proved reluctant to accept such a sensitive project, fearing financial losses—in particular when exporting the film to one of Egypt's biggest markets, Saudi Arabia. There the representation of Christians is only rarely welcomed and images of churches, crosses, and so on have been prohibited. No wonder the project was not realized for years. Only in 2003, when it had become politically more opportune to present Copts on the screen, did it finally find a production company willing to support it. This was, perhaps unsurprisingly, the partly state-owned Media Production City administered under the auspices of the ministry of information.

The final result, directed in the event by Munir Radi, followed the usual appeasing formula, but was not necessarily approved. One comment came from an *Al-Ahram Weekly* reporter, who was particularly annoyed by the film's allusion to the 1919 revolt in a scene where an old Christian man reminisces about his part in the demonstrations as a pupil, along with his Muslim schoolmates (Elbendary 2003).

"Whenever national unity is up for discussion 1919 is invoked as the paradise lost. This particular reading of Egyptian history has been systematically promoted of late, and comes hand-in-hand with a broader revisionist reading of prerevolutionary Egypt as a golden age of 'liberalism.' That it was paradisaical is a point of contention; that it might somehow be regained by such mediocre attempts as *Film Hindi* is beyond belief."

In fact, the film overstated its case in asserting the absence of difference and the profound love between the two friends, whose ultimate proof of friendship is demonstrated in a mutual act of sacrifice. As both of them dream of solving their sexual problems by marriage, they find themselves—and their future wives—in competition for the same flat, which each of them finally gives up for the sake of the other. The final version of the film, unlike the script, displays an ambivalence in its treatment of Christian 'difference': not only is Samuel now called 'Atif, a secular name that works for both religions, but also the depiction of Christian rituals is inaccurate in showing 'Atif confessing his sexual fantasies at the altar, an action that is flawed on two counts, since the altar is not the correct place for confession in Christianity and Protestants do not confess to priests, at least not in a ritualized manner.

Not all projects experienced the same setbacks as *An Indian Film*. Some works by either Christian or Muslim directors dedicated themselves explicitly to advocating the common discourse of national unity, among others Khairy Beshara with *Abrakadabra America/Amrika shika bika* (1993). Here for the first time he included a Christian character, a young man who tries to emigrate, just as his Muslim compatriots do, but without giving this personality any further religious specification. The young man is only revealed as a Christian right at the end of the film during the funeral of a fellow emigrant, when he prays and crosses himself instead of reciting the Qur'an. This depiction is very close to Haikal's statement, which can be read metaphorically as confining differences exclusively to the places of worship, or in other words to the religious service.

One year later a spectacular feature film reached Egyptian screens insisting on the very discourse that used Islamist terrorism as a narrative backdrop. *The Terrorist/al-Irhabi* by Nadir Galal, starring the most commercially successful Egyptian star, 'Adil Imam, received much attention and was released in 1994 under heavy police protection. It deals with a militant Muslim fundamentalist who has a change of heart after he is cordially received in the house of a liberal bourgeois family. There he meets, among others, a Coptic neighbor whom he first—without knowing his real religion and ultimate sign of the presumably even national fabric—tries to rope in for his extremist ends. Finally, a *rapprochement* takes place when both men sit together watching a football match on television. When the national team wins, the difference between them indeed turns out to be minimal: while the Muslim yells '*Allahu akbar*' the Christian crosses himself, and thus the film proclaims that Copts and Muslims are inseparably related through patriotism, united in the struggle against extremism. It goes without saying that the message here is overtly rhetorical and tied into the politically affirmative stance of the film.

The same applies to Amali Bahansi's *The Switch/al-Tahwila* (1996), which was also aimed at discrediting Sadat's regime. It used Christian symbolism to express the suffering of the protagonist Hilmi, interned under Sadat in a desert camp. While being tortured, Hilmi looks up at a window frame in the form of a cross. The next sequence depicts his family in church, sadly taking part in the ceremony of a holy day while he is missing. The Copt Hilmi is, as a sign of ultimate injustice, deliberately mistaken for a Muslim and detained in his name. The film thus underlines the coherence of Muslims and Copts even under persecution and reduces the difference to the religious rite only. As a result each can be mistaken for the other because there is neither ethnic nor linguistic difference.

Between Separatism and Pluralism

If up to the 1980s few Egyptians were still willing to point out any differences in public, the pressure created by the tide of Islamist assaults in the early 1990s was most probably responsible for the fact that difference and assimilation became a topic on screen. This, together with the increasing isolation and isolationism of the Coptic community, led to the creation of a Coptic counter-public *(Gegenöffentlichkeit)* in the cinematic field.[8] After some amateur films shot on Super 8 and 16 mm during the 1980s, an entirely professional Coptic feature film production evolved in 1987, starting with

Magid Taufiq's *Bishop Abraam/al-Anba Abra'am* (1987). Ten years later, more than sixteen long feature films had been produced on video, directed mainly by Magid Taufiq, a television director, and Samir Saif, one of the most popular directors of the Egyptian film industry. Two churches, in Cairo and Helwan, offered funding for the first productions. Since then, the financing of each film has relied completely on the sales of the previous one. The biggest revenues came from sales to Coptic churches in Canada and the United States. Toward the end of the 1990s even secular-oriented Khairy Beshara joined in, directing a (Protestant) fiction episode film and several documentaries on religious topics.

These specifically Coptic productions are not allowed to be sold in public; nonetheless they must obtain shooting permission from both the Coptic Pope and state censorship. They are supposed to be distributed only to churches and were confiscated once when they appeared in a public bookstore ('Abd al-Gawwad 1995, 32). Productions have been almost exclusively

St. Dimyana/al-Qiddisa Dimyana, 1990

Christian, directed by Copts and performed by Christian actors, most of them professionals, who work in television or in the film industry. The majority retell the lives and ordeals of Egyptian saints and martyrs, like St. Antonius (Anthony), St. Dimyana, St. Abra'am, St. Musa the Black, St. Menas, St. Abanub, and others. Plots are highly schematic and repetitive in terms of storyline and pivotal climax, usually ending with a graphic Christian martyrdom, that is, they are related to the legendary models of persecution, torture, and death. In general, they emphasize the Christian readiness to sacrifice, describing how the early believers became targets of Roman and Berber persecution and attacks and how, supported by their faith, they received supernatural powers to overcome unspeakably cruel treatments, eventually starting to work miracles after their bloody deaths. Only few Muslims appear in these works, mostly in the more recent saints' lives, as in *Bishop Abraam*, and *Bishop Barsum the Naked/al-Anba Barsum al-'Iryan* (1990) by Samir Saif where the Muslim rulers come to honor the holy men after hearing about their glorious deeds.

In spite of their schematized structure, the stories draw their legitimization from historical events and personalities as well as existing places. They line up present-day Copts with their historical predecessors, confirming their religious and (sectarian) national identity. How this identity can be interpreted may be explained by a response given to me by a priest involved in the production. When I told him that I was carrying out research on minorities in Arab cinema, he answered, "We are no minority. We are the origin."

Ideologically, these stories by no means feed a pluralist conception of the Egyptian nation. In fact the Coptic glorification of the church's historical personalities can be seen as an equivalent to the Islamist *salafiya*, which eulogizes the lives and deeds of great figures of the past. It runs parallel with the Islamic emphasis on the utopia of early Islam (Talhami 1996, 94); however this is undoubtedly a utopia on the defensive. For Hanna Grace interpreted this unprecedented tide of Christian martyr films as a response to the Islamist threat to the Coptic community during the early 1990s. The audiovisual revival of legends of Egyptian martyrs who suffered under the

Romans or Byzantines could also be read as a direct translation of the Coptic conviction of having entered a new era of martyrdom (*'asr al-shuhada,'* as Copts have dubbed the time from the second to the fourth century AD in Egyptian history) (Grace 1997, 9).

Coptic fears were likely to be emphasized even more by public and official reactions to any expression of difference or violations of the codex of national unity. In 1994 a Conference on Minorities in the Middle East, in which Egyptian Copts were supposed to take part, aroused a highly charged political debate in the Egyptian media. Organized by the private sociological Ibn Khaldun Research Center headed by Saad Eddin Ibrahim and the Minority Rights Group in London, it was at first meant to take place in Cairo but was then transferred to the neutral Limassol in Cyprus. Many Copts refused to participate, arguing that they were not a minority. One of the main critics of the conference was Muhammad Hasanain Haikal, the former editor-in-chief of the official daily paper *al-Ahram*. He attacked the notion of a Coptic minority heavily. In his opinion, the conference represented the first step to foreign intervention in Egypt's internal affairs (Köhler 1994).

At the end of the 1990s further aggravations occurred. The discussion of the situation of Egyptian Copts by the U.S. Congress in summer 1997 was countered by official Egyptian statements that Coptic U.S. citizens were falsely accusing Egypt of massive persecution and extermination of their community and resulted in fierce, partly justified, reactions in the press. Some voices went so far as to equate the extremist Coptic lobbying with treason by associating its agents with Zionism (al-Banna 1997). The same link was openly pointed out again by Al-Jazeera (November 21, 2005) during a direct program transmitted from Washington reporting on the Second Coptic Immigrants Conference. It gave evidence that Michael Munir, leader of U.S. Coptic immigrants, co-scripted an article with a former Israeli ambassador on the occasion of the conference.

Already in 1997 the widely read political (governmental) magazine *Ruz al-Yusuf* had drawn a similar connection. It described the activities of the Coptic American Committee, which seemed to be responsible for the

statements, as marginal while it accused the Committee of receiving political and financial Jewish support. In its July 21, 1997 issue it presented the
following headline, "The coalition of Jews and Copts in the Diaspora." The
same issue stated further, "Human rights regulations can never disregard the
rules of the homeland. While we ask for equality and justice for everybody,
we ask at the same time that no element of the homeland becomes a toy in
someone else's hands."9

Yet these remarks, which were obviously aiming to dismiss and control
Coptic dissent and political activity at the same time, were not universally
accepted. Some more moderate voices were disseminated by the same channels. Three years earlier, in 1994, Muhammad al-Sayyid Sa'id criticized
Haikal and others by writing in *Ruz al-Yusuf*, "It is easier and safer for a
writer to flatter people's national and religious instincts by stating that all
problems we meet are but the results of a Western, a Zionist, or a satanic
conspiracy."10 And indeed the Copts' anxieties when faced with Islamist
assaults were rarely addressed at that time and still form a serious problem.
According to the Coptic Research Center for Social Studies, in two years
alone, between 1992 and 1993, around thirty Christians were killed by radical Islamists (along with a far larger number of Muslims) (Murqus 1995,
11). In the 1980s and 1990s, encroachments had been undertaken mostly by
radical Islamist elements; with the al-Kushh massacre in 2000 the violence
witnessed a certain mainstreaming spreading also to the 'masses' ('Abd al-
Fattah 2003, 291). To name only the most recent incident, in 2005, a furious
mob besieged churches in Alexandria because a Christian youth had
authored a play for an audience of churchgoers that was said to insult the
Muslim faith. This crisis eventually escalated in April 2006 with the stab-
bing to death of a churchgoer by fanatics and the injury of several others in
the same city.

Naturally, the Egyptian media disseminated such incidents very cau-
tiously, at the very least in order to preserve the country's internal peace,
although the spread of new and alternative media has made it more difficult
for the ministry of information to hide and channel crucial information. This

led also to the fact that in addition to the constantly cited unity, the notion of pluralism *(ta'aduddiya)* started appearing in the Arab and Egyptian media discourse, in particular after September 11. Thus, with the turn of the millennium, the readiness to address conflicts in the relations of the two communities rose. That made Samir Murqus, who is also an active figure in current Muslim–Coptic dialog, describe the current phase in Egyptian political life as one of restructuring citizenship. Yet he has also been warning that equal citizenship was a precondition for political reform, particularly in view of ongoing clashes.

Doubtless, the mounting polarization on the streets points to the fact that the sociopolitical organization of Egyptian society is the main factor that has generated separation between the different communities. The lack of real political participation and the difficulties in establishing secular political institutions involving citizens regardless of their religious affiliation, are among the reasons for separatism. In addition, economic pressures and poverty have led to the latent social mobilization of the different communities, thus antagonizing the elites of the communities and the state leadership and promoting particular confessional and ethnic identities at the expense of a general national identity and all this has led also to a temporary muting of the Coptic voice.

A Muted Community or Religious Hetero-glossia?

The silencing of Coptic 'difference' for the sake of national unity has ironically converged at times with historical attitudes of Arab-Christians, who tended to draw the least possible attention to their religious affiliation in public. For centuries it has been the task of *dhimmi*s to behave as unobtrusively as possible in order not to hurt, as 'Adel Khoury put it, "Muslims' religious sentiment and their feeling of superiority" (Khoury 1994, 105). Thus, they were not allowed to ring bells, to pray loudly, to build their church steeples higher than Muslim buildings, or to hold public processions using crosses. Quiet adaptation and constant afffirmations of loyalty have also dominated the official discourse of the Coptic church. Since the 1960s, the modern secularist orientation seems to have overridden or in some cases even eclipsed inherited self-denial, albeit leading to a similar result, which is the absence or conscious refusal of Christian symbolism and imagery in public representations.

Following the same ambiguity, the right of a Christian to represent his/her 'side culture' in public was not always taken into consideration. The case of Youssef Chahine's feature film, *The Emigrant/al-Muhagir* (1994), clarifies this. Muslim fundamentalist circles sued Chahine after the screening of this film, accusing him of flouting the Muslim convention that bans any visual representation of the prophets, with the story of young Ram bearing strong resemblance to that of the prophet Yusuf (the biblical Joseph). During the trial, the fact that the director of the film was himself a Christian was never referred to, not even by the director himself; nor did anyone mention his possible right to deal with the figure of Joseph from the perspective of his own religious heritage. The public discussion of the case remained restricted to a solely Muslim framework.

The discourse of national unity also reflected on the attitude of Christian filmmakers. It at times increased their reluctance to make reference to their religious affiliation, perhaps in part because so far they have faced no problem with professional integration. Some of the foremost Egyptian directors are Christian by birth. Youssef Chahine and Yousry Nasrallah, for example, are known abroad as unconventional supporters of the *cinéma d'auteur*. Henri Barakat is considered one of the most prolific Egyptian directors and left his distinctive stamp on the Egyptian musical and melodrama of the 1950s and 1960s. Samir Saif has made a name for himself as a commercially successful action-film director since the late 1970s. Khairy Beshara and Daoud 'Abd El-Sayed distinguished themselves as committed directors of New Egyptian Realism films that first came to light in the 1980s.

When interviewed, secularly oriented directors Khairy Beshara and Daoud 'Abd El-Sayed justified their lack of interest in representing their community by their disgust with any religious fundamentalism, be it Muslim or Christian. Both directors defined themselves explicitly and unexceptionally as Egyptians. Beshara even went so far as to claim that his religion may be Christian, but his culture is Islam.[11] His opposition to religious fundamentalism was expressed in a rather ironic scene in his comedy *Strawberry War/Harb al-farawla* (1994): a team of burglars, two men and two women enter a bank. They are disguised as Coptic nuns and priests. Yet the men wear their beards in the same way as Muslim fundamentalists do, growing it only on the chin, not on the upper lip. Muslim/Christian confessional confusion is further confounded when, at the time of Muslim prayer, one of the nuns calls for a prayer-mat!

Only very few Egyptian filmmakers showed the way to a real 'heteroglossia' or a representation of inclusive difference, as Youssef Chahine began to do in the late 1970s, something his financial independence, attained through his foreign coproductions, allowed him. His semiautobiographical films *Alexandria—Why?* and *An Egyptian Fairytale/Hadduta misriya* (1982) are some of the few Egyptian feature films that use explicitly Christian symbols—though negatively depicted. In one of the brief sequences that recapitulate childhood traumas the director as a boy is seen horrified at the sight of a sculpture of the crucified Jesus; in another the (child) protagonist inadvertently sets fire to the crib and fears to be punished with death "for having burnt Jesus."

In Chahine's personal cinematic universe, ethnic or confessional deviations have been consciously paired with friendship and love. In *Alexandria—Why?* the hero's best friend in school is a Jew. Among his further acquaintances we find a Marxist female Jew who marries a Muslim comrade as well as an Egyptian (homosexual) patriot who falls in love with a British soldier. With this, the film makes an unmistakable plea for a peaceful coexistence of faiths and the inclusion of the Other. The strategy he uses is to diminish differences while feeding the almost stereotypical image of a traditional tolerance of Arab–Muslim culture.

In contrast, Yousry Nasrallah (whose films are produced by Chahine's company) did not make any reference to his own Christian upbringing in his first film *Summer Thefts/Sariqat sayfiya* (1988), although the story is quite obviously autobiographical. However, with the upcoming tide of Islamist assault, religious, sexual, and ethnic deviance became more outspokenly an issue in his second film *Mercedes/Marsidis* (1993). The Christian affiliation of his (Marxist!) chief protagonist is suggested first by a visit to a church during the wedding of relatives. An assertion of difference is made in this film on a rather allegorical level during the scene of a bus ride where the hero, al-Nubi (the Nubian) encounters a Muslim fundamentalist. The latter is astonished by al-Nubi's white hair and asks if it is natural (literally: God-made). When the protagonist says yes, the man asks him to dye it in order to make him look like everyone else.

The representation of a relatively natural and equal common life between Muslims and Copts, in other words a life that does not submit to the rhetoric of national unity or display any overt political correctness, has remained rather exceptional. It has occurred mainly in the work of a few Muslim filmmakers, for example in the documentaries made by Ateyyat El Abnoudy, such as *Rhythms of a Life/Iqa' al-haya* (1988), *Responsible Women/Nisa' mas'ulat*, (1994) and *Girls' Dreams/Ahlam al-banat* (1995). One of the first to introduce a deliberately Coptic element in some of his fiction films as early as the late 1980s was screenplay writer and director Ra'fat al-Mihi, for example in *Broken Images/Li-l-hubb qissa akhira* (literally 'love has a last story,' 1986) and *Dear Ladies!/Anisati sayidati* (1990). In *Broken Images* the Muslim protagonists entertain a cordial relationship with an old Coptic woman. Unlike in *The Terrorist*, for example, this character is not idealized nor does she carry any explicit message but appears naturally, in passing. In addition, the funeral of this old woman offered, for the first time in the history of the Egyptian cinema, the opportunity to represent a Coptic sermon realistically in a fiction film.

A more recent film that also falls into this category is the comedy *Cultural Film/Film thaqafi* (2000) by a first-time director, Muhammad Amin. It depicts three young male friends, one of them Christian, who are searching for a VCR in order to watch a blue movie. But as they go from places that range from the homes of friends to a Muslim center, they do not succeed in

Ahmad 'Id (right) in *Cultural Film*, 2000

finding a quiet spot to view their 'cultural film,' as they call it. The Christian character oscillates between complete similarity and (relative) difference expressed primarily in the design of his parents' home, something that does not work him into an explicit statement about national unity but rather allows him to represent one facet of Egyptian reality.

In general, the increasing number of films and also television serials featuring Coptic families since the turn of the millennium is an aspect of Egyptian filmmaking that has been backed by the ministry of information. The official discussion of problems of coexistence, though, was not always welcomed by members of the Coptic community. They tended to read film characters allegorically as representatives of the whole Coptic community, as two recent examples show: the television serial, *Season of Roses/Awan al-ward* that was authored under official protection, and the fiction film entirely dedicated to a Christian family, *I Love Cinema/Bahib al-sima* (2004) by former Christian, now a Muslim convert, Usama Fawzi. Both caused a stir in the Coptic community.

After the previously mentioned killing of almost twenty-four Copts in the village of al-Kushh in Upper Egypt in 2000, the ministry of information shifted its policy toward promoting the representation of Copts more openly in Egyptian television, including dramatic works. Hence, the idea "to write something about Coptic–Muslim co-existence" was proposed to the scriptwriter Wahid Hamid personally by the Minister of Information Safwat al-Sharif (Hani 2000, 74). Eventually, the serial was aired during Ramadan in 2000, starring top cinema star Yusra. Yet, although its screenplay was written by one of the most acclaimed Egyptian cinema scriptwriters and it was directed by Coptic filmmaker Samir Saif (who has also a history as a director of Coptic saint films), *Season of Roses* resulted in strong protests from the Coptic community. Three legal complaints were filed against the makers of the serial, accusing them of misrepresenting Copts. The affair escalated to the point where Pope Shenute III intervened in an attempt to contain the conflict.

The drama, dwelling as usual on a version acceptable to Muslims, presented Yusra as the offspring of a mixed marriage between a Coptic woman and a Muslim man. The heroine's parents had faced tremendous pressure from their respective families: now she herself turns out to be unable to find a suitable match because of her mixed religious background. Tellingly, the Coptic protest that Hamid's script initiated was eventually contained, not through an enlightened public discussion on the topic but politically through the intervention of the head of the Coptic community. Instead, the debate was turned away from the serial's initial subject, namely inter-faith marriage, toward the question of individual artistic freedom, censorship, and liberalism. Along the way, criticism was dismissed as fanatic by drawing parallels between the serial and Youssef Chahine's trial over his film *The Emigrant* and by calls for freedom of speech and opinion for members of both communities. Yet the real reasons for Coptic alienation were not addressed, nor were the Copts' own conservatism and isolationism.

No wonder that the next crisis occurred only four years later. In contrast to *Season of Roses*, *I Love Cinema* directed by Usama Fawzi and authored by Hani Fawzi (the two are not related) had no official backing. On the contrary, the censor, at first hesitant to allow the film, proposed consulting the Church to avoid offending any sensitivities. However, this was strongly opposed not only by producer Is'ad Yunis but also by a number of Coptic and Muslim liberal intellectuals, alarmed by the fact that this would create a precedent and diminish the state censorship's independence of religious institutions, namely the Church and al-Azhar. With the backing of the ministry of culture the film was eventually released and did as expected meet strong reservations from the Coptic side.

The film was regarded as "a demeaning portrayal and a ridiculing of Christian doctrines" as the *Al-Ahram Weekly* reported. Over one hundred Copts demonstrated in Cairo's main cathedral in mid-July 2004 "demanding that the film be removed from theaters and the production crew be tried in court for contempt of religion. Eleven priests, a Coptic lawyer and reportedly one Muslim lawyer have filed a lawsuit against the film, calling for its banning" (El-Rashidi 2004). Interestingly the protests disregarded the fact that the film was actually set in a Protestant family and that the church depicted was also not Coptic-Orthodox.

The resistance with which the film was met was due to several factors. One of them was that it openly discussed the issue of Christian fundamentalism and that it showed actions in church that were considered immoral and disrespectful, such as a couple kissing in the church tower and a brawl during a wedding ceremony. The plot is framed by the adult Na'im reminiscing about his childhood in Shubra, a Cairo neighborhood that is home to a large number of Christians, on the eve of the 1967 defeat. The main conflict in little Na'im's life arises from his father 'Adli's strict piety. Not only does his father fast most of the year, avoiding cohabitation with his beautiful wife, a painter turned headmistress (played by Layla 'Ilwi); he even forbids his family from attending movies because he considers them sinful *(haram)*.

Just as in *An Indian Film*, scriptwriter Hani Fawzi intended to portray the atmosphere of his own Protestant upbringing in that very Cairo neighborhood

(Shubra). He included a tremendous variety of humorous situations and a range of characters affiliated to the main protagonists, their conflicts, animosities, and sympathies, as well as festive occasions, furnished with a 1960s atmosphere. Na'im's situation changes eventually when his father is punished for his strict morals—first, by his superiors at work (he refuses to tell a lie in a situation where everyone else would have done so) and next, when he discovers that he is seriously ill. All this softens the patriarch's attitude to the extent that he eventually takes his son to the movies and allows his family to acquire a television set.

Yet the film is also eager to connect its narrative and the problematic of the family to its temporal framework, namely the Nasserist period, as the point of departure for subsequent malaises. This is underlined in the finale when 'Adli takes his son on a bicycle ride along the seaside. Evidently seized by a stroke, he continues pedaling so as not to disturb their shared moment of happiness. Simultaneously the soundtrack plays reports of the military defeat by Israel. It thus establishes a crucial connection between the defeat and the father's fading authority and strength, which demands to be read as an allegory of Nasserism's waning as a cohesive social power, in turn the source of fundamentalism and sectarianism.

Mahmud Himida in
I Love Cinema, 2004

Indeed as director Fawzi explains, "there are many nuances to the story that [I] would have not been permitted to include in a film directly representing contemporary Egypt and because the historic distance allows for a contemplation of the root causes of the problems we face now. The narrator, the adult Na'im, provides a showing on the religious, political, family, and school institutions of that period that have shaped the present" (El-Assyouti 2004). While the film's actual dissection of the roots of the interrelated problems of fundamentalism and confessionalism remains hazy, it offers a somewhat atmospheric, dense, and personal portrayal of a decisive period in recent Egyptian history, asserting Christian Egyptian roots in the *same* historical framework and sociopolitical conditions, or in other words, as occupying the same *time* and *space* as that of their Muslim compatriots.

The Nubians: Servicemen of the Nation

Doubtless the cinematic organization not only of space but of time is of tremendous relevance to the representation of cultural, racial, and territorial difference and this holds true even more in narratives that either dislocate Egyptian characters from their homeland or portray communities linked to specific geographic locations that mark the country's territorial borders, such as the Arab Bedouin tribes and the Nubians. Thus Egypt's religious Others have found themselves inscribed into the spatial dimensions of the territorial inside–outside (something that could not be upheld in the Coptic case but became even more true for Jews), the geographic passage from South to North (Upper–Lower Egypt), East to West (Orient–Occident), and separated additionally through the linguistic divide of proper and broken Arabic (differentiating Egyptians from Nubians).

In his study 'DissemiNation' Homi Bhabha introduced Mikhail Bakhtin's notion of the chronotope, a narrative space-time configuration as a locus where national difference gets constructed. In using Goethe's travel book *Italienische Reise* he showed how the latter instrumentalized the time-space nexus in order to set apart home- and host-land (Bhaba 1990, 294).

Film scholar Hamid Naficy in turn based his attempt to classify transnational filmmaking on the same notion, claiming in regard to space that in "transnational genre, it is the enclosed claustrophobic spaces, often in the form of prisons, which both express and encode the (melo)drama of transnational subjectivity" (Naficy 2003, 211). A similar 'claustrophobia' produced on the temporal level by the long take and editing pace, and which has helped to cement the paternalistic 'poor foreigner' discourse in some Turkish-German films can also be observed.[12]

Hence it is striking to see that when Egyptian films shift their action from Egypt to abroad, particularly in the most recent 'glocal' (global-local) film stories that I will introduce later, they do not show any altering 'chronotope' when dealing with alien places. This however does not mean that the *mise-en-scène* is not applied to create difference, as in the case of the Nubian minority, who became inscribed into the film industry's farce repertory, while they were spatially and geographically extracted from the nation's body through a voyeuristic lens among others. Very much instilled into the near-folkloric farce canon of early Egyptian cinema, their representation has been highly schematized, and altered only slightly over the years despite the fundamental changes that occurred in the real-life community in the course of the twentieth century. Stressing at first Nubian servility and marginality, it shifted gradually to become a marker of Egypt's modern, developed, and 'white' identity.

Historically, Nubia (al-Nuba) was largely dominated by Egypt. Nubian kings achieved rule over Ancient Egypt only for a relatively short period after 715 BC during the Twenty-fifth Dynasty. In general, it remained in an adjunct and marginal position, squeezed and divided between Egypt and today's Sudan. In modern times, Nubia's affiliation to Egypt has been politically justified by the need to preserve the unity of the Nile valley. At times that also included Sudan, a concept that developed as a consequence of Egypt's military occupation of Sudan, dating back to the days of the viceroy Muhammad 'Ali, who conquered the region in 1821. From 1884 to 1898 Egypt's rule was challenged by the Sudanese al-Mahdi movement and then reintroduced nominally by the Anglo-Egyptian Condominium which was in turn terminated by Sudanese independence in 1956. Since then, Nubian territory has been divided between the two modern states of Egypt and Sudan.

Egyptian Nubians fall into three different tribes: the Fedija, the Kenuz, and the Arabs. Fedija and Kenuz each have their own language while the Arabs use Arabic for communication. The Nubian tribes converted to Islam quite late, in the fourteenth century (Hamid 1994, 38), after having been Christians for centuries, which made them preserve many ancient Egyptian and Christian rituals and customs. In 1960, before the resettlement, their population was estimated at approximately 120,000, out of a total of twenty-six million Egyptians (Fahim 1983, 10).

Nubians have in general a darker skin color than the average Egyptian, a fact that placed their ethnicity under scrutiny. One of the most extensive anthropological Egyptian studies on New Nubia claims that, although there has been miscegenation with black Africans and Arab Bedouins, Nubians have still kept the characteristics of the 'white race' or Caucasians[13] to which Egyptians supposedly belong (Hamid 1994, 38), a specific category that forms part of the colonial legacy. The category 'Caucasian' first gained currency in the first half of the nineteenth century through Samuel George Morton among others, who was the first anthropologist in 1830 to construct an alleged relation between brain size and racial affiliation (Banton 1998, 50). In fact, modern racial categories as a whole are a product of colonialist discourses, developed for the first time in Linnaeus' *Systema Natura* in 1735. He distinguished between races by their 'colors' and linked the latter in turn to different civilizational levels (Fluehr-Lobban 2004, 142). Subsequent codification of white, red, yellow, and black races is in reality challenged by enduring variety and miscegenation, while it has for a long time tried to conceal the fact that such categories serve social rather than biological ends. This did not prevent independent North African states from adopting colonialist categories of racial separation too, which made the first Sudanese census in 1956 for example distinguish between Arabs and Africans (Fluehr-Lobban 2004, 146), a distinction that destabilizes the country to this day.

Apart from the question of census, Bernard Lewis suspected that in pre-colonial times, until the nineteenth century, what has subjected Nubians occasionally to slavery has been their dark skin (Lewis 1992, 12). Their geographic marginality, living at the borders of the Ottoman Empire, seems a more plausible argument though. For it has to be noted that contrary to Christian Europe, Islam had a more reformist approach, banning the slavery of fellow-Muslims and disregarding their color (Fluehr-Lobban 2004, 153). Notwithstanding, the Arab system of slavery—although far less cruel than the Western—indicated a less favorable attitude toward black Africans. In contrast to white slaves they were mainly used for hard and domestic labor and were rarely offered the chance to advance socially (Lewis 1992, 12, 54).

The racial and cultural classification can be also traced linguistically, for the Nubian is sometimes carelessly called *barbari* and moreover confused with the Sudanese. The term Sudan shares the same root with the Arab word for black, whereas *barbari* derives from the Greek *barbaros*. Unlike in European languages, *barbari* has in Arabic a linguistic rather than a cultural connotation (Fahim 1983, 10). Thus, the black Nubian, referred to in Egyptian colloquial as *barbari*, signifies an incomprehensible black coming from somewhere south of Aswan.

For a long time, Nubians have immigrated to Egyptian and Sudanese towns. A Nubian quarter (Harat al-Nubiyin) has existed for centuries in Cairo along with a Jewish (Harat al-Yahud) and a Christian quarter (Harat al-Nasara) (Kerkegi 1967, 212). Emigration increased considerably after the construction of the first Dam in 1902. It intensified again after the two subsequent elevations of the Dam, in 1912 and in 1933. In 1960, before the last big exodus started, already more than 50 percent of all Nubians were living outside Nubia (Fahim 1983, 13) turning Nubians into a sort of sacrificial lamb for Egypt's modern agricultural and industrial development.

Most of Old Nubia, the traditional homeland of the Nubians, today lies buried under the water of Lake Nasser, which extends around five hundred kilometers upriver from Aswan, reaching one hundred and eighty kilometers into Sudan. Because of the High Dam, inaugurated in 1971, almost the entire Nubian-Egyptian population was resettled in 1962–63 by the Egypt-ian government to a barren region located further to the Northwest near Kom Ombo, close to Arab-Egyptian settlements and far from the shores of the Nile which had formed, since ancient times, a substantial part of Nubian mythology, tradition, and economy. This displacement caused a serious dis-ruption in the communities' cultural, economic, and communal life. Questions have been raised by community representatives as to why the resettlements were not located along the shores of the lake, suspecting that the choice of place was not simply a result of centralist state mismanage-ment but intended to disintegrate Nubian identity for the sake of Egypt's territorial interests (cf. Al-Jazeera 2005).

The notion of Nubia's having been put 'in service' to the Egyptian nation in real life, bears a striking resemblance to Nubians' on-screen posi-tion. The Nubians who populated Egyptian movies until the 1960s, women and men, worked either as nannies, servants, doorkeepers, or waiters in prosperous bourgeois surroundings, the homes of beys and pashas, reflect-ing the reality that the most common profession of Nubians in Egyptian cities at that time was to serve in homes, hotels, and restaurants. They were usually portrayed as naive, honest, kind-hearted, and humorous, also easy to belittle, because they did not speak proper Arabic. These traditional notions reveal the paternalistic, almost racist, attitude toward the Nubian.

The first Nubian principal character was performed by the comedian 'Ali al-Kassar. Even though he was not Nubian himself, for decades he was referred to as 'Egypt's *barbari*.'[14] Originally, he developed this character for theater and performed it on screen for the first time in 1935, in Alexander Warkash's film *The Doorkeeper/al-Bawwab*. The *barbari* 'Uthman became so popular that his character was even used until the late 1940s in several animated films advertising soap and other cleansing agents, such as the film spot '*Ali Uthman's Light/Nur 'Ali 'Uthman* (1949) by Frenkel. In the fol-lowing years al-Kassar featured in a dozen different films mostly directed by Togo Mizrahi and all dedicated to this Nubian personality, with three of them set in the fantasy atmosphere of the *One Thousand and One Nights*

(Bahgat 2005, 205). They were generally characterized by their extreme 'farce' form, that is, dramatic fragmentation through sketches.

It goes without saying that dark skin color, naiveté, and a strong accent were central to 'Ali al-Kassar's comic character 'Uthman. A typical *karagöz* (a Turkish *Punch*) figure, he was usually portrayed as blind to any consequences of his behavior, ready to misunderstand and misinterpret anything and always in search of trouble, as in *Lend Me Three Pounds/Sallifni thalatha gunayh* (1939) where he gets kicked out consecutively from different workplaces, among them a dentist's clinic where he messes up everything by assuming the role of the long awaited doctor, ready to give patients a disastrous treatment. Yet at the very end he manages to achieve a lucky resolution to his financial problems by winning a boxing match.

Apparently, 'Uthman is not only honest, kind-hearted, and naive, but he has a vivid imagination that lands him in trouble. In Mizrahi's film *Seven o'Clock/al-Sa'a sab'a* (1937) he works as a courier for a company in Alexandria. One night, burglars break into his bedroom and steal a sum of money belonging to the bank, which sets the police on 'Uthman's trail. After

'Ali al-Kassar in *'Uthman and 'Ali*, 1939

an adventurous flight he wakes up to find that it all was a dream. With this character al-Kassar drew very clearly on popular *fasl-mudhik* and shadow-play traditions that inspired style and plot construction (cf. Shafik 1998, 70); much less on any classifications related to the modern 'census.' Nonetheless, racial attributes inspired by Eurocentrism sneaked into the fabric of some of his films due to its director's *mise-en-scène*.

In one section of the film where 'Uthman drives south to home, we see a so-called Nubian dance, presumably celebrating a wedding. The simple performance, comprising a drummer and a dancer, differs considerably from modern oriental dance or the *varieté* dances usually presented in Egyptian cinema at that time for the sake of spectacle. In this case it functions rather as a cultural marker, yet the film's ostensible 'ethnographic' endeavor does not result in a realistic depiction. Although the music displayed in this scene seems close to Nubian music, neither the way the dance is performed nor the set design for the surroundings is authentic. Rather, the architecture, furnishing, and decoration of the house hosting the celebration resemble the house of an Upper Egyptian notable. The guests do not join in dancing as Nubians usually do during marriages but watch the performance and comment on it, thus sharing the point of view of the (voyeuristic) outside spectator on an 'indigenous' people.

Moreover, since Mizrahi's artificial staging of supposedly Nubian culture, a similar spatial cinematic configuration has been repeated numerous times, transforming the Nubian into the object of a presumably 'white' Egyptian gaze, still displayed in Egyptian cinema in 1963 for example, when the public 'discovery' of the real Nubians started because of the construction of the High Dam and the resettlement plans. *The Naked Truth/al-Haqiqa al-'ariya* (1963) by 'Atif Salim deals with a young female tourist guide from Cairo who falls in love with an engineer working on the construction of the High Dam. While accompanying Europeans to tourist sites, she meets the Nubian Ramsis (performed again by a 'white' actor), whose behavior is rather funny and childish. In his village, the tourists watch a Nubian dance performed by the inhabitants. The *mise-en-scène* is very reminiscent of colonial jungle films that show white people entering a native village. In Salim's film, Egyptians join the tourists in surrounding the Nubians and observing their performance. In this folkloric scenario, which installs the apparently black and indigenous Nubians as the object of the white gaze, Egyptians are equaled with fair-skinned Europeans.

This combined spatial and cultural positioning of Egyptians vis-à-vis Nubians is based on a long tradition reaching back into post-independence that was expressed also in relation to Sudan (with Nubia as an intermediate territory) and is clearly related to Egypt's territorial claims on the region. Quite tellingly a cartoon that Beth Baron has unearthed, published in the Egyptian magazine *al-Lata'if al-Mussawara* in 1932 depicts Egypt as a fashionable white lady, contrary to black, meager, and bare-breasted (primitive) Sudan (Baron 2005, 73). In her 1995 dissertation *The Colonized Colonizer*, Eve Marie Troutt Powell gave insight into the historical roots of this juxtaposition by analyzing the image of the Sudanese along with the Nubians in Egyptian writings until the 1930s.

According to her Egyptian nationalists' ambiguous view of the Sudanese was due to the fact that the Sudanese were on the one hand, exactly like Egyptians, the victims of British domination, while on the other, Sudan was still nominally subject to Egyptian military expansionism. This ambiguity was expressed in the perception of Nubians and Sudanese as younger uncivilized brothers, while simultaneously supporting their nationalist cause against the British. Local culture was neither studied nor considered. Egyptian writers preferred to invent the image of Nubians and Sudanese than to reflect their reality. The black *barbari* or Nubian, who appeared in Egyptian fiction of that period in the role of a naive and spontaneous servant, confirms Egyptian paternalism clearly and was adopted by Egyptian cinema without any further questioning.

By the early 1960s, because of the necessity of its evacuation, Old Nubia became the object of increasing interest to Egyptian documentary filmmakers, most notably Saad Nadim. He tried to document as much as he could, particularly of the old monuments. However, out of more than a dozen documentaries, only one, entitled *A Story from Nubia/Hikaya min al-Nuba* (1963), dealt directly with Nubia's inhabitants. But even this film did not let Nubians speak for themselves. In its visual representation it relied primarily on paintings by Northern Egyptian artists of life in Nubia, and not on material shot in the region.

In contrast, Youssef Chahine's Russian-Egyptian coproduction *The People and the Nile/al-Nas wa-l-Nil* (1972) must be in a sense considered a marginal exception. It included a more realistic depiction of Nubians in a film plot that was, however, again centered on academic professionals visiting Nubia from northern Egypt at the time of the construction of the High Dam: an intellectual, an engineer, a doctor, and a novelist. In the following, very few filmmakers, such as the Palestinian Ghaleb Chaath and the New Realist Khairy Beshara for example, two socially committed filmmakers, departed from the caricaturist image of Nubians and blacks in their films. They included popular Nubian singers in their films—Muhammad Hamam in *Shadows on the Other Side/Zilal 'ala al-janib al-akhar* (1971) and Muhammad Munir in *Necklace and Bracelet/al-Tawq wa-l-iswirra* (1986)—but without any further references to the Nubian community. Instead they chose to depict them as regular Egyptian characters, without resorting to ethnic or cultural comic stylization.

Filmmakers of Nubian origin willing to address the problems of their community came to the fore only in the early 1990s. Two of them, Sabir 'Aqid and Ahmad 'Awad, studied at the Film School in Cairo and have not made the transition to commercial cinema so far. They were encouraged in their work by the late Mustafa Muhammad 'Ali, the first Nubian to attain a really high position in the field of cinema. He became head of Egypt's National Film Center and the Higher Film Institute during the late 1980s and encouraged Nubian students to deal with their own community in their graduation projects.

In fact the eventual appearance of Nubian academia and arts in relation to the silver screen reflects the profound changes that have occurred within the Nubian community, both within and without today's Nubia. While Old Nubia was dominated mostly by old people who had been left behind, New

Nubia is said to be vibrant with young people aspiring to higher education who work primarily in white-collar and professional jobs, which allow them to assume more importance in community affairs (Fernea 1994, 157). These young people have been looking for, and producing, new forms of cultural expression. The most obvious sign of this is the appearance of a new popular Nubian music that has conquered Egyptian broadcasting. The most acknowledged musician so far is Muhammad Munir, who has appeared since the late 1980s in several Egyptian feature films (at first in those directed by Khairy Beshara) but then also in Youssef Chahine's *Destiny/al-Masir* (1997); not necessarily representing his community, but offering at least a musical subtext of what has become an increasingly important means to express modern Nubian identity (Fernea 1994, 157).

A sociological study undertaken in 1980 showed that "the spatial transplantation of families has apparently not resulted in a fragmentation of the social, psychological, and cultural spheres of Nubia's social organization. While a shift has occurred in the latter's material aspects, the basic Nubian character has continued to be shaped by many of Nubia's old values and traditions" (Geiser 1980, 62). The obvious struggle of the Nubian community to preserve its culture on the one hand, and on the other, to create new forms of genuine cultural expression, led Robert Fernea to predict "an increasing politicization of this ethnicity in the years ahead" (Fernea 1994, 158). But Egyptian popular cinema has so far remained on the whole unaware of and unaffected by this.

Since the resettlement, the High Dam and the Old Nubia have become central themes in modern Nubian culture. Numerous songs, as well as contemporary Nubian literature, have chosen to reflect these themes as a decisive turning point in their community's history and to negotiate through them some of "the self-reflective sense of being a Nubian" (Fernea 1994, 158). The two films made by Nubian film students, *The Dam/al-Sadd* (1990) by Sabir 'Aqid and *The High House/al-Bayt al-'ali* (1991) by Ahmad 'Awad also deal with the effects of the High Dam on their community, and clearly reflect the struggle for Nubian identity.

'Aqid's *The Dam*, for instance, belongs to that category of films that focuses on the trauma caused by the destruction of Old Nubia. The director displays the traditional architecture, costumes, and rituals prevalent before the construction of the dam. Without commentary, he illustrates in a rhythmical animation the literal drowning of a culture. His powerful combination of drawings with traditional Nubian music manages to reflect a sense of loss and grief, thus suggesting what Robert Fernea underlined, namely the conviction of many Nubians that they can never be compensated for what they have lost in Old Nubia, in the material as well in the cultural sense (Fernea 1994, 158). It is notable that although it was realized by a young director who was born after the resettlement and raised far from his origins, in the cities of Suez and Cairo, no references are made in this film to modern Nubian life. This orientation toward the past seems to cry out for acknowledgement of what has been inflicted on a community for the sake of the nation; but it is also an attempt to redefine Nubian identity. None of this has made its way into popular cinema though.

In spite of the deep changes that Nubians experienced due to the building of the High Dam, they were not a significant presence on the Egyptian screen during the 1970s and 1980s. Popular Egyptian cinema did not abandon them completely: it clung to their traditional inscription into the comic farce canon. Since the 1990s, however, the role of blacks or Nubians has changed considerably in quantity and quality. They were not always put at the service of Egyptian characters, but instead they began to be instrumentalized as catalysts for East–West encounters, most notably in *Terrorism and Kebab/al-Irhab wa-l-kabab* (1992) by Sharif 'Arafa, starring comedian 'Adil Imam as a white-collar worker on a mission to al-Mugamma', the large government office building in downtown Cairo; frustrated by its bureaucracy, he unwittingly ends up as a hostage-taker.

Among Imam's hostages is a black man, who repeatedly prefaces his remarks with: "In Europe and the developed countries . . ." whenever he wants to criticize or suggest something. The comic effect is here of course the carnivalesque reversal of 'social' positions: to hear the reproach of

Yusra in *Terrorism and Kebab*, 1992, with the black man in the background.

underdevelopment from a Black-African and not from a white man comes as an unexpected surprise. This motif appears like an allegorical quintessence of Egyptian national self-definition, caught between civilization and progress and its opposite pole, backwardness and underdevelopment. Thus, whenever the question of backwardness is raised and an imaginary encounter with the 'developed' West conjured up, the black man appears— either as a reminder of Egypt's transitional status or as a confirmation of its basic alignment with what the West stands for.

A similar configuration is also found in *An Upper Egyptian at the American University/Sa'idi fi-l-gam'a al-amrikiya* (1998) directed by Sa'id Hamid (a director of Sudanese origin). The main protagonist Khalaf (Muhammad Hinidi) leaves his upper Egyptian village for Cairo, having received a scholarship to study at the American university there. The gap between him and his fellow students is all too evident. He differs from them in everything: language, clothing, behavior, and thinking. Yet he is quickly initiated into 'modern' Egypt through his urban friends there on the one hand, and encounters with 'hostile' Westerners on the other. An Afro-American student who is always bumping into Khalaf offers the opportunity for comic exchange but is also used to heighten the sense of the peasant-protagonist's sense of alienation. A comparable comic moment is provided by a young black prostitute and her small community of African women camping on a houseboat on the Nile. Samara (derived from *samra'*, literally 'the dark one') is kind enough to take in desperate Khalaf when he gets kicked out of his Cairo accommodation. The spectacular highlight of this part of the story is a cheerful song entitled "Shukulata" ('chocolate') that "turned brown, black, got burned but is a sweet potato." Here Khalaf appears in a Nubian dress and dances to a Nubian-inspired rhythm with the women, who are wearing West-African-style dresses and haircuts. Samara even falls in love with Khalaf because 'he is so kind to her.' But at the end the hero goes off with his fellow-student, the fair-skinned Egyptian Ziyada (Mona Zaki).

Despite Samara's positive role as Khalaf's host, she nonetheless provides the subject for some 'good' jokes that mock her skin color. The first time Khalaf meets her, she is presented to him by his roommates as a welcome surprise upon his arrival to Cairo. When they are alone in the bedroom she switches off the lights, which makes Khalaf ask, "Why did you turn off the light? You're dark enough already." Later, he tells his friends, "Everyone enjoys red nights, only I had a black night" (note that 'black night' in Arabic is a metaphor for bad luck and turmoil, while 'red night' signifies amusement and fun).

As a whole, the recent revival of the issue of ethnicity and color in Egyptian cinema in this context cannot only be perceived within the limits of generic traditions or as an attempt to align Egyptians with the white race, but seems also to indicate a revived need to reaffirm the outline of the nation in an increasingly globalized world. This can be observed in another recent film that does not fit into the comic category. 'Amr 'Arafa's *Africano/Afrikano* (2002), starring Ahmad al-Saqqa and Mona Zaki, revives the old stereotype of the black domestic worker, though in a rather transnational context. The film introduces Badr, a young Cairo veterinarian who has no opportunity to practice his profession properly, but to his surprise receives a visit by his uncle's lawyer from South Africa telling him that his relative left him a considerable inheritance. However, in order to be able to acquire his legacy, a large safari park, Badr has first to win the heart of his uncle's daughter Gamila, and to fight an intrigue of Gamila's foreign stepmother, who wants the park for herself. In this struggle Badr is assisted, among others, by his brother-in-law 'Isam and his uncle's black driver, who turns out to speak Arabic because he studied at the Islamic university of al-Azhar in Cairo!

The film includes a number of racist jokes made by the brother-in-law, who at the same time provides a comic relief to the hero's sober personality. When they first arrive in South Africa, they visit a hotel. Walking down a corridor, 'Isam observes a group of black Africans disappearing around the corner. He asks, "Is there an electricity cut down there?" alluding to their dark skin color. On another occasion he snoozes in the car and gets very frightened on waking to see the driver's black face looming over him at the

Ahmad al-Saqqa and Mona Zaki in *Africano*, 2002

window. He nicknames the driver 'Bakkar,' the title of a children's television series aired annually during Ramadan, featuring the adventures of a Nubian boy called Bakkar. In addition to these allusive verbal and mimetic jokes, the film includes, just like *The Naked Truth,* a scene reminiscent of exotic colonial jungle movies, depicting a 'negro village' that treats our heroes to a folkloric feast of singing and dancing, dressed in an awkward mish-mash of all kinds of African-style costumes.

Glocal Self-Assertions

It may be suspected that films like *Africano* share in the general attitude of Egyptian society, which is still lacking in any substantial self-awareness regarding ethnic racism. It seems, moreover, as if the opportunity for Cairo lower-middle-class men to ascend and imagine a positive future abroad brings about the necessity to symbolically reenact the encounter with the nation's own suppressed or excluded Others, or in other words to reframe them within the 'glocal' nexus according to the common national narrative. This reenactment becomes apparent in *Hello America/Halu Amrika* (2000) by Nadir Galal, which appeared in the context of a whole tide of 'Egyptian hero goes global' films starting in the mid-1990s. This new wave seemed to respond to the new global village situation engendered by, among other things, the introduction and spread of satellite television, first and foremost Arabic transnational news channels in the early 1990s.

As I stated earlier, it has to be emphasized that those films in particular, although they narrate emigration and travel stories, do not display any recognizable shift in the time-space configuration between home- and host-land that differs from the transition from poor to rich, from the cinematic representation of an Egyptian lower-class environment to bourgeois surroundings common to social ascent stories. If we compare, for example, two 'migration' films starring 'Adil Imam, *The Terrorist* (1994) and *Hello America,* both by Nadir Galal, the migration of the hero from the overcrowding and bustle of his home alley to the spacious streets and villas of the more privileged neighborhood is staged similarly within and without Egypt in terms of *mise-en-scène* and set design.

While in *The Terrorist*, its deprived radical Islamic protagonist leaves Upper Egypt to become stranded in Cairo's bourgeois milieu, *Hello America* features two U.S. immigrants Bakhit ('Adil Imam), a former member of parliament (dismissed because of his honesty) and his fiancée 'Adila, two characters who had already appeared in *Bakhit and 'Adila/Bakhit wa 'Adila* (1997) by Nadir Galal, and who had exposed nepotism in parliamentary elections. As Bakhit originates from a poor neighborhood and has no financial means to wed 'Adila, they search for a solution. This time the couple decides to try their luck with Bakhit's cousin who lives in New York. He and his family, however, have not retained the traditional Egyptian values of family solidarity, generosity, and hospitality. Instead, they exploit Bakhit and 'Adila as cheap labor, eventually turning them onto the street. Here they experience the ups and downs of life in America. After becoming homeless they are roped in to work for an Islamist center that rewards Bakhit by arranging his marriage to an African-American so that he can get a visa. However, Bakhit is lucky: he gets hit by a car belonging to the daughter of the U.S. presidential candidate, and with the help of his cousin he sues the girl and her father. With the prospect of winning a multimillion dollar case, Bakhit is transformed into a major political player in the U.S. elections. This situation is not to last though, for the cousin has managed to cheat the couple out of the game, and Bakhit and 'Adila end up on the streets again.

Hello America certainly includes an indirect and complex response to Hollywood's perception of the Arabs, incorporating some motifs of American 'hate-and-terminate-the-Arabs-films' (Shaheen 2001, 6). In this context the American preoccupation with terrorism is dissected as mere hysteria in one of the film's most hilarious scenes in which American special agents mistake a glass of pungent Egyptian cheese *(mish)* in Bakhit's possession for a virus bomb. Yet regarding the theme of social ascent the message of the plot is clear: the protagonists are caught in a vicious circle so that at the finale they arrive where they started.

In between, the narrative negotiates several crucial issues, the most pivotal being the relation to home and tradition in a time of increased mobility and globalization. Central in this respect is the attitude of Bakhit's cousin and family as expressed also in spatial terms. They have lost all sense of solidarity and hospitality according to the *awlad al-balad* code of honor. Moreover, they have abandoned the code of Egyptian morality by allowing their daughter to receive her boyfriend in her room, even explicitly approving her loss of virginity. The successful Egyptian immigrants' 'Western' attitudes and possessions, their prosperity, their egotism, their vast villa and garden, are strongly constrasted to the densely populated lower-class neighborhood from which Bakhit, the *ibn al-balad* originates, with its crowded cafés and alleys, and the closeness of neighbors and friends, who gather when Bakhit leaves to bid him a cheerful send-off. Lower-class Egyptian solidarity and affluent bourgeois Westernization and alienation are shown as opposite extremes. In this the film follows the same strategy as *The Terrorist*, where a comparable polarization with respect to space is achieved between Upper Egyptian alleys and Cairo's fancy suburbs.

Moreover *Hello America* is, like *An Upper Egyptian at the American University*, quite explicit in its (re-)positioning of the 'white' Muslim protagonist toward the nation's Others. In a highly coded way it creates in relation to immigration and globalization a meaningful triad between the United States, the black minority, and the Copts in a sketch that implies Bakhit and a Christian-Egyptian passerby on the streets of New York. In addition the film draws a clear distinction between fanatic and moderate Muslims, the latter represented by Bakhit, while the Islamists are portrayed as demagogic, opportuntistic frauds. The Islamist center in the film is first introduced when Bakhit takes his little nephew to the Friday prayer to discover that the mosque's Shaykh is delivering a condemn-the-American-devil sermon. Bakhit, in a movement of fear holds his hand over the mouth of the little boy who wants to shout out his protest loudly, but later, Bakhit and his fiancée resort to the same Shaykh when they are thrown out of his cousin's home. In the following scene Bakhit is shown collecting donations on the street, and instead of his usual blue jeans and T-shirt he wears an Islamist dress and a long beard, while 'Adila is covered up with a chador. Bakhit stops a passing pedestrian, asking him in Arabic, "Brother, you are Egyptian, right?" The young man replies, "By Jesus, I don't even have a dollar." Of course this particular scene is meant to dissociate Egyptian identity from religious affiliation, while the narrative otherwise remains centered on its Muslim hero.

Bakhit's masquerade is soon terminated, for the Shaykh offers a solution to his plight in the form of marriage to an American woman. Expectantly Bakhit waits for his bride with a bouquet in front of the registry office, but when the Shaykh arrives with her, Bakhit is in shock. His future wife turns out to be a huge, stout, coarse-looking black African, much bigger than himself, who immediately asks for payment in exchange for the service she offers. As they walk toward the stairs, Bakhit tosses his flowers in disgust into the street. Later, at the woman's home, male and female roles are confounded as she forces him to share the bed with her and finally rolls on top of him in a suggestion of sexual rape, with Bakhit helplessly caught underneath her. In a subsequent scene, Bakhit barely escapes her violent rage, which leaves her whole home in ruins.

In all her appearances the Afro-American, portrayed as a corpulent, ugly, and sexually aggressive woman is equated with a quasi-animalistic sexuality. Physically she stands in contrast to Bakhit's fiancée's milky white complexion, blond hair, and petite fragility (actress Shirin). Herewith, the film displays a strong degree of ethnic racism toward or 'demonization' of its black protagonist and simultaneously overt political correctness toward the emigrant Christian as a fellow citizen, insisting in the face of the implied Islamist threat that the presence of non-Muslim (Christian) Egyptians has to be considered.

As mentioned earlier, *Hello America* depicts Bakhit's temporary social rise from a marginal Third World parliamentarian into immigrant into a pivotal player in U.S. presidential elections. No wonder it includes highly comic cinematic allusions to American political thrillers, such as the plane scene, the CIA investigation, and U.S. political intrigues. With this the film clearly follows the subversive quasi-anthropophagic (with respect to Western culture) and carnivalesque strategies of cultural resistance as sketched out by Robert Stam and Ella Shohat, which also allude to the ironic mimicry of Western generic elements in a comic framework (Shohat and Stam 1994, 302). The fact that it applies the style of the carnival confirms its preoccupation with the issue of power, domination and its subversion of power. Resistance in this case, however, displays a strongly essentialist and not necessarily deconstructive anticolonial moment, if we think of the representation of the Afro-American. The film tries to resort to the (supposedly) positive quintessence of Egyptian culture, which includes human loyalty and hospitality among other qualities, in order to expose American culture as governed by fierce materialism, sexual libertinage, and racism. However, it excludes the American (and its own) socially marginal groups—that is the black African, or, read in the Egyptian context, the Nubian.

Moreover, in the course of the action Bakhit's dream to solve his economic problem does not materialize. As the film's ending clearly signals, social equality is a goal too hard to achieve. Most other immigration films do not share this view. They may even be read as an assertion of Egyptian supremacy and predisposition to success. One of the films that forms a precursor to this type of narrative is the previously mentioned *An Upper Egyptian at the American University* (1998) by Sa'id Hamid, starring the then relative newcomer Muhammad Hinidi. The film was so popular that it initiated a whole Hinidi-cycle (series) and turned out to be a prelude to the arrival of a new generation of stars that has been taking over the Egyptian film industry and to the 'new comedy' that appeals also to the shopping-mall audience.

In addition *An Upper Egyptian at the American University* heralded the subsequent production of a series of fiction films that freed the Egyptian cinema from its seclusion and its confinement to its homeland. Formerly, shooting on location outside Egypt was, if it was done at all, confined to neighboring Mediterranean countries, that is, Lebanon and Greece. While Lebanon was recurrently chosen for shooting (due also to the strong presence of Lebanese distributors) between the 1940s and 1950s, Greece became more fashionable during the 1980s, being still relatively affordable for limited Egyptian film budgets. 'Exotic' places and characters were sought at times, to name only a very early example, Amina Muhammad's *Tita Wong/Tita Wong* (1937) starring herself as a Chinese girl (which was shot of course in Egypt). However, in the late 1990s, Egyptian films quickly surpassed even the Northern European borders to more distant locations, such as the U.S., Brazil (in a film that remained uncompleted), South Africa, and even Thailand. Yet, as much as those films capitalize on the spectacularity of their attractive locations, on the narrative level they seem to insist, through plot and character traits, on their 'genuine' Egyptian-ness, something *An Upper Egyptian at the American University*, the first one in the series, demonstrated in an exemplary way. The film's form is highly stylized, including farce sketches, musical numbers and a lot of stereotypical characters; however the inner Egyptian social fissure, the gap that the hero eventually manages to bridge, is complemented by an element of conflict, projected onto international relations, embodied by the strongly Americanized Sirag, a teacher at the university, who mutates into the hero's fiercest opponent, with the confrontation ignited over their opposed standing on the Palestinian question. Sirag, clearly marked as pro-American, tries to subvert the students' efforts to mobilize in solidarity with Palestine and organize a demonstration on campus. Eventually, the malicious teacher gets exposed and the students succeed in launching their protest.

On the formal level the Upper Egyptian's passage from south to north and his subsequent 'acculturalization' are equivalent to a passage from farce to drama on the level of *mise-en-scène*. While his father's farm, with which the film begins, and its inhabitants are depicted in a strongly caricatured way, as a conglomeration of odd people and customs who even at times manage to frighten the absent-minded Khalaf, they are clearly opposed to the more realistic treatment of Khalaf's Cairo environment, starting in particular with the highly dramatic problems of his two flat-mates caught in difficult emotional and economic situations and ending with the very serious political on-campus fight for the Palestinian cause.

The film does moreover prolong the old motif of the ever-present Zionist that had been already introduced by Nadia al-Gindi's espionage films,

like *Mission in Tel Aviv* (1992) nurtured by the post 1948-phobia of the foreign conspiracy *(mu'amara)* against the Arab world. If there is no Zionist or
Israeli adversary visible then at least a plot waits to be uncovered, as in the
recent action film *Mafia/Mafya* (2002) by Sharif 'Arafa that resolves the
mystery of a planned terrorist attack on the Pope's life during his visit to
Egypt—as an Israeli plan. The same motif (including the passage from farce
to drama) is present also in one of the most popular new 'globalizing' comedies, *Hamam in Amsterdam/Hamam fi Amsterdam* (1999) by Sa'id Hamid.
It presents the character of Yuda, an Arabic speaking Israeli. He tries to
hamper the Egyptian hero's steep ascent from marginalized immigrant to
successful hotel employee to no avail. Hamam's success is coupled with his
insistence on his Egyptian identity, but also with his moral conviction, that
sets him in (friendly) opposition to the second lead of the film, Adriano,
played by Ahmad al-Saqqa whose career as an action film performer, starring later in *Mafia*, *Tito/Tito* (2004) and *The War of Italy/Harb Italya* (2005),
was initiated with this film.

    Adriano is introduced as an Egyptian Christian. He is the one who
accommodates Hamam when the latter, in a scene reminiscent of *Hello
America*, has left his familiar crowded Cairo alley to be thrown into the
street by an inhospitable Egyptian uncle. Riding a motorcycle, wearing the
obligatory leather suit, and always seen in the company of his Dutch girlfriend, Adriano is characterized as strongly Westernized. On top of this, his
eventual entanglement with organized crime leads him to a violent confrontation with his adversaries including near-fatal car chase. All this makes
him embody the young immigrant whose absence from home has led him
astray. The same motif is also used as a starter for the conspiracy of *Mafia*.
Here al-Saqqa gets stranded in an undefined Western country (actually shot
in South Africa), falls prey to a sinister gang, and is eventually used by the
Egyptian state security as a special agent to prevent a foreign-planned terrorist attack in Egypt, later revealed as an Israeli plot.

    Adriano and Hamam's alliance in *Hamam in Amsterdam* starts with a
highly expressive verbal exchange and remains unchallenged throughout the

whole film also vis-à-vis the Jew. The insistence on this kind of triangular constellation at the representational level demarcates the borders of national in- and ex-clusions, expelling the Jew while insisting on Christian-Muslim fraternization, as the film seeks also to underline in its dialogue. In one instance Hamam starts a conversation by telling Adriano to praise the Prophet *(salli 'ala al-nabi)*, but then pauses and notices the big cross dangling from a chain around Adriano's neck. The latter follows his gaze, smiles when he realizes the reason, and says,

"O God, praise him *(Allahhuma salli 'alayh)*."

Hamam replies with the beginning of a traditional verse, "'Issa [Jesus] is a prophet."

Adriano continues, "Moses is a prophet."

Hamam: "Whoever has a prophet . . ."

Adriano: ". . . shall praise him."

At the same time Hamam is placed in a strongly pan-Arab context. At work he makes friends with a North African colleague who agrees to marry him at the end of the film. The accommodation Adriano finds for him, a flat shared by several immigrants, houses among others a Lebanese and an Upper Egyptian. On one occasion the flow of action pauses with the men standing in front of a large photograph stuck to the wall of their living room depicting the Dome of the Rock in Jerusalem, while the film score launches into an emotional song about how the "unity of homelands will wipe away all differences; it suffices to be a human." It is most telling that this unity excludes the Jew but explicitly includes the Christian Adriano.

Tellingly, in *Hamam in Amsterdam* the internal national appeasement, that is, the alliance with the Egyptian Christian as well as the loyalty displayed between different immigrants from the Arab world—is coupled with the direct confrontation with an Israeli. Yuda, a colleague at the Dutch Hotel in which Hamam eventually finds work, is shown in constant opposition to the funny and sympathetic Egyptian. Yuda tries to discredit Hamam at every opportunity, leading eventually to Hamam's temporary dismissal from work. He continues to threaten Hamam's interests to the very end, trying to prevent

Ahmad al-Saqqa and Muhammad Hinidi in *Hamam in Amsterdam*, 1999

him from acquiring a restaurant at an auction by putting in a higher bid. In contrast, the Egyptian merely refuses to shake hands with him, explaining that he is going to befriend him only if peace prevails. He is unwilling to listen to Yuda's attempts to tell him about Anne Frank's fate (a famous Dutch-Jewish adolescent girl sent to the gas chambers by the Nazis). Moreover, after having been so strongly affected by his adversary's mean tricks, Hamam takes several opportunities to degrade and insult Yuda by slapping him or ordering cockroaches for his meal, because he is "just a worm."

In contrast Yuda shocks Hamam on their first encounter by describing a visit to 'our' (that is, Yuda's) pyramids, referring to a frequent claim that Jews consider themselves to have built the Pyramids, based on their alleged intentions to found a Greater Israel extending from the Euphrates to the Nile. This spatial reference is not unintentional as it alludes to the territorial and geographic aspect of the Egyptian–Israeli conflict, completing on the symbolic level the final extraction of the Jew from the national body. Yet we need to ask why it is in these emigration narratives that allusions to Egypt's internal and external Other recur so often.

I would assume that what necessitates this resurgence of the encounter with the internal Other is the moment of liminal uncertainty caused by globalization, for as Homi Bhabha says, the "paranoid projections 'outwards' return to haunt and split the place from which they are made. So long as a firm boundary is maintained between the territories, and the narcissistic wounded is contained, the aggressivity will be projected onto the Other or the Outside" (Bhabha 1990, 300). Thus it is the prospect (or should we say the fear) of a possible global interaction that asks, at the very moment when it puts national borders at stake on the imaginary level, for a reaffirmation of the self vis-à-vis the internal Other.

Examining the new wave of Egyptian popular films that go global, and comparing them with other films that remain 'local,' as stated earlier, no recognizable shift or difference in the construction of the familiar and foreign space/time unit can be found. This convergence of inside and outside is underscored by other elements: not only are foreigners mostly played by Egyptian performers, but also most of the secondary characters themselves are not an integral part of the host land, but family members who emigrated long ago or characters who originate from other Arab countries. It is they who are made to represent the negative aspect of Western culture, in the case of *Hamam in Amsterdam* for example or *Hello America*, thereby familiarizing the Other's space (or reducing its threat?) while at the same time exporting the confrontation with the internal Other, be they the Islamist, the Copt, or the Jew.

Thus it seems that those films, despite the choice of their location and the fact that their protagonists depart for new shores, never reach from the national to the '*inter*-national' state, in the sense of Frantz Fanon's paradoxical statement: "National consciousness, which is not nationalism, is the only thing that will give us an international dimension" (Fanon as quoted in Bhabha 1990, 4). Instead the Egyptian works in question remain loyal to national(ist) strategies of difference and exclusion, achieved (among other means) through overt stereotyping of the so-called Other with which the real encounter and *inter*-relatedness can largely be prevented.

CHAPTER 2

The Allegorical Nation

The Fe-male Nation

Having undertaken the cinematic examination of the 'terror of the space or race of the Other' in correlation with modern nation formation, it still is necessary to take a look at narratives with an overt and explicit sense of 'nationness' as expressed through anti- and postcolonial allegories. In the 1980s Frederic Jameson had proposed to understand the relation of nation and narration through the device of the allegory, particularly in the Third World context, an allegory clearly distinct from unequivocal symbolism though: "If allegory has once again become somehow congenial for us today, as over against the massive and monumental unifications of an older symbolism or even realism itself, it is because the allegorical spirit is profoundly discontinuous, a matter of breaks and heterogeneities, of the multiple polysemia of the dream rather than the homogenous representation of the symbol" (Jameson 1986, 73). Jameson even went so far as to suggest reading postcolonial narratives in general as allegories of the nation, for "the telling of the individual story and the individual experience cannot but ultimately involve the whole telling of the collectivity itself" (Jameson 1986, 85–86), or to put it differently "the story of the private individual destiny is always an allegory of the embattled situation of the public third-world culture and society" (Jameson 1986, 69).

Subsequently Jameson's view has been contested as a "hasty totalization," because it was "impossible to posit any single artistic strategy as uniquely appropriate to the cultural productions of an entity as heterogeneous as the 'Third World'" (Shohat and Stam 1994, 271). Ella Shohat and Robert Stam have thus pointed out that the "allegorical tendency available to all art becomes exaggerated in the case of repressive regimes, perhaps, especially where intellectual filmmakers, profoundly shaped by nationalist discourse, feel obliged to speak for and about the nation as a whole" (Shohat and Stam 1994, 272). In their contemplation of mass-mediated Eurocentrism and Third World responses to it they first of all singled out "allegories of impotence" as one type of the (exaggerated) allegories that have been expressed by the formerly (or still) colonized. In the case of popular Egyptian cinema, too, it would certainly be futile to read every film narrative in relation to the nation, for the detection of allegories alone would be insufficient, regarding the varied and multi-layered forms through which meaning gets constructed.

In the following I have therefore preferred to focus first on 'exaggerated' national allegories and on cases where the image of the nation oscillates between metaphors of male and female, domination and subjugation, offense and defense. Interestingly, as we saw earlier, the narrative attempts at singling out those who are on the margins of the nation, those who may or may not be admitted to its body, or briefly the Other, are largely imagined as being male. In other words, the encounter with the external and internal Other has been pictured usually as a male affair, signaling that the nation is to be defended by men from men or opened up for men by men, thereby coding the nation indirectly as female. In contrast, narratives which picture the encounter with Europeans or the Western Other are more likely to imagine them, as can be seen in the quite recent *The Danish Experiment/al-Tagruba al-danimarkiya* (2003) by 'Ali Idris or in *Love in Taba/al-Hubb fi Taba* (1992) by Hisham 'Abd al-Hamid, as female herewith indirectly re-coding the Egyptian nation as male. This has been a quite consistent feature since the first Egyptian film *Awakening of the Conscience/Wakhz al-damir* (1931) by Ibrahim Lama, which featured a treacherous European wife almost destroying her Egyptian husband's family.

In the more recent *Love in Taba* and *The Danish Experiment*, it is seductive Western women (complemented by a female Israeli in the case of *Love in Taba*) who lure Egyptian men into disastrous sexual relationships. Read allegorically, *The Danish Experiment*, for instance, presents the European woman as a source of national 'division,' something that is also underlined by linguistic usage. In Arab political rhetoric, social unrest that threatens national unity is commonly dubbed *al-fitna*, that is, *al-fitna al-ta'ifiya* (confessional division). In traditional Arab literature the same term was also used to describe 'chaos' provoked by female sexuality, a connotation the film plot of *The Danish Experiment* uses extensively to get its national allegory going.

The film, considered a comeback for senior comedian 'Adil Imam ('Abd al-Fattah 2003, 46), featured him in the role of a father of four adult sons who gets nominated Youth Minister. In this position he has to receive a foreign guest, Anita Gutenberg from Denmark, a self-declared 'sex prophet' and holder of a Ph.D. in 'sexology' who wants to improve Middle Eastern sex education. Questioned on the curriculum of her studies, she states that the "first year teaches ninety positions." Yet it is not Anita's profession but rather her seductive Barbie-like appearance, blue eyes, and long blonde hair and a lot of revealing dresses that prove a source of chaos in the minister's household. An echo of this appears in the film's title: read with a slightly different vocalization it bears in classical Arabic a second meaning, namely *tajriba* (temptation) instead of *tajruba* (experience, experiment).

Indeed it turns out that not only his four unmarried sons but the minister, too, is seduced by Anita's appearance. This is made visible in a highly voyeuristic scene in which she sunbathes in the minister's garden in her bikini as men hang like apes from neighboring trees to catch a glimpse of her body. "You cannot do this in Egypt, it's an Eastern country," the minister desperately explains. However, instead of replying, she hands her sun block over to him and points to her naked shoulder. The minister is unable to resist and rubs her with the cream, an occasion to show several closeups of his hands caressing her lower back. At the end, it is the minister who wins Anita's heart even though his much more attractive sons have fallen earlier for her sex appeal. He decides eventually to enjoy his life, quits his job, and plans to leave with her to Europe. However, at the very last instant at the airport, when his sons gather to bid him farewell, he realizes his mistake: "I love my sons. I love Egypt." The final shot of the film depicts him coming up a hill with his four sons, their wives, and his grandchildren, emphasizing that Anita has not succeeded in planting the seeds of *fitna* between the members of the Egyptian family, father and children.

The constant reference to Eastern values in the face of this European female's seduction is not incidental, as the film certainly desires to be understood as a cultural and political allegory of the East–West encounter, yet it does so in a highly spectacular way with little by way of narrative. Love stories between eastern men and occidental women as a device through which

'Adil Imam in *The Danish Experiment*, 2003

to discuss the problematic of cultural difference have a long history, not only in popular local cinema but also in modern Arabic literature, where examples abound as Rotraud Wielandt has demonstrated (1980). Commonly, the issues of modernity, acculturation, and at times moral values were brought up in these kinds of narratives, to mention only the most famous literary example, the Sudanese *Season of Migration to the North/Mawsim al-hijra ila al-shamal* (published in 1969, not adapted for the screen), some of which have also found their way to Egyptian film, like *The Lamp of Umm Hashim/Qandil Umm Hashim*, which was adapted for the screen in 1968. In contrast *The Danish Experiment* touches only superficially upon this issue. In a number of highly artificial scenes it is much more concerned with exposing the physical assets of its European heroine at the expense of more serious character traits or narrative situations. All this is backed by a strongly stylized farce-oriented *mise-en-scène* and performance. The exclusive coding of woman as the embodiement of sexuality finds its explanation at first in the binary stereotype of a morally restrictive East versus an absolutely permissive West.

Imagining the Egyptian nation (or self) as male in the face of a female West can certainly unfold an "empowering" effect if understood in Bill Nichols' sense, namely as "wish-fulfillment." How this wish or desire may get pushed to its limits, and what effort it takes to maintain a male self in the face of a powerful foreign military threat to and presence in the region, engenders a kind of popular allegory of impotence that was vividly put into action in the black comedy *The Night Baghdad Fell/Laylat suqut Baghdad* (2006) by Muhammad Amin (who also authored the script). Inspired by the recent U.S. invasion of Iraq, the plot presents in a highly ironic twist the 'American threat' as an all-sexual metaphor of mutual penetration. It revolves around a schoolmaster who believes that after the fall of Baghdad, Egypt is under immediate threat of occupation by U.S. forces. As his country's leadership is obviously unwilling or incapable to act, he decides to invest his own money in Tariq, a student of supposed genius, with the aim of developing an effective defensive weapon.

Tariq, ugly, lean, and unfocused swears to sacrifice all his efforts and even his 'desires' for the mission. Yet, despite new comfortable accommodation and all the necessary equipment, his drug addiction and sexual deprivation prevent him from making headway. When the schoolmaster attempts to settle the matter by wedding Tariq to his patriotic daughter (she agrees only for the sake of Egypt!) he turns out to be unable to perform in bed. His impotency is traced back by a psychiatrist to his fear of the coming American invasion. His young wife eventually finds the cure by disguising herself as a GI, thus inciting his sexual aggression and even igniting his creativity to develop a defense weapon. At this point the CIA intervenes and tries to bribe the schoolmaster and his protégé. As the two refuse to cooperate they are declared insane and hospitalized. In a final climax the film shows the American army smashing the gate of Tariq's and the schoolmaster's hospital, as they in turn are joined by their family and friends using the young man's weapon for resistance.

The film, with its highly comic *mise-en-scène*, and its uncountable sexual allusions and *doubles-entendres* is keen to expose Egyptian technological 'backwardness' and military vulnerability (represented metaphorically by male sexual impotence) on the one hand, but calls for patriotic resistance on the other. The codification of U.S. military aggression as a sexual assault is, last but not least, achieved by allusions to the abuses in the Iraqi Abu Ghraib prison and by the staging of one of the most widely circulated stills—the American female soldier pointing her hands in a gun-like gesture toward the lower parts of naked Arab prisoners—culminating later in the rape of the schoolmaster's daughter through a nightmare experienced by her father. This is also reinforced on the verbal level: when the schoolmaster fails to secure the support of an important businessman and the development of the invention seems stalled, he orders his family and friends to kneel down in front of cardboard GIs they were using earlier for military training and to beg in English, "Please don't fuck me, please don't fuck me!"

Thus the work regenerates and mobilizes an all-too-familiar gendered national iconography at the moment of national crisis, namely that of the

The Night Baghdad Fell, 2006. The nightmare of Abu Ghraib.

raped nation. In the face of the symbolic military threat of a U.S. invasion the young man loses his sexual power, which his wife can only reanimate by applying a trick and inciting his self-defense and 'savior' instinct. Being able to penetrate the U.S. soldier (his wife in disguise), he is eventually able to assume his masculinity, a masculinity that is as much as the image of the raped nation built on Fatima Mernissi's 'explicit' gender model of the dominant male opposed to the subjugated female. On the political level *The Night Baghdad Fell* doubtless reads very overtly as an allegory of impotence of a subordinated people in the face of a dominant imperial power, an impotence that the film text struggles hard to overcome and transgress. Such a struggle, even though in a much more sublime manner, has also been visible in numerous male resistance figures fighting for independence, to name only the most known examples, *Land of Peace* (1957) and *A Man in Our Home/Fi baytina rajul* (1961). The sacrificial attitude of these characters was likewise mirrored in the woman-in-service-of-the-nation image as will be described later.

Indeed the metaphor of the raped nation must be considered one of the most pivotal representations of national allegories during decolonization, like the spectacle *Layla, the Bedouin/Layla al-badawiya* (produced in 1937 and released in 1944 under the title *Layla, Daughter of the Desert/Layla bint al-sahra'*) by Bahiga Hafiz who also played the female heroine Layla, the beautiful daughter of an Arab tribe's leader. In secret she admires one of her male cousins but is captured instead by the soldiers of the Persian king. Her refusal to become the king's concubine and a failed flight from the harem are met with physical torture and an attempted rape. Soon, however, the tribesmen led by her beloved cousin manage to rescue her from the hands of the tyrant king. Doubtless, the splendid and mighty Persian royal court in this context as opposed to the simplicity of the Arab tribes invites an allegorical nationalist reading that is further underlined by the film's finale. Here Layla, the courageous liberated Arab virgin, is carried on the shoulders of her kin as a symbol of liberty and cultural resurrection, recalling Delacroix's famous painting *La Liberté guidant le peuple* (1830) as well as the Marianne figure of the French Revolution. It is unclear whether French-educated Hafiz drew her allusion directly from the above-mentioned source or from local ideology. The fact is that nationalist iconography since the turn of the twentieth century has used, first the image of an ancient Egyptian queen, then the peasant woman, and occassionally the modern 'new' woman to represent the Egyptian nation (Baron 2005, 57), which was additionally linked to the rape of the nation motif.

The same motif was still reproduced almost forty years after *Layla, the Bedouin* in 'Ali Badrakhan's adaptation of the folktale *Shafiqa and Mitwalli/Shafiqa wa Mitwalli* (1978). In contrast to the literary original that focused primarily on the issue of female aberration and family honor, the cinematic adaptation of *Shafiqa and Mitwalli* made a much stronger political statement. In the tale, Mitwalli is conscripted from his village to help dig the Suez Canal, leaving behind his sister Shafiqa. She is soon forced to prostitute herself, and Mitwalli kills her upon his return. In the cinematic version the meaning shifts to the iconographic motif of the seduced/raped nation, for the film finale sees Shafiqa's upper-class slave trader and lover shooting Shafiqa before her brother can clear his reputation by doing the same.

Bahiga Hafiz in *Layla,*
,the Bedouin, 1937

As Beth Baron stated in her study, the rape allegory entered nationalist
anticolonial rhetoric in the wake of British assaults on Egyptian villages during the 1919 unrest, triggering the interrelated concept of family honor that
is to be defended through the struggle against occupation and colonial domination (Baron 2005, 45). This indicates that colonialism must have acted as
a pivotal catalyst for the transformation of women into the embodiment of
the nation. Indeed female passivity and weakness were made operational in
the fight against social underdevelopment, injustice, and political domination in other parts of the Arab world, not only on the Egyptian screen (cf.
Shafik 1998, 62).

One of the most widely circulated cinematic variations on the raped
nation allegory, namely that of the (female) nation under siege was presented
in Youssef Chahine's strongly political and highly fragmented film-narrative
The Sparrow/al-'Usfur (1971). Enriched with several parallel stories and
numerous subjective moments such as fantasies and nightmares, this
panoramic film introduces a group of friends who are all linked together

through their close relation to Bahiya, an elderly woman who hosts them and tries to lift their spirits whenever they feel depressed. The group comprises the journalist Yusuf, who traces the dealings of an arms mafia, as well as Shaykh Ahmad, a kind of leftist fundamentalist, Johnny a pessimistic drunkard, and Ra'uf, the fiancé of Bahiya's daughter, son of an important state official. They become united, first in helping the journalist with his investigation and second in their eventual common experience of a collective debacle.

In a scene reminiscent of the real events of June 9, 1967, the protagonists watch the 'President' make a momentous televised speech and feel shocked by the quick and unexpected military defeat. This is in fact the film's most dramatic and pivotal moment. It uses real historical footage showing Nasser's sad face and strongly measured voice in his 1967 speech, incorporating the emotional quintessence of that specific historical era and reviving the emotional commitment to his personality on and off the screen. While the leader declares his resignation, Shaykh Ahmad sobs uncontrollably and Bahiya gets up and hurries out shouting, "No, we are going to fight, we are going to fight." Doors and windows open behind her through which people flood into the streets. In the background the corrupt official shouts into the phone, "Who are those people, if they are not ours, who are they?"

Bahiya's character is clearly metaphorical. She stands for 'Mother Egypt.' This allusion is further backed by the Shaykh Imam song that frames the film and starts with the lines *Masr yamma ya bahiya* ('Egypt, O mother beautiful'). The ending of *The Sparrow* evoked quite clearly the allegory of a female nation, a nation in this case that is not just in danger of losing its leader but which finds itself betrayed by the new class of functionaries. Unwilling to accept her own defeat, Bahiya asks her leader to stay on, insisting on her determination to fight. The call to arms inherent in this scene was the reason why Chahine's film was prohibited by Sadat's censor. For President Anwar al-Sadat (the new self-declared 'Father of the Nation' who came to power in 1970) wanted to conceal Egypt's future military intentions in order to take Israel by surprise and was not interested in any spontaneous war cry. Thus *The Sparrow* was only released in 1973 after the October War.

In tracing the iconographic genesis of the construction of the Egyptian nation as a woman, Beth Baron proposed that this representation developed in the course of the struggle for national independence was possibly facilitated by the coding of *Misr* (Egypt) in Arabic as a feminine noun; while on the other hand the formation of this particular iconography *(Egypt as a Woman)* was hampered on the visual level by the fact that most elite women did not expose their face in public until the 1920s (Baron 2005, 58). Furthermore Baron underlined that Egyptians did not develop a more abstract notion of Mother Egypt akin to Mother India, choosing instead to give certain women the role of 'Mother of Egyptians' in the course of the fight for national independence, such as Safiyya Zaghlul, the wife of the national leader Sa'd Zaghlul (Baron 2005, 78).

In any event, the coding of the Egyptian nation particularly before and in the immediate aftermath of national independence was predominantly female, as reflected in the melodramatic *Layla, the Bedouin.* This applies also to the postindependence female liberation narratives depicting women in the service of the nation, as well as modernist-oriented works that disseminate the motif of the mother as the Dark Continent, as we will see later. In general, when picturing the homeland as oppressed or threatened by occupation and assaults (rape) whether from the outside *(Layla, the Bedouin)* or from within *(The Karnak/al-Karnak)* the cinematic narration was more likely to focus on a woman; however, if the homeland was to be liberated or defended most probably a male hero would be installed, as in numerous post-independence national liberation narratives. Only during the 1990s did another version start to emerge, with the notable examples of Nadia al-Gindi's 1990s espionage films, where the heroine embodied, on behalf of her nation, both sexual vulnerability and the capability to fight back.

In general female-nation narratives such as *The Sparrow* the role of the threatened woman usually called for a man in the role of savior. This duality remained recurrent, particularly in correlation with the historical figure of Nasser as it was presented among others in *Nasser 56/Nasir 56* by Muhammad Fadil (1996). In a pivotal scene we see Nasser after the nationalization of the Suez Canal being visited by an old peasant woman all in black (Amina Rizq). Handing him the shroud of one of her male relatives who died during the digging of the Canal and whose body was never retrieved, she tells him that only now does she feel the 'honor' of the deceased reestablished and has no need to keep the shroud any longer. This particular image of Nasser as the 'son' of Egypt defending his maternal nation is reinforced by a number of misconnected phone calls by an old woman who wishes to speak to a relative but who always ends up on Nasser's personal phone, and eventually, when she is convinced that he is the president, gives him her blessing.

Incar-nation

Analyzing Nasser and his "actions within the links between leadership, charisma, power and ideas" (Hassouna 1990, 136), Moustafa El-Said Hassouna suggested that Nasser "incarnated the defeat as completely as he had incarnated the nation" (Hassouna 1990, 330). Notwithstanding this national setback, or *naksa* as the 1967 defeat was termed, his followers were still remembering his achievements, such as the nationalization of the Suez Canal, the land reform, the construction of the High Dam, running water and electricity in many villages, public schooling, and so on. Consequently, as expressed in *The Sparrow* many considered the Egyptian army defeated, but not the nation (Hassouna 1990, 344), a view that still reflects on the 1996 production *Nasser 56* starring Ahmad Zaki in the role of Nasser.

For a long time, the Egyptian film star Ahmad Zaki had cherished the dream to perform the roles of three extraordinary historical personalities: president Gamal 'Abdel Nasser, singer 'Abd al-Halim Hafiz, and president Anwar al-Sadat. Indeed the three form a highly iconic triad of recent Egyptian history and are closely linked to past national glories: Nasser had led the country into independence and successfully confronted the West with his anticolonial politics, while 'Abd al-Halim had sung to the glory of the new era representing a young modern generation grasping for a different life under a new revolutionary leadership. Sadat, the last in this succession, had turned the devastating defeat in 1967 into a national victory by challenging

Israel successfully in 1973, even though he eventually aligned himself with the former enemy by signing the Camp David Accords and by initiating the antisocialist Open Door policy that had a number of far-reaching and controversial social and economic consequences.

A fact that additionally strengthened this on- and off-screen bond was that Ahmad Zaki's own persona and offspring bears some resemblance to those he embodied in cinema. He not only originated from the same village in al-Sharqiya province as singer 'Abd al-Halim Hafiz, but like Nasser, he came from a modest middle-class rural Muslim background, and like Sadat his physical appearance looked more African than Arab. In fact, because of his dark skin and curly black hair Zaki was dubbed the Black Tiger (al-nimr al-aswad) after the title of one of his early popular films, directed by New Realist 'Atef El-Tayeb in 1984, in which he assumed the character of an Egyptian immigrant who attains fame in Germany due to his boxing talents and eventually—supported by his German wife Helga—installs himself successfully as a businessman.

Ahmad Zaki featured in quite a number of committed films by New Realist directors in the 1980s, often representing a deprived young urban male, but he also appeared in some highly popular films, such as the musical Crabs/Kaburya (1990) by former Realist Khairy Beshara. In this film, which included several musical numbers involving Zaki, he again featured as a young have-not who uses his boxing talent, this time as an entertainer for a prosperous couple bored by their own luxury, so that the boxer and his group of friends offer a welcome opportunity not only for entertainment but also some emotional adventures. The popularity of this film and its leading player may be measured by the fact that the special haircut Zaki had in it was soon copied by young urban, particularly lower-class men and became known as the kaburya haircut.

Eventually in 2005, Ahmad Zaki was able to realize his dream (at least in part, for he died of cancer during the shooting of 'Abd al-Halim's biopic). Before that, he had first adopted Nasser's personality in Nasser 56/Nasir 56 (1996) and four years later Anwar al-Sadat's in The Days of Sadat/Ayam

Ahmad Zaki in *Crabs*, 1990

al-Sadat by Mohamed Khan (2000). Apart from Zaki's personal interest, the timing of this wave of film biographies seems not necessarily accidental (it was complemented by another biopic directed by Muhammad Fadil the director of *Nasser 56* in the same decade and dedicated to the female national icon, 'star of the Orient' Umm Kulthum, who was also thoroughly linked to the Nasserist project). Some possible reasons could be the more visible interference of foreign powers in the region, beginning with the U.S. which had just undertaken its first military intervention in the Gulf, and also the continually desperate situation in Palestine.

Nasser On- and Off-screen

Colonel Gamal 'Abdel Nasser (1918–70), president of the first Egyptian Republic is one of those charismatic or quasi-charismatic leaders of the colonial and postcolonial era of the twentieth century, comparable to Ghandi, Sukarno, Castro, Peron, whose fame rose in the wake of their nation's independence and/or were intrinsically linked to the fight for national liberation. Nasser, like almost all of the 'Free Officers' (the movement responsible for toppling the Egyptian royal house in 1952) was of petit-bourgeois origin. He thus belonged to a newly admitted minority in the Egyptian army. Moreover, he witnessed the disastrous Palestine war personally in 1948 on the battlefield. The defective arms supposedly provided to the army by the Egyptian government were then later perceived as one of the direct reasons for the Free Officers' conspiracy and eventual coup against the *ancien régime*.

Upon the coup of July 23, 1952, Colonel Muhammad Naguib became the first president of the newly created republic. In 1954 he was replaced by Nasser who had been able to garner a stronger following. Nasser's message focused first of all on the revolution, implying social reform and fighting the corruption embodied by the monarchy and foreign domination. He did not, however, promote democracy but assumed authoritarian rule by dismantling political parties and imprisoning Muslim Brothers and communists. In the following years Nasser attained an immense popularity not only in Egypt but also in the whole Arab world to the extent that he became a symbol of non-alignment, pan-Arabism, and Arab socialism. This popularity was due to several achievements in the field of foreign policy: the Czech arms deal, the deconstruction of the Baghdad Pact, the nationalization of the Suez Canal, Egypt's liberation from Britain and France, and his success in withstanding the Eisenhower Doctrine which was heading to fill the colonial vacuum left behind by European colonial powers. All this brought together the masses of Egyptians and Arabs behind him (Hassouna 1990, 311).

However, during the mid-1960s conditions changed drastically. The merger of Syria and Egypt into the United Arab Republic was initiated in 1958 and failed in 1961. Moreover, Egypt's high political aspirations were undermined by its economic problems and turned against it. In particular, its military involvement in Yemen's war against U.S.-backed Saudi Arabian influence weakened Egypt to the extent that its military confrontation with Israel in June 1967 ended in disaster, with three quarters of Egypt's air force destroyed, 12,000 men left dead, and Sinai, the Golan Heights, Jerusalem, the West Bank, and Gaza occupied.

This event was a major blow to Arab and Egyptian self-confidence. As a response Nasser proclaimed his resignation on June 9, 1967, a move that was not accepted by the masses, who took to the streets and asked their *rayyis* ('chief') to stay. This and Nasser's funeral in 1970 when again millions bade him goodbye were taken as a clear sign of Nasser's charismatic personality, which had allowed him to embody the nation and preserved him a strong following in and outside Egypt despite his authoritarian rule and his more than evident failure to fulfill the hopes he had raised. According to one of his comrades, 'Ali Sabri, "by playing the historically decisive role of realizing earlier Arab hopes, he had in effect translated disembodied ideas into concrete realities, giving them in the process distinctive shape and specific form" (as quoted by Hassouna 1990, 341).

Moustafa Hassouna argues that Nasser's (actually disputed) charisma[15] developed primarily because he lived in a time of crisis, a crisis due to coercive external factors, such as colonialism and the strong need for social change that called for Nasser's self-proclaimed revolution. "Egypt, in the middle of the twentieth century, experienced certain factors that fermented a revolutionary atmosphere; the pressures of industrialization, the dislocations of the World War II coupled with the loss of the Palestine war [in 1948]. Thus to the majority of Egyptians revolution meant on the one hand, the negation of Egypt's colonial past and, on the other, promise of political community" (Hassouna 1990, 121).

Yet Nasser's image had only few mythical or, to be more precise, visual-symbolic aspects. Contrary to Indonesia's Sukarno for example, an intersection between him and a legendary figure is only marginally documented, primarily in cinema through Youssef Chahine's historical spectacle *Saladin Victorious* (1963). Apart from that, Raymond Baker once alluded in his political study to the Arab perception of "Nasser the new Saladin, savior of all Arabs" (Baker 1978, 39). Maybe he was influenced by Chahine's film, but it is almost certain that the Saladin allusion was not widely exploited or constantly repeated in the media.

In addition, the promotion of Nasser's ideas and his image during his lifetime was rather word-oriented. He had not only inherited an articulate scriptural propaganda machine traceable to the Fatimid and the al-Azhar universities that supplied libraries on five continents with books and pamphlets (Hassouna 1990, 248), but Egypt at that time published more newspapers and magazines than any other Arab country and Radio Cairo, Voice of the Arabs, and Voice of Islam reached out to the whole Arab world, disseminating every speech and action of Nasser. Starting from 1960 Egyptian television also played an increasingly important role as an official mouthpiece.

It is claimed that Nasser himself strongly rejected symbolic deification along with his visual representation. Even though his photographic image seemed everywhere, no statues of him are found and his face was never printed on postage stamps (Hassouna 1990, 313). In fact, with this rather scriptural orientation Nasser was much in line with Muslim iconoclasm and the traditional orthodox Sunni rejection of spiritual superhuman beings, such as priests and saints (though the latter were sought for and adored in practice nonetheless). This may be one of the reasons why Nasser's alignment with mythical figures and religious symbolism was so weak and why allegorical (and charismatic) interpretations of his persona remained rather absent from the silver screen during and long after his lifetime.

In view of such iconoclastic inclinations Youssef Chahine's Saladin film, produced in 1963 and equipped with clear allusions to Nasser, deserves an even more thorough analysis. Two years after the failure of the United Arab Republic it affirms Nasser's incarnation of the pan-Arab ideal through the allusion to a strong heroic figure from the Arab Muslim past, one of the first historical figures studied in Egyptian primary classes. By means of this confluence the film works out certain character traits ascribed to Nasser that would be reproduced in later cinematic representations.

The plot of *Saladin Victorious* (1963) was based on a screenplay developed by three acclaimed Egyptian novelists and scriptwriters, Naguib Mahfouz, Yusuf Siba'i, and Galal Sharqawi (along with the filmmaker 'Izz al-Din zu-l-Fiqar who was supposed to direct the film at first). It was coproduced by private producer Assia Daghir and the National Film Center due to its immense budget. It became one of the most remarkable historical movies of the Egyptian film history, thanks to Chahine's skill in handling fierce battle scenes, but also because of the careful set and costume design carried out by Wali al-Din Samih and Shadi Abdessalam.

However, the film was not accurate in describing the details of the Crusades but offered a rather apologetic nationalist statement, depicting the Kurdish warlord Salah al-Din al-Ayyubi as a pan-Arab national hero defeating the crusaders, not simply by means of his military skills but by his high moral standing, most notably his righteousness and wisdom. The comparison between Saladin and Nasser, the great leader who unites the Arabs to defeat the foe, while at the same time displaying magnanimity and religious tolerance, was persuasively made through the calm and thoughtful performance of the main actor, Ahmad Mazhar.

The allusion to the present time and especially to Nasser was achieved first of all on the linguistic level by using Nasser's family name *Nasir*, meaning 'victorious,' for the film's title. Contrary to Saladin's heroic

Ahmad Mazhar in *Saladin Victorious*, 1963

figure, the crusaders appear as a crude mixture of reckless and morally corrupt adventurers originating in different European countries, most notably
France and Britain. The latter are in the forefront of the confrontation.
Richard Lionheart in particular is singled out as the strongest adversary.
Whereas the different national affiliations of the crusaders are emphasized,
the Kurdish origin of Saladin is never alluded to. In contrast his Muslim
and Arab identity is underlined through dialog and action. Several character traits (which were ascribed to Nasser as well) are worked out:
simplicity in dress and personal comportment that strictly avoided any luxury, and magnanimity. In one scene where the crusaders, all dressed in
splendid robes, are awaiting Saladin, they mistake him for a messenger
because his dress does not differentiate him from his companions. In
another instance Saladin awaits Richard Lionheart on Arab soil, but on his
way Richard is wounded by the arrow of treacherous crusaders who want
to prevent the meeting and any consequent peaceful agreement. However,
the following night Saladin passes unrecognized into the crusaders' camp
in order to cure Lionheart personally and to convince him of Arab fairness
and good intentions.

The idea of national liberation is explicitly evoked through Saladin's
eventual success and his ability to persuade Lionheart to withdraw (just as
Nasser was able to press for British military withdrawal in 1955). With this
the film was able to draw clear parallels by building up the magnificence of
a legendary figure from the Muslim past and re-coding it to evoke a present
leader. This re-coding is clearly mythological, if we understand mythology
as an essentializing narrative that is emptied of history and filled with nature,
to take up one of Roland Barthes' ideas (cf. Shafik 1998, 176). Even though
Nasser is said to have resented his magnification or 'deification' by visual
and symbolic means, yet his peculiar relation to Egyptian cinema as such
was later used to underline another myth, namely Nasser the 'reluctant dictator' (cf. Hassouna 1990, 137).

In general, Nasser was as fond of going to movies as anyone of his
generation (and like other Free Officers—including Sadat, who is said to

have almost missed the coup d'état in July 1952 because he was attending a screening). Joel Gordon states in his book that both leaders were active cinemagoers, careful to attend the premieres of new feature films (Gordon 2002, 41). During Nasser's reign in 1959 the first national film school, the Higher Film Institute, was established. Its entrance was decorated with a huge photograph showing Nasser using a film camera, suggesting the leader's personal fascination with the medium. Nasser moreover approved the nationalization of Egyptian film studios and movie theaters and the foundation of a public film sector, even though this nationalization came quite late—in 1963—in comparison with others.

Egyptian film historiographers like 'Ali Abu Shadi (Abou Chadi) have reproduced a number of stories in this context, telling of the first premiering of a film Nasser attended in his capacity as head of state. The work in question was *God Is With Us/Allahu ma'na* (1955) by Ahmad Badrakhan, a film that had been withheld until then by censorship but was released upon Nasser's personal orders (Abu Shadi 1998, 170). It featured an officer who had lost an arm and numerous friends in the Palestine war of 1948 because of the defective weapons issued to them. Back home the injured man investigates the case in order to win redress, but is soon to discover that the whole political elite bears responsibility. The reason why *God Is With Us* was prohibited—despite the fact that it laid the blame on the deposed monarch for the loss of the war—was trivial: one of the officers depicted in the film resembled Colonel Naguib, who had just been replaced by Nasser. It is said that when the president in power learned about the film he watched it and subsequently ordered its release (Abu Shadi 1998, 170).

In 1955, the year when *God Is With Us* was screened, the revolutionary government issued a new censorship law annuling some of the restrictions of the pre-1952 situation, where it was prohibited by law not only to depict the social situation as hopeless, but to represent features of a political struggle at all (Shafik 1998, 34, 132).

It also declared the new law's objectives: "to protect public morals, to preserve security, public order and the superior interests of the state"

(Lüders 1988, 227), formulations open to individual interpretation and arbitrary abuse. The new government's anti-imperialist and anti-Zionist stance led to the prohibition of dozens of foreign 'Zionist' films, even though censorship was relatively permissive regarding foreign art films. Many provocative films, such as some of Pasolini's and Fellini's works, passed the censor. At the same time, censors were oversensitive to any depiction of the system and its leader even if it was highly allegorical or unintentional, as happened to filmmaker Tawfiq Salih in the 1960s with his film *The Rebels/al-Mutamarridun* (1966), which was banned temporarily even though he claims to have always backed Nasser and his ideas (Lüders 1988, 143). His film pictured a rebellion in a desert sanatorium aborted by human failure and corruption and was therefore read as a negative comment on the July revolution.

What seems crucial in this context is that Nasser's interference in film releases has not been interpreted or read in terms of arbitrary and individual authoritarian rule but was portrayed rather as generosity and fairness, as the case of another prohibited film suggests. *Something Frightening/Shay'un min al-khawf* (1969) by Hussein Kamal produced by the Public Film Organization was set in an Egyptian village dominated by a criminal gang. Oppression mounts as the village beauty Fu'ada is kidnapped and forced to marry 'Atris, the head of the gang. Two years after the 1967 debacle the film was banned by the censors as an allegory of Nasserist rule taking Egypt by force. But the president interfered, saving the film without even a cut. According to 'Ali Abu Shadi, after watching the work the president asked the censor if he considered his government a gang and Nasser its leader. The censor denied both. Nasser then replied, "if we were like that we really would deserve to be burnt," alluding to the violent end of the gangsters in the film (Abu Shadi 1998, 171). This anecdote (cited by Abu Shadi without any reference to its source) again suggests Nasser's magnanimity. By being more liberal than his subordinates—something that is clearly belied by the restrictive measures of his regime since 1954—he could easily be stylized into a 'reluctant dictator.'

Postmortem Charisma

Even if we assume that films like *The Rebels* or *Something Frightening* did not allude to Nasser personally or did not have his political system in mind, by 1967 the failure of Nasser's ideas as well as his policy had become clear. While some true believers still perceived him as having built an egalitarian society, harsh critics blamed him for having wrecked the once prosperous Egyptian economy and replaced a 'liberal' monarchy with a dictatorship and enabled the formation of a corrupt state bourgeoisie largely composed of technocrats and army officers.

This schism was clearly reflected in Egyptian films. It was Chahine with a script written by Lutfi al-Khuly who first tried to rescue Nasser's image from beneath the rubble by underlining his tragic heroism in *The Sparrow* (1971). However, not everyone was sympathetic to Nasser's legacy. Other films, such as *Miramar*, *Adrift on the Nile/Tharthara fawq al-Nil* (1971), *The Process 68/al-Qadiya 68* (1968), *Visitor at Dawn/Za'ir al-fajr* (1973), and *The Karnak*, some of which had been temporarily banned under Nasser, drew a more or less ferocious picture of conditions under Nasser. *Miramar* (1969) by Kamal El-Cheikh, which was only released after Nasser's death in 1970, and Salah Abu Seif's *The Process 68* criticized the revolution and its party, the Arab Socialist Union, through negatively depicted film characters. But whereas *Miramar,* and Hussein Kamal's *Adrift on the Nile*, the former scripted and the latter adapted from a text by Naguib Mahfouz, focused on the inner corruption of Egypt's intellectual and political elite, *Visitor at Dawn* by Mamduh Shukri (released in 1975) and *The Karnak* (1975) depicted the abusive side of the regime. In particular *The Karnak* (1975) by 'Ali Badrakhan went so far to associate the past regime with torture and rape by telling the story of a politically active student couple who are seized by the state security forces in an attempt at brainwashing.

In *The Karnak* the portrait of Nasser that decorates the walls of the protagonist's home later witnesses her rape at the hands of his state security. Some non-Egyptian productions made the portrait embody the positive side of Nasserism, alluding to the most important ideas Nasser stood for, such as

Su'ad Husni in *The Karnak*, 1975. State security raping the heroine.

pan-Arabism and the notions of *israr* (persistence) and *karama* (dignity) that were of utmost importance to Nasser's rhetoric (cf. Hassouna 1990, 340). Examples abound particularly in some *auteur*-films of 'new Arab cinema,' to name only *Kafr Kassem/Kafr Qasim* (1974), directed by Lebanese, Borhane Alaouié and *Dreams of the City/Ahlam al-madina* (1984) by the Syrian, Muhammad Malas.

These positive values shine also through two recent cinematic Nasser biographies, *Gamal 'Abdel Nasser/Jamal 'Abd al-Nasir* (1998), and *Nasser 56* (1996) by Muhammad Fadil, a major box-office hit and widely distributed in other Arab countries. Based on thorough research the latter recounted the detailed chronology of the events that lead to the nationalization of the Suez Canal in 1956. With its sympathetic depiction of Nasser's character and the strong focus on his subjective views it reflected a call for positive uncritical identification with his character. Ahmad Zaki's naturalist performance and immense popularity certainly added to the credibility of the representation and increased the sympathy for the character he portrayed. As in *The Days of Sadat* Ahmad Zaki tried in this film to imitate the expressions, mannersims, and voice of the late leader. This insistence on an almost documentary faithfulness to reality, that is, its *real*-ization of the subject, was further enhanced by the film's balanced *mise-en-scène* and its use of high contrast black and white photography that facilitated the insertion of archival footage. The script, too, was eager to depict Nasser as people loved him to be, a truly sober, uncorrupted man, who lives with his wife and children in a modest villa, a workaholic who cares only for the needs of his country, but who is nevertheless often seen in the film with a loving wife and well-behaved children.

Nasser 56 excluded the experience of the defeat entirely in focusing on a decisive moment in the life of Nasser and Egypt as a whole: the year 1956, when he reached the peak of his political career and popularity because of the nationalization of the Suez Canal and the pan-Arab and anticolonial euphoria this caused in the rest of the Arab world. The plot starts with the leader's attempt to fight back after he has learned of the refusal of the World Bank to finance the construction of the Aswan High Dam, which was planned not only to control irrigation but also to provide the country's main electricity supply—a refusal the film interprets as an attempt to hamper the country's economic growth and industrialization.

Subsequent events offer a detailed account of Nasser's clandestine plan to nationalize the Suez Canal, run by France and Britain. At first a senior Egyptian canal engineer is summoned to Cairo—in the middle of the night and still in his pajamas—to cooperate on the plan, which is successfully executed, after several sleepless nights. The film ends with the immediate results of this success: cheering masses on the one hand and, on the other, the bombs of the tripartite attack by France, Britain, and Israel falling on Egyptian soil. It is particularly this ending which has caused an American reviewer to wonder, "Why the story should end before peace was restored (by the U.S. working through the UN) is a mystery, though a sequel could be on its way."[16]

In fact, there was no sequel on its way, and the choice of ending is not such a mystery. Dramatic 'lapses' or unresolved endings are not necessarily unplanned but may be indicators of a possible implied meaning. Indeed, the film concludes with a highly telling image, a moment of utmost challenge and danger matched with a strong insistence on national defense and persistence. It is most probable that Egyptian television (ERTU—Egyptian Radio and Television Union), the producer of the film that had it released first in cinemas, sensed a need for this kind of allegorical representation. And they were not proven wrong, for Fadil's adaptation was received enthusiastically and turned out to be very successful at the box office in and outside Egypt, a fact that was certainly not only due to the popularity of its leading player, Ahmad Zaki.

Interestingly, only two years later, to be precise on September 28, 1998, the twenty-eighth anniversary of Nasser's death, another film biography followed, *Gamal 'Abdel Nasser* directed by Anwar al-Qawadri, a Syrian filmmaker, starring a relatively unknown Egyptian actor (but with a stronger physical resemblance to Nasser) in the title role. In contrast, this film biography did not focus on the most pivotal period but reenacted the late leader's

Ahmad Zaki in *Nasser 56*, 1996

life chronologically, starting with the Palestine war in 1948 and ending with his sudden death in 1970. While *Nasser 56* was praised as a good historical drama that "concentrated on character, and how Nasser's character shaped his approach to historical events" (Darwish 1999, 47), *Gamal 'Abdel Nasser* enjoyed little popularity and was, according to a Middle East reporter, "roundly rejected by critics and historians alike" for "dangerously rewriting history" (Darwish 1999, 45). In addition, it was criticized for engendering "personality cult propaganda of the worst kind" (Darwish 1999, 47). The magazine's criticism of this aspect of *Gamal 'Abdel Nasser* seems a little disingenuous, given that *Nasser 56* was hardly a demystifying film, but just as eager to cinematically reconstruct a legendary Nasser.

More than al-Qawadri's comprehensive Nasser-portrayal, *Nasser 56* concentrated almost exclusively on those historical events that made Egyptians and Arabs sculpt Nasser into a savior from colonial oppression and a representative of lost historical greatness. *Nasser 56* conferred on its protagonist exactly those attributes ascribed to Nasser in *Saladin Victorious*: his uncorrupted simplicity in dress and personal comportment, his class loyalty, his relentlessly unselfish pursuit of national interests, his boldness in the face of political pressures and dangers, and his ability to concert and successfully plan political conspiracy and action. In sum, the film evoked the image of cheering masses in response to Nasser's accomplishments. Even the fact that Egypt was saved from further damage and fresh occupation in 1956 only because of UN and Soviet interference was omitted in the film. So was the fact that in exactly that period the regime laid the foundation of its authoritarian rule, whose effects still plague Egyptian society until today.

All this may be seen as a clear indication that *Nasser 56* not only 'mystified' Nasser but also revived the identification of his persona with the nation. The reasons may be personal: like most film stars, Ahmad Zaki was interested in representing strong, positive heroes. Also the director Muhammad Fadil belongs to an older generation, educated during the Nasserist period; and he has proven social commitment in some of his other television films, such as *Climbing the Palm Tree/Tali' al-nakhl* (1986) for instance. The fact, however, that *Nasser 56* was followed by the Syrian-directed *Gamal 'Abdel Nasser* seems to indicate a certain need in the 1990s to revive the image of a strong unvanquished nation, represented through a leader who was willing to boldly face some of the malaise of his country and of the whole Arab world. A deep sense of crisis has the region in its grip, due to constant setbacks in the Palestinian question and the increasing neo-colonial domination of the Middle East, after the first U.S. intervention in the Gulf region along with globalization that has in fact reduced the accomplishments of the Nasserist period almost to nil. Considering all this, the attempt to rein-voke the Nasserist glory is understandable; even though it seems little more than a compensatory escape from the pressures of reality into a sense of uncontested national identity and unity.

In its essence Nasser's cinematic image got constructed through the explicit insistence on difference between self and other, nation and colonial power, male and female, galvanizing moments of defense and offense at the same time. Yet more implicit allegories of the nation got created through other forms of 'difference,' namely through polarizing social and geographic spaces, spatial passages, or social ascent stories. In them, as we saw earlier, male heroism becomes coded as the sign of either progress or persistence of the nation particularly in the more globalized context while simultaneously including or excluding of Egypt's internal Others, most notably religious and ethnic minorities, Jews, Copts, and Nubians.

PART 2

Gender

CHAPTER 3

Feminism and Femininity

I n general the status of women and the issue of gender inequality have been among the most negotiated and controversial questions relating to modern Arab-Muslim culture. Since the late nineteenth century they have become an integral part of many either competing or complementary ideological discourses spreading in the Arab world in general and in Egypt in particular. Numerous informed studies have been published during the last decade dealing with the situation of women in the region on the one hand while reviewing the history of feminist development and thinking on the other. Some of them, such as Leila Ahmed's groundbreaking *Women and Gender in Islam*, Valentine Moghadam's *Gender and National Identity*, and Lila Abu-Lughod's *Remaking Women* have introduced critical and deconstructive notions, not only to gender problematic as such but also to detach the discussion of feminism from its original Eurocentric orientation.

Thus, strongly concerned with Western and local discourses that have defined and interfered with women's issues, the main achievement of these publications was to deconstruct the modernist approach to gender, placing it in its proper historical, or to be more precise, into its colonial setting while at the same time unveiling its affinity to contemporary Islamist thinking.

Reviewing and comparing Islamist and modernist discourses they were able to work out their common undercurrent, often heavily gendered antagonization of East and West, progress and underdevelopment, acculturation and traditionality. This kind of critical approach has however not found its way so far into any studies on Egyptian cinema.

It has even to be admitted that only a very limited number of academic studies has been published on women and Egyptian cinema. The most widespread and representative works are not academic but descriptive historical accounts, largely based on textual analysis that do not take up (Western) film theory in general and feminist film theory in particular. This becomes clear when discussing the most prominent examples. First Samir Farid published in 1984 an article, *Surat al-mar'a fi-l-sinima al-'arabiya* ('The Image of the Woman in Arab Movies'), tracing the activity and presence of women directors, producers, and actresses in early Egyptian cinema. In a subsequent study for the United Nations carrying the same title, "The Image of Woman in Arab Movies" (1985), he attempted to analyze the representation of women. In a kind of swift cross-cut through Arab film history he summarized quite descriptively female models and themes discussed in relation to women. He did not, however, discuss or relate to any major film theoretical approaches, not to speak of feminist film theory. The more recent publication by Mahmud Qasim carrying the vague title *al-Mar'a fi-l-sinima* ('The Woman in Cinema,' 1998) has remained even more descriptive; like "The Image of Woman in Arab Movies," this book has been informed by quasi-sociological forms of analysis. The author has concentrated on the textual level in exclusively discussing (stereo)typical character traits of mainstream cinema's heroines.

A profoundly academic study was in contrast Mona Hadidi's doctoral thesis, "Dirasa tahliliya li-surat al-mar'a al-misriya fi-l-film al-misri" ('An Analytical Study of the Image of the Egyptian Woman in Egyptian Cinema') presented in 1977, which was followed in 1986 by Safiyya Magdi's similar study "Surat al-mar'a fi-l-sinima al-misriya" ('The Image of the Egyptian Woman in Egyptian Cinema'). Eventually in 2003 a comparable work appeared—Ihsan al-Sayyid's "Surat al-mar'a al-misriya fi sinima al-tis'iniyat" ('The Image of the Egyptian Woman in the Cinema of the 1990s'), which covered all crucial films made in the 1990s, but ignored recent developments in international feminist film theory. All three studies followed the same trend of early feminist film criticism that concentrated mainly on the stereotypes with which women were represented in the media (cf. Hollows 2000, 20). The shortcomings of this, in comparison to today's theoretical approaches, is apparent, particularly in al-Hadidi's case: despite a consistent methodology and at first sight convincing results, the application of sociological methodology to film characters generates a reductionist equation that leads to confusion between representation and reality. As Joanne Hollows remarks, "these problems with 'the images of women' research are also related to the problems with content analysis which concentrated on '*what* the media showed' rather than '*how* they produced meaning'" (Hollows 2000, 23).

One way to stick to the 'how' in the production of meaning is to examine sexual difference as it shapes and is expressed through various popular film genres, such as melodrama, thriller, action film, and involved star personae (see Chapter 4); and second—bearing in mind the critical objections and qualifications of the earlier mentioned sociopolitical contributions—to read against the grain of earlier textual analyses. In other words I will look at the rhetoric of films that deal explicitly with the women's question in order to reevaluate the feminist legacy of 'committed cinema,' particularly those films that explicitly raise the question of gender inequality, and to compare them with negotiations of femininity undertaken in works authored by women, be they directors or actresses. In fact, these films that stem from different historical periods are not as coherently feminist as their earlier labeling suggests. To investigate how and to what extent they have uttered feminist concerns may enable us, first, to understand some of the current discourses and concerns and, second, to detect whether there is a proper feminist film or even a genuine *sinima al-mar'a* (women's film) as proposed by some Arab researchers like Gene al-Muqadasi (2001).

Advocating Female Labor

Feminism and femininity were first polarized through the idea of female labor. The Nasserist period brought about a distinct, though not really dominant, politically committed cinema that voiced nationalist, socialist, and also feminist interests, in often contradictory ways. The most acknowledged realist directors were the most active in adhering to this agenda. Yet, except for Salah Abu Seif who did present explicitly 'feminist' topics, it was mainstream directors, to name most prominently Henri Barakat and Fatin 'Abd al-Wahab, who took up the issue more frequently. The first was known for his excellent melodramas and musicals, and the second directed some of the most popular and well-made comedies of the period. And even Abu Seif, like others, authored a large corpus of mainstream productions along with a number of 'realist works.'

These more outspoken 'feminist' films advocated quite explicitly female education and professionalization, rejecting seclusion and ignorance while juxtaposing these binarisms to a nationalist framework in which female liberation was regarded as operative in achieving national independence and economic progress. Accordingly, in most of the narratives, women's liberation was only occasionally discussed in terms of individual independence and self-determination. Moreover, the vision of femininity and female liberation that leaked through these 'feminist works' did not essentially qualify religious and patriarchal moralism. Even though most of these films did not bar transgressive cinematic pleasure, they tended to exclude polysemic female identities at the same time. Motherhood, particularly, was constructed as the antithesis of the educated working woman. No wonder that some narratives even ventilated male anxieties particularly with respect to questions of female labor and independence.

This is not to say that women's labor and independence were not discussed before 1952. Yet they still did not carry any explicit 'feminist' superstructure. *The Lady's Game* (1946) by Wali al-Din Samih, for example, presented belly dancer Tahiyya Carioca in one of her early film roles. Nagib al-Rihani featured as Hassan, a poor man who works at the Isaac

Stores. One day he is forced to shelter a young entertainer whom he later marries. She becomes an acclaimed movie star, a fact that alienates her increasingly from her modest husband, to the point where she asks for a divorce after having been courted by a prosperous Lebanese. However, Hassan surprisingly acquires a fortune and reunites with his wife in a happy ending. *The Lady's Game* emphasized the necessity of an economic balance between the two spouses. It is not as much the wife's labor or her profession that unbalances her marriage but her social position, her income and, last but not least, her independence. The last is expressed in her physical mobility, which allows her to travel to Lebanon and meet another more attractive man. In a way this film, just like most Egyptian melodramas, expresses the aspirations of social ascent through gender difference. Yet it also pays attention to cultural peculiarities, as it is the poor husband's humiliation vis-à-vis his failed role as family provider that triggers the schism between the spouses. The man, who is robbed of his leading position in the family, is perceived as the one who has the biggest trouble accommodating female independence and economic potency positively. The roles of housewife and working woman outside the home are moreover regarded as mutually exclusive, if not morally opposed to each other, for they are presented as an alternative between performing in front of other men or remaining faithful to the (economic and spatial) confinement of one's own home and spouse.

Even after 1952, this very conflict between marriage and work outside the home remained virulent enough to offer the stuff of witty comedy, as can be seen in the work of one of the most talented comedy directors of the time, Fatin 'Abd al-Wahab. Two of his consecutive comedies reflected the ideological development and constraints negotiationg the idea of women's position between family and profession during the Nasser era. While his *Professor Fatima/al-Ustadha Fatima* (1952, screenplay by 'Ali al-Zurqani) was still overtly hostile to the idea of women in pivotal professions and positions, the subsequent *My Wife the Director General/Mirati mudir 'am* (1966) expressed its reservations in a much more subtle way.

The plot of *Professor Fatima* concerns the conflict ignited between two neighbors, an educated white-collar worker and an illiterate trader, because of a wall the latter wants to erect in order to prevent his daughter from being pestered through her window by the neighbor's son, 'Adil. What adds a comic effect to the quarrel is the fact that the illiterate trader tries to compensate for his inferiority to his educated neighbor, by means of his only daughter. He sends her to the same law school as the neighbor's son 'Adil, and when she graduates he acquires an office for her in the same building. Yet it turns out that Fatima (performed by Fatin Hamama) is able neither to attract customers nor to win any lawsuits, even though her own ambitions make her almost lose the admiration of 'Adil, who rejects the idea of her trying to win anything—other than his heart.

However, fate intervenes. 'Adil falls prey to a conspiracy involving one of his clients, a beautiful but greedy woman who succeeds in killing her husband and putting the blame on 'Adil. Once he is behind bars and under sentence of death, the two fathers unite forces and back Fatima, who works out a scheme that makes the culprits admit their deed before court. Thus she wins her first and only case, not by skill in collecting evidence or argument in court (here she is only able to affirm emotionally her belief in the innocence of her beloved, almost bursting into tears) but by female guile that eventually leads her to the safe haven of marriage. While the plot first emphasizes Fatima's intelligence and worthiness of higher education, showing her getting better grades than her admirer, she is thereafter constantly denied any success other than in female qualities, or, to be more precise, she is denied any achievement that would show her as capable of assisting her future husband in more than emotional support.

Yet the film specifies the female ideal even further on the moral level. Fatima is clearly distinguished from the femme fatale type of the cold-hearted unfaithful wife and murderess, who involves 'Adil maliciously in her plot. She visits 'Adil several times in his office, arousing Fatima's suspicion, and mocks academic women with their 'thick glasses' (Fatima, needless to say, wears glasses).

In contrast, *My Wife the Director General*, directed by the same Fatin 'Abd al-Wahab, drew its comic effect from the admittance of a woman to a leading position. Realized fourteen years later than *Professor Fatima*, and most probably because its screenplay was written by the progressive playwright Sa'd al-Din Wahba, this film seems more able to imagine professional women, even though it leaves doubts as to whether the assumed conflict between leadership, power, and femininity may be realistically resolved.

It features the singer Shadia as a dedicated employee of a public construction company, who works with her husband in the same department. However, their mutual love and marital relationship starts to be challenged the day she is appointed director general. She imposes strict order and encourages her department to fulfill its plan to construct a building complex in a short time. She even fines her husband when he arrives at work late one day. Her husband, however, starts jeopardizing her ambitions by criticizing her for not fulfilling her marital duties, such as cooking varied dishes. The film ends with the wife teaching her husband a lesson. He fails to show up for a public speech, where she talks about the role of women and praises the support of her husband. At this point, she asks to be transferred to another department, a fact that is very much regretted by the employees. Furthermore, she stops communicating with him, while still seeing to her duties in the household. Eventually the husband realizes that he has to make a choice between perfect housewife and good companion, so paving the way to the happy ending.

Despite its conciliatory ending the film does not accommodate women's new professional role and their access to power unequivocally. In one telling scene the husband is asked to attend a party organized for directors and their wives. As his wife is the only female director he is the only man who is invited as spouse. His awkward position is expressed first of all in spatial terms. While the men involve his wife in a professional discussion, the husband steps alienated to the side. He decides to join the women's group at the other end of the room, but discovers that they are talking about cooking. As he is not able to contribute anything valuable, he decides to return to the men

Shadia (right) and Salah zu-l-Fiqar in *My Wife the Director General*, 1966

with the same discouraging result. Eventually he stops in the middle, where two Nubian waiters are engaged in a vivid debate. But again he is unable to participate, for they don't speak Arabic. Thus, the husband is cast out, with no place at all.

Through the association of professionalism with social power the film makes an important point. It perceives gender roles as a result of the social structure, or in other words as a cultural construct, rather than a given continuum. At the same time the film relies on one basic assumption, which is responsible for the somewhat utopian and carnivalesque character of the narrative: that women's access to power results automatically in the disempowerment of men. The party scene underlines this unmistakably. Replaced by his wife in the men's world, the protagonist aligns himself automatically with the marginalized: women and blacks. The message is that the only option for a man is to be in power. Despite the husband's eventual coming to reason regarding his wife's position, that scene reveals not only how bitter is the pill he has to swallow, but also works strongly against the grain of the film's overall feminist message.

Serving the Bourgeois Nation

Crucial to the 'feminist films' of the immediate post-independence period in the mid-twentieth century is that they were exclusive in terms of class and profession. In fact they ignored the variety of women's work outside the modern bourgeois context and ranked academic and white-collar jobs much higher than other kinds of work. They helped to polarize labor in terms of class, income, and status. In relation to women this polarization may seem more crucial as it intersects with morality, in that some professions, like working as a servant, seem morally more questionable than others. In the past, work opportunities for women were confined to certain traditional professions, such as midwife, weaver, baker, marriage broker, bath attendant, servant, greengrocer, peddler, entertainer, and prostitute (Ahmed 1992, 1, 5). Hence, women's call for education has been much more compelling than the mere call for work, as it is first of all literacy and formal education that opens up more 'prestigious' working opportunities and allows a raise of status and income. No wonder, then, that the modern demand for women's rights and their need to work has been directed primarily at the middle and upper classes who are, ironically, in a better financial position to restrict women's activities to the home. For working class women, by contrast, this ideal is at odds with the reality of their daily life, as in Egypt—just as anywhere else—lower-class families could not survive without female (largely informal) labor, particularly in the countryside.

Regarding cinematic representations of labor, whether in quasi-feminist films or in clear-cut mainstream films, they remained relatively limited in scope. The female entertainer in *The Lady's Game*, for instance, is a typical cinematic character of the period before 1952, along with the maid, the nurse, the Bedouin or peasant girl, and the housewife. This cast did not alter drastically during the Nasserist period, although the representation of academic women started to increase, along with rising numbers of female academics in real life. Female enrolment had risen to 7 percent in 1950 (Badran 1995, 151) while it most probably reached parity in some fields in the course of the 1970s.

Notwithstanding the rising number of educated women entering the work force under Nasser, Mona Hadidi pointed out in her study that leading female characters of the films of the 1960s and 1970s tended to be specified less in terms of profession, namely more than 50 percent were either house-wives or not further specified. If specified, they were associated with typical female professions, such as those of secretary, nurse, teacher, and ocasion-ally journalists or doctors (Hadidi 1977, 130). More recent roles are the clerk and the shop vender. The elite businesswoman appeared during the 1980s and tended to occupy an ambiguous position, as she would embody negative aspects just like men of the same profession, primarily greed, cleverness, and abusive power.

The number of positive heroines in 'traditional professions' increased to my knowledge only after independence and preferably in realist films, to name only the rural seasonal worker in *The Sin/al-Haram*, the greengrocer in *The Thug/al-Futuwwa* (1957) or the soft-drink vender in *Cairo Main Station/Bab al-Hadid*. The at first absent, and later reluctant or ambivalent representation of traditional female professions, and the emphasis on 'mod-ern' professions cannot be considered an accident. It is a natural by-product of the modernist discourse that sets progress and scientific knowledge apart from underdevelopment and 'ignorance.'

In her study of a crosssection of popular fiction films between 1972 and 1983 Safiyya Magdi came to the following conclusions: in that decade women were largely presented in a position adjunct to men as wives, moth-ers, daughters or sisters, and were usually preoccupied with looking after the needs of men (Magdi 1986, 41). Working women were largely presented as working either because of economic needs or for fun, but not as fulfilling any special role or following a certain vision (Magdi 1986, 55). While mar-riage was presented as finding its ultimate fulfillment in procreation, the behavior of mothers could be summarized as love, sacrifice, care—and the spoiling, particularly, of sons—with her main interest focused on finding a suitable match for her adult children (Magdi 1986, 46–47). The only honor-able exception, in Magdi's eyes, was the film *The M Imperium/Imbiraturiyat mim* (1972) by Hussein Kamal after a screenplay by Ihsan 'Abd al-Quddus, starring Fatin Hamama as a bourgeois single mother and working woman who is able to teach her children a lesson in solidarity, independence, and self-reliance.

With their focus on white-collar professionalism, feminist-oriented films of the post-independence era amalgamated female and national liberation with the privileged position of the middle class. One of the most acknowledged 'feminist' Egyptian movies, *The Open Door/al-Bab al-maftuh* (1963) by Henri Barakat, is a case in point. The film's bourgeois heroine studies at university, where she is advanced by her future husband, a serious and sinister professor. After marriage she is expected to remain at home and to fulfill her duties as housewife. Increasingly suffocated, she manages finally to separate. Through the character of the much older husband, the narrative and *mise-en-scène* introduce right from the beginning the idea of gender inequality, defined first in terms of age and knowledge and second in terms of male dominance. However, upon her final release the heroine does not choose to pursue her stalled carrier but decides to go instead to the Suez Canal to help defend her country.

Female liberation and the *prise de conscience* are thus aditionally mapped out as part of the nationalist agenda. Upper-class feminists had participated actively in the national uprising in 1919 that ended in nominal independence in 1922. In 1923 the Egyptian Feminist Movement made its first public declaration during an international congress in Rome. Six years later, in 1929, it already claimed 250 members (Badran 1996, 91–99). Moreover, very much aware of national interests, they initiated for instance an anticolonialist battle within the International Woman's Suffrage Alliance during the 1930s (Badran 1996, 13) at a time when nationalist rhetoric chose to make women embody the Egyptian nation. Yet as Beth Baron has remarked, "although a woman symbolized the nation, women were pushed aside in national politics" after the revolution in 1919 (Baron 2005, 80). Indeed the interaction of early Egyptian feminism with the national cause seems comparable to the French Revolution model, as described by Valentine

Fatin Hamama in *The Open Door,* 1963

Moghadam. The French Revolution leaders mobilized women in large numbers to create an "image of a national alliance of comrades in arms, mothers,
sisters, and children" (Moghadam 1993b, 75). Upon establishing the republic they soon abolished the venues of women's active participation and
promoted the woman-in-the-family model instead, which was in turn similar to the Victorian idea of women educating the nation.

This is exactly what occurred in Egypt, where after the acquisition of
nominal independence in 1922, feminists found themselves suddenly not in
alliance, but in confrontation with Egyptian men over their right to vote.
However, after the nationalist *coup d'état* in 1952 and 'final' independence,
Egypt shifted temporarily to flirt with the "Bolshevik model" that views
"woman as part of the productive forces, to be liberated from patriarchal
controls expressly for economic and political purposes" (Moghadam 1993b,
77). Woman's housewifely existence was never as harshly rejected in Egypt
as it was by the Bolshevik revolutionaries; still at least the idea of a female
labor force was advocated.

How the orientations of preindependence were mainstreamed and spiced with some socialist understanding becomes pretty clear in *The Open Door*. The film did reject the woman's housewifely existence on the one hand, but created a strong link to national liberation on the other. Based on Latifa al-Zayat's quasi-autobiographical novel of the same title, the work was discussed by Maggie Morgan regarding the positioning of the post-independence autobiographer in the face of his/her emerging nation. As Morgan pointed out in her 1998 thesis, al-Zayat's alter ego indicated the symmetry of the self with the nation that was to be deconstructed if not destroyed in subsequent Egyptian autobiographical narratives. In fact the immersion of the female self in the nation's whole is the key for the protagonist to transcend the confinement of her gender role, first as daughter and student and later as spouse and housewife. Education plays a pivotal role in this, being the essential catalyst for woman's new role outside the home.

How to canalize female education and public labor into serving the nation was also central to *I Am Free/Ana hurra* (1959) by Salah Abu Seif, set in preindependence Egypt and adapted from a novel by Ihsan 'Abd al-Quddus, a narrative that tries to qualify the very notion of female freedom. Amina has been brought up by her uncle and aunt. Because of their restrictiveness she decides to go and live with her open-minded father where freedom becomes to her a goal in itself. She is ready to sacrifice anything for its sake. After graduating she takes a job in a company where again she feels upset by any limitations she is confronted with, until she meets the journalist 'Abbas. Through him and his political interests she realizes that liberty is based on responsibility. The fight for national independence develops to become their common interest. They issue political pamphlets for which they eventually get arrested. The conflict between female subjectivity and the needs of the community, and more importantly the 'nation,' are once again resolved in favor of the latter. Moreover, the danger of women 'breaking loose' touched on in this work recurs in other quasi-feminist films such as in *I Don't Sleep/La anam* (1957) and *The Closed Path/al-Tariq al-masdud*, both written by Ihsan 'Abd al-Quddus.

The novelist Ihsan 'Abd al-Quddus, son of Fatima al-Yusuf, a theater
actress but also the founder of the political magazine *Ruz al-Yusuf* that carries her name, has coined numerous narratives centering around the issue of
female identity. His heroines are not necessarily positive; they rather seem
to strive to accommodate personal freedom within an already unbalanced
family dyad, such as the heroine of *I Don't Sleep* directed by Abu Seif, an
ill-mannered young girl (Fatin Hamama) who deliberately destroys her
father's happy marriage. In the case of *I Am Free*, the absence of a mother
who could balance the father's *laissez-faire* seemed crucial to the protagonist's misguided understanding of freedom. In a way the al-Quddus serial
expressed male anxiety in the face of the need to accommodate women's
new role as much as it tackled gender equality. As a consequence it even
enhanced some of the mechanisms of inequality, particularly by constantly
invoking moral aberrations and damaged families.

Ravaged nuclear families are in fact the major reason for those heroines'
distress. This applies to an earlier adaptation (in 1958) by Abu Seif of a novel
by al-Quddus, *The Closed Path*. This film presents Fatin Hamama in the role
of Fayza, a responsible and caring young student trying to come to terms with
her father's death, which has left her and her mother without any financial
means. As the mother transforms their home into a private gambling hall,
which attracts even a well-known and much admired novelist, the daughter
feels increasingly alienated. Fayza decides to abandon her mother for a job as
a teacher in the countryside, but is again dragged down by the dishonesty and
double standards of her surroundings. She has to leave after the father of one
of her students accuses her of being involved with his son. The young woman
returns to the city ready to succumb to her mother's way of life but is saved
in the last moment by the novelist, who now wishes to marry her.

In *The Closed Path* a binary and morally coded notion of freedom is
embodied by Fayza and her mother. In the absence of the father, in other
words, of a protective authority, the latter takes the easier way to improve
her situation by opening her house to gambling, a practice prohibited by
Islam. The former tries to remain 'respectable' until she is almost corrupted

by a ruthless environment only to be saved at the last minute by a man—
one more allusion to women's weakness and moral vulnerability that needs
to be advised by an enlightened, balanced masculinity. Al-Quddus' story
line and likewise Abu Seif's cinematic interpretation do in fact—and contrary to the 'liberal' reputation of the film—treat female liberation with
suspicion. Freedom is discussed in moral terms. Liberation comes down to
a question of individual social behavior and moral comportment rather than
a structural problem.

The anxiety expressed in Abu Seif's adaptations of novels by al-Quddus
are certainly due to the difficulties of the writer and filmmaker in accommodating women's new professionalism and mobility (in a spatial sense as
well) with the conservative moral understanding of the virgin–whore
dichotomy. The gambling hall motif is strongly significant: it may be read as
a kind of brothel substitute, as both 'institutions' open up the private
'female' space of the home to strange male visitors in exchange for money.
In fact, it functions almost as a metaphor of prostitution, through which a
female body gets exposed to other men and penetrated in the absence of its
legal proprietor. Crucial to *The Closed Path* is that it hides its moral bias
behind the façade of supposedly feminist rites of passage. Accordingly it still
gets cited, until today, as a pro-liberation film, along with *The Open Door*, *I
Am Free*, and *I Don't Sleep* (Abu al-Magd 2001, 7). Moreover, the narrative
of this and all the other films relies essentially on the absence or the inability of the mother to support or provide a positive role model for daughters,
who are thus burdened with seeking a whole new role for themselves.

Misery Feminism

Only some 'developmental' oriented 'feminist' works, such as *My Wife the
Director General* and *I Am Free* presented active, self-confident women, in
contrast to the more prevalent 'melodramatic mode,' which preferred presenting women as victims of patriarchy. Quite a number of the works
touching on gender equality have given rise to a paternalistic brand of misery feminism, like the 1975 production by Sa'id Marzuq, *I Want a*

Solution/Uridu hallan that capitalized on the decades-old convergence of feminist and melodramatic tradition. It was considered one of the major feminist films of the age, as it discussed the injustice produced by some specific regulations of the Personal Status Law. Durriya, the childless wife of a diplomat, is no longer able to accept her husband's numerous abuses, and files a petition for divorce. She manages to separate from her husband (Rushdi Abaza), starts to live her own life, and falls in love with an artist whom she wishes to marry. Legally she has the right to be divorced if her husband does not touch her for a fixed period of time. Her spouse however thwarts her plans. He raids her house and eventually calls in false witnesses in order to produce evidence that he has not left her, with the result that Durriya loses her case after years of struggle.

Durriya was performed by mega-star Fatin Hamama who had starred in innumerable romantic weepies during the 1950s and 1960s, but appeared, too, in some of the earlier 'feminist' works such as *The Closed Path, I Don't Sleep*, and *The Open Door*. In the 1970s and 1980s she appeared in several socially committed films such as *Mouths and Rabbits/Afwah wa aranib* (1977), *The Night of Fatima's Detention/Laylat al-qabd 'ala Fatima* (1984), and *Bitter Day, Sweet Day/Yawm murr, yawm hulw* (1988). As in her early melodramas *Date with Happiness/Maw'id ma'a al-sa'ada* (1954) and *The Call of the Curlew/Du'a' al-karawan* (1959), her more 'realist' characters combined the determination to fight in the face of almost insurmountable obstacles with an appearance of delicate fragility. Hence, despite its very up-to-date subject, the film *I Want a Solution* builds on Hamama's well-established melodramatic on-screen persona on the one hand and on a decades-long generic film tradition on the other. The latter opposes heroine and ill fate, woman and social conditions, with its narrative constantly juggling between the conflicting pairs. The plot structure relies essentially on the moral binarism that contrasts the violent wickedness of the husband's character with the likeable helplessness of the heroine.

The feminist-oriented works of the 1970s were, in spite of their individual importance, marginal, at least in terms of quantity; so were the films

Fatin Hamama and Rushdi Abaza in *I Want a Solution*, 1975

produced during the preceding decade which addressed feminist issues explicitly. What has to be noted though, is a shift in topics and orientation: while the 1950s and 1960s focused on problems of work and education, the 1970s began addressing problems related to the inequitable Personal Status Law and other legal issues obstructing women in Egyptian society. This was also reflected in the shift of official interests, not least because Jihan al-Sadat, the then first lady, participated actively in the public discussion that preceded the issuing of the new Personal Status Law in 1979.

The emphasis on women's powerlessness did not cease, though. This becomes apparent in the 1985 production, Inas al-Dighidi's first film *Pardon Me, Law!/'Afwan ayuha al-qanun*, similarly concerned with the law and jurisdiction. The story was presumably based on a real case. It deals with a university professor who is harshly sentenced for shooting her husband and his mistress. Surprising them in her own bedroom, she loses control and fires at them with her husband's gun. Unable to win the case in spite of her female lawyer's brilliant defense, she is sentenced to fifteen years' hard labor although, as we learn in the course of the events, her father-in-law (Farid

Shawqi) who had committed a similar crime years ago, killing his unfaithful wife, was released after one month. Ironically, this very father-in-law mutates into her fiercest opponent and manages to deprive her of the custody of her child. Comparing both cases, father and daughter-in-law, the film clearly draws attention to the inequality of sentencing that turns the heroine into a victim of patriarchal society.

After the good reception given to this film, woman director Inas al-Dighidi, who had worked as an assistant for veteran directors of melodramatic and realist cinema, made a sequel, entitled *The Challenge/al-Tahaddi* (1988). Here she took up the story at the point when the heroine, released from prison, attempts in vain to regain custody of her child. Both films are in fact the thread melodrama is made of: a woman's happiness threatened by the overwhelming power of a patriarch, and here again set against the backdrop of a society's unequal application of the law. The problem with this kind of narrative is that it leaves, contrary to expectation, little liberating or transgressive space. *I Want a Solution*, for instance, contains some "transgressive fantasy" to use Yvonne Tasker's words (Tasker 1993, 1, 7), unfolding in the heroine's inspiring relationship with the artist, and in parties with her girl friends; yet the failure of her attempt to break out curtails, if not thwarts, these fantasies. The tension between power and powerlessness is resolved in favor of the latter. For the narrative and the *mise-en-scène* are subjected far too much to the 'woman as victim' discourse.

Indeed, they come close to what Valentine Moghadam detected in the academic arena as 'misery research' in contrast to the 'dignity research' that underlines women's active role (Moghadam 1993b, 7). We could take the argument further and say that cinematic misery feminism represents in its essence a paternalistic view that positions women as objects of male power, in other words as victims of society, patriarchy, and so on, thus negating actual (even if relative) female abilities to negotiate their position and induce change.

It is noteworthy that the same discourse surfaced also in non-Egyptian Arab post- and anticolonial productions, for instance the Tunisian *Sejnane* (1974) and the Kuwaiti *Cruel Sea/Bass ya bahr* (1971). The affinity of their plot structure—not *mise-en-scène*, though—to melodrama is evident. Surpisingly the melodramatic genre has offered its audience a much larger spectrum of transgressive fantasies than clear-cut 'committed' or realist films did. Particularly the recurrent utopian happy ending, which attempts to negotiate the individual's social positioning regarding class and gender, has to be considered as part of the transgressive power of the genre. No wonder the pragmatism of the realist perception that usually refuses utopia and may even amount to social pessimism has deprived films like *I Want a Solution* or *Pardon Me, Law!* of these transgressive powers.

Effemination, Sacrifice, and Arranged Marriage

Western film theory has unearthed a strong link between melodrama and women (Altman 1999, 71) to the extent that the genre was often dubbed 'women's film' with its often tragic stories of love, seduction, and family conflicts, in which woman played an essential part. In the case of Egyptian film, whether dwelling or only touching upon the problematic of economic deprivation, its stories did focus on women and men alike, as numerous musicals prove, for instance *The White Rose/al-Warda al-bayda'* (1933) or *Tears of Love/Dumu' al-hubb* (1935) both starring singer and composer Muhammad 'Abd al-Wahab. Yet in these works, just as in the melodramas that centered on female characters, what was negotiated was not simply class difference, but more importantly the idea of love marriage put at the mercy of social prohibitions and restrictions.

Indeed, the refusal of arranged marriage in favor of the bourgeois family ideal, namely "a conjugal marriage based on love, a mother dedicated to raising her children, a wife frugally managing her household, and an attentive father" (Baron 2005, 33) had been increasingly on the agenda of women's associations and was advocated through the women's press from the turn of the century. Film melodramas quite evidently helped to mainstream this ideal further, for as much as their stories had a tendency to focus on class difference, it was precisely the vision of marriage based on love that was presented as the needle's eye through which those social limitations could be transgressed.

Thus, producer 'Aziza Amir's *Layla* (1927) and, five years later, *The White Rose* (1933) by Muhammad Karim became prototypes of Egyptian melodrama, the first focusing on a peasant girl who was seduced, only to find a better-off match after leaving home, and the second being a kind of male *Dame-aux-Camélias* drama, depicting a poor male hero who tragically falls in love with an upper class girl whom he eventually gives up for her own good. While *Layla* was considered to signal the advent of a national cinema, *The White Rose* was the first musical to be exported to neighboring countries. Numerous successive films have been shaped according to this schema—including the films presenting the singer 'Abd al-Halim Hafiz, whose songs, more than any others, were linked to Nasser's nationalist aims, and who at the time embodied postrevolutionary youth. He starred in, among others, *Love Appointment/Maw'id gharam* (1956) by Henri Barakat, and *The Empty Cushion/al-Wisada al-khaliya* (1957) by Salah Abu Seif. The majority of his films were directed by Hilmi Halim and usually presented him in the melodramatic persona of an poor, unfortunate singer aspiring to fame and in love with a rich girl, as in *Love Story/Hikayat hubb* (1959). Even though plots of this kind may have become outdated since the 1980s they

Muhammad 'Abd al-Wahab in *Tears of Love*, 1935

recurred occasionally in several later musicals, though combined with more 'realist' *mise-en-scène,* as for instance *Ice Cream in Glim/Ice Cream fi Glim* (1992) by Khairy Beshara with pop star 'Amr Diyab, and *Round Trip to Ismailia/Isma'iliya rayih gay* (1997) by Karim Diya' al-Din featuring singer Ahmad Fu'ad.

In concentrating on the point of view of the victim, melodrama has certainly been more capable of reproducing "the patterns of domination and exploitation existing in a given society" (Elsaesser 1985, 185), yet it used to do so in a fairly gendered way. If men were to appear as victims, their features had to be feminized to a certain degree in order to connote passivity and powerlessness. This may be one of the reasons for the slightly 'effeminate' appearance Christophe Ayad assigned to the first generation of stars (Ayad 1995, 138), who appeared during the heyday of Egyptian melodrama. Indeed, most male stars of early melodrama, Badr Lama at first, the singer and composer Muhammad 'Abd al-Wahab, and later Farid al-Atrash, 'Imad Hamdi, and even 'Abd al-Halim Hafiz looked neither tough nor muscular. It has to be suspected that the genre was thereby able to resolve the paradox of male victimization by maintaining a quasi-'feminine' aura in keeping with the traditional dichotomy of male activity and female passivity. During the late 1950s new, more muscular stars came to the fore, like Rushdi Abaza and Farid Shawqi, who embodied both physical strength and aggressive virility (and, in the case of Farid Shawqi, with a clear lower-class connotation). They quite tellingly featured in action-oriented genres, such as gangster films.

This apparent shift from an overall 'feminized' look toward a stronger polarization of gender after independence—in terms of features and body language—has inspired cultural critic Mohamed 'Aziza to bring an anti-colonial perspective to his evaluation of the genre. He suggested reading the victimization of the individual in melodrama as an allegory of the weakness and dispossession of Arab society in the face of the colonizing West (cf. Aziza 1978, 15). Indeed, 'Aziza's remark reflects a sense of the genre's preoccupation even though it fails to reveal its ideological complexity and strong preoccupation with class.

The question of 'effemination' aside, the fact that women did play an equally important role in Egyptian melodrama did not prevent the genre from helping to pave the way for what would later become a paternalistic brand of misery 'feminism,' emphasizing women's plight in patriarchal and capitalist society from a male perspective. For what makes fallen women positive figures regardless of moral issues is that, to quote Ann Kaplan, "the narrative is structured so as to put the spectator in the position of finding the 'sacrifice' (with its suffering and subsequent death) 'beautiful' and 'admirable.'" This effect, accompanied by the heroine's "desire for an unsatisfied desire," or in other words her search for an impossible love, is described by Kaplan as neurotic (Kaplan 1983, 47).

In 1930 Muhammad Karim brought his first melodrama *Zaynab/Zaynab* to the screen. It bore witness to a more enlightened and progressive view of gender relations that arose from local modernist but also colonialist-oriented criticism of Muslim culture. The original model for the film, first published in 1914, was a *Bildungsroman* by Muhammad Haikal that reflected the thinking of a considerable current in Egypt's elite. Popular enough to be adapted to the screen again by Muhammad Karim in 1952, *Zaynab* was on several levels typical of Egyptian melodrama.

Its first film adaptation is unfortunately not available for viewing, yet analysis of the novel's narrative construction in modernist terms proves illuminating. An innocent, loving girl who is forced into an arranged marriage suffers to the extent that she loses her life. Three character traits define the female heroine here: passivity, purity, and the ability to sacrifice. The dramatic conflict of the film is generated through forbidden love in the first instance, but in a second and even more important one, through the virtue of the girl's character torn between faithfulness to her love and obedience to her parents. The plot of *Zaynab* and the heroine's character traits as such are not enough to mark the story as specifically Egyptian. Specific, however, is the emphasis on arranged marriage as a sign of oppression and gender inequality. This topic continued to be tackled by numerous films after independence and is still topical until today. The film *Request for*

Obedience/Inzar bi-l-ta'a by 'Atef El-Tayeb, as recently as 1993, shows a couple struggling for their marriage against the wishes of the girl's parents.

Arranged marriage was a central problem in the real lives of the first Egyptian feminists, most notably Huda Sha'rawi (Badran 1996, 35) whose biography was eventually made the subject of an Egyptian television serial in 2005. This preoccupation in early melodrama reflected, first of all, if we think of *The White Rose* for instance, the concerns of upper-class women who were the first to be mobilized for the feminist cause (though this is not to say that it did not play a role in the life of lower-class and rural women). In their life, arranged marriage had an important and certainly also devastating social and economic function, namely to secure and sustain their families' wealth and position, facilitated through female seclusion in the harem, which ceased with the advent of the twentieth century after the abolition of slavery, as described by Beth Baron in the first chapter of her book (2005). True, this particular seclusion was not as common or feasible among the lower classes. Yet it was against the background of their own class experience that enlightened elite modernists and feminists started to advocate the ideal of Western bourgeois love-marriage as opposed to arranged marriage.

Love-marriage was promoted under the pretext that spouses were not held together through power and domination but through respect and companionship. This very concept, however, was rooted in the colonialist critique of Muslim society. For in general the oppression visualized in the seclusion and veiling of Muslim women had become a "centerpiece of Western narrative of Islam in the 19th century" and modeled into a kind of "colonial feminism" (Ahmed 1992, 150–51). In particular the veil, behind which women were "buried alive" (Ahmed 1992, 154) was denounced as a visible sign of backwardness and uncivilized behavior. Missionaries and anthropologists described Muslim marriage as based on sensuality and not on love, rendering woman a "prisoner and slave rather than . . . companion and helpmeet" (Ahmed 1992, 154). Hence colonialists, prominent among them the British administrator in Egypt, Lord Cromer, (who at home, ironically, was a founding member of Men's League for Opposing Women's

Suffrage), "captured the language of feminism and redirected it, in the service of colonialism, towards Other men and the cultures of Other men"
(Ahmed 1992, 151–52).

Some or all of the assumptions of colonial feminism were taken up by
the native elite, among them the writer Qasim Amin whose demands and
criticisms set the agenda for women's issues in Egypt and elsewhere in the
Middle East to this day. The enslaved as well as the victimized woman were
both part of this agenda. Their presentation in Egyptian melodrama is not
surprising, given the cosmopolitan upper- and middle-class background of
early filmmakers on the one hand, and historical events on the other. Thus
the modernist thinking that was mainstreamed subsequently through the
emerging seventh art shaped also the polarization of mothers and daughters
as representatives of two different social (and ideological) models.

Mothers: The Dark Continent

While in modernist-oriented Egyptian films, progress has been bound to the
iconography of the daughter, either as victim of past traditions or as carrier
of a modern future, the realm of the mother came to embody the worst of
native tradition. The devaluation of premodern female spiritual knowledge
went along with a dismissal of the traditionally strong position of mothers,
particularly in the rural household that used to comprise (and often still
does) an extended family. The insistence on mothers' ignorance instead,
however, bore some signs of psychological sublimation. The film *The Lamp
of Umm Hashim* (1968) by Kamal 'Attiya, starring Shukri Sarhan and Samira
Ahmad, has offered a master narrative in this respect.

The film was adapted from a novel by Yahya Hakki and is one of the
few to discuss the conflict between mythical and rational thinking. It presents a young doctor who returns from Europe to work in his home town. He
has just had a stimulating experience in Europe with a cultured European
woman. At home, he finds his mother expecting him to marry his friendly
though uneducated cousin. The doctor feels alienated, even more so when
he discovers that his cousin has an eye disease but resorts to traditional

healing. The mother drips the holy oil of Umm Hashim's lamp in the girl's eyes, damaging her sight even further. The son reacts with anger, destroys the lamp, leaving the whole neighborhood in shock. While his cousin's condition deteriorates he gradually assumes responsibility for countering their ignorance. He delves into specialized studies so that he can cure the girl. Eventually, he is reconciled with tradition, acknowledging the importance of Umm Hashim's lamp for his people and accepting the marriage with his cousin.

Yet, this ideological dispute around the compatibility of the mother's world with modernity conceals what the narrative is unable to hide completely. The problem that faces the doctor upon his return is not simply that of ignorance but the fact the mother has chosen a bride for him. This hits him even harder, as he has just given up his beautiful educated European girlfriend. However, to conceal the issue of power in the mother-son relationship, the narration displaces the conflict to the developmental dichotomy between (popular) religious tradition and science, superstition and rational thinking, Egyptian man and European woman. Traditional healing is, in this context, equated with a wrong and even destructive concept of knowledge. The hero's reconciliation at the end is close to a tactic, allowing him to acknowledge that people have difficulty giving up their tradition, but at the same time to adopt and use Western science to his own benefit. Women (except for the European), and in particular mothers, are on the negative side, on the side of backwardness, ignorance, and superstition. They are made to represent the discarded 'native' tradition. What furthermore shines through this denunciation is the new disciplinary or 'colonizing' role that the modernist project has allocated to the mother. Stripped of her former managing position in the extended household, she had to be reinvented as the agent of the nation-state who helps to reconstruct the modern nation.

This process of recoding maternity dates back to the turn of the nineteenth century and the colonial era. Already in 1899 Qasim Amin had published his famous book *Tahrir al-mar'a (The Liberation of Women)*. In it he advocated first and foremost the necessity of female primary education, a request that was not much in dispute, even among many conservatives, for "it is impossible to breed successful men if they do not have mothers capable of raising them to be successful" (Ahmed 1992, 156). This was moreover very much in line with British thinking, for the Victorian value system considered the home the natural and proper place for women. Hence, through the gendered schism of public and private sphere, "[w]omen's role in this scheme was to stabilize society from within by exerting a moral influence on household members" (Traube 1992, 123). This did not prevent the British administration—despite its lip-service to the liberation of the Muslim woman—from curtailing female public education in its Egyptian colony (Ahmed 1992, 153).

In contrast to the traditional woman, the educated mother and housewife has been regarded as a major condition for national development and progress. "Within the nexus of anticolonial nationalist struggle, then, mothering took on a supplemented value: that of inculcating nationalist virtues in the face of colonial oppression" (Shakry 1998, 131), as did Safiyya Zaghlul for instance when her husband, the nationalist leader Sa'd Zaghlul, was deported in 1918 by the British. But this stance could easily be combined with misogyny. While seemingly speaking in favor of educating and unveiling Egyptian women, Amin simultaneously dismissed them as untended, unattractive, mindless, and obsessed with monitoring their husbands (Ahmed 1992, 157).

Crucial to this coding of ignorance is that it is made to negate the existence of any premodern forms of knowledge, while rational science acquired through schooling has been perceived as the centerpiece of modern development. Consequently women as the most colonized part of society were represented as the most in need of development and education, thereby being transformed into society's 'Dark Continent'[17] keeping their original (relatively) powerful position particularly for their sons (within a nonetheless male-dominated society). "[M]isogyny represses woman into her maternal role and by that very fact sets up a veritable 'kingdom of mothers'" in which "the mother appears as an effective, unconscious recourse against the castrating intentions of the environment," writes Abdelwahab Bouhdiba (Bouhdiba 1998, 214–23).

This meant, according to Bouhdiba, that the premodern patriarchal society could be turned "at the very heart of the private, personal life" into a maternalistic one (Bouhdiba 1998, 223). It may be assumed that the modernist dismissal and attack on 'traditional' motherhood had to be even stronger in view of the special position mothers held in the extended patriarchal family and the specific psychological formation of men due to the privileged mother-son relationship. To bear a son, as Bouhdiba but also Fatima Mernissi have illustrated, has commonly been the married woman's key to prestige and to the exercise of power within the family (Bouhdiba 1998, 216; Mernissi 1987, 132–52).

Salah Abu Seif's film *Youth of a Woman/Shabab imra'a* (1956), which was criticized for its misogyny, may be perfectly well understood in the light of Bouhdiba's interpretation, as its symbolic arrangement demands a psychological reading along the lines of maternalism. The narrative is constructed as an oedipal drama: Tahiyya Carioca performs in the role of an elderly femme fatale, an independent woman who runs a mill in a lower-class neighborhood. She agrees to take a young student from the countryside into her house, then seduces him with the result that he neglects his studies. All his attempts to liberate himself from her grip fail. The film ends with the woman's violent death at the hands of one of her employees, an old, obviously broken man who confesses to the student that he had been ruined earlier in exactly the same way.

Control is the key to understanding the female protagonist here. Monopolizing the young man's emotional and sexual life, she even thwarts his romance with his young cousin by blackmailing him into marrying her instead. He is only set free and able to return to the girl when his seducer is killed. The character of this elderly vamp thus bears much resemblance to the image of the nurturing but also possessive mother. The son is too weak to unite with another woman unless this (symbolic) mother is destroyed. Crucial, too, is the weakness of the symbolic father-figure whose revolt, crystallized in the killing, comes rather late and as an act of despair. Hence, the drama of *Youth of a Woman* should in reality be called 'Youth of a Man' as it represents in fact a male coming-of-age story.

It could be also read as an allusion to what Abdelwahab Bouhdiba calls the Arab Oedipus. To him the Judar myth from *One Thousand and One Nights* represents the Oedipus complex of Arab society: less guilty, but fatal in its denial of feminine essence on the one hand, and its confinement of women to the maternal role on the other. In search of treasure, Judar has to dry up a river, pass through seven doors, experience death seven times, and take advantage of a propitious astrological conjunction to enter the last room, in which he meets his mother. He has to order her to undress. This is the most difficult part, asking his own mother to strip herself naked. The first time he falters, but the second time he does not. As soon as she removes her last garment, she vanishes. At that, the treasure appears—but it is worthless, a shadow. Back in the world, the young man finds his real mother has been begging in the streets ever since he left her to search for the treasure. Judar is not a guilty or violent Oedipus: his 'crime' was committed only in fantasy but in Jungian terms he is haunted by "the anima in the form of the mother-imago" (Bouhdiba 1998, 227).

In the face of the powerful symbolically charged narrative of Judar, and *Youth of a Woman,* the ideological superstructure of 'feminist films' seems even more a step toward dethroning the maternalistic aspect of motherhood. I would even argue that this was all an attempt to redistribute notions of power in relation to gender. To suggest female powerlessness as uttered through melodrama and misery feminism was just one appropriate strategy to achieve this; another was to relegate mothers to the realm of ignorance and superstition.

In 1995, 'Ali 'Abd al-Khaliq presented in his *The Ladies' Threshold/'Atabat al-sittat* an educated middle-class housewife, performed by Nabila 'Ubaid, who desperately wishes to conceive. After a long odyssey through the waiting rooms of doctors she learns about a *shaykha,* a female healer woman. She pays the *shaykha* a lot of money to have a *zar* celebrated,

Shukri Sarhan and Tahiyya Carioca in *Youth of a Woman*, 1956

a ritual close to African possession cults, in which spirits who are believed to have taken possession of someone get appeased. During the *zar* she is made to lose consciousness, which gives the *shaykha* a chance to inseminate her with the sperm of one of her assistants. Eventually the woman gets pregnant. To her dismay, her husband accuses her of infidelity and repudiates her: he has known all along—but has never admitted to her—that it is he who is unable to procreate.

Thus the heroine is tricked twice, by the *shaykha* and by her husband. Her major fault, as presented by the film, is that she resorts to the kind of fraud the *zar* stands for—and this in spite of her elevated social status and education. But what really makes her drop scientific knowledge overnight is her wish to join the realm of motherhood, the ultimate female ideal and setback at once. The tradition to which she resorts to achieve this goal is simply dismissed as humbug and as a means for its practitioners to make money. No way is offered to think of it as a female-oriented spiritual practice which places the human and her body in a specific metaphysical relation. Premodern forms of knowledge and spirituality are hence fiercely rejected and devalued. The sole positive knowledge women should cling to is objective science.

Gateway to the Repressed

Indeed, one of the most negatively depicted traditional practices related to the female (and maternal) realm has been the *zar*. This fundamentally therapeutic celebration used to comprise almost exclusively women (except for the musicians), who would gather under the guidance of a female *shaykha* to eat, drink, sing, dance, fall into trances, and sacrifice an animal. The *shaykha*'s task is to call upon the demons that have presumably caused the illness, trying to appease them in order to relieve the patient. The sources of these practices are possibly ancient, and have East African origins, among others (Littmann 1950, 50). They continue to be used by Christians as well as Muslims (Littmann: 1950, 57). A belief in demons is not necessarily opposed to Islamic (nor to Coptic Christian) teachings despite the fact that orthodox Muslim belief has tended to dismiss it, along with the veneration of the saints, as *shirk*, or polytheism (de Jong 1984, 495), while the Coptic Church is opposed to the popular practice of *zar* (although priests used to resort to practices of exorcism). Consequently, in the late nineteenth century the *zar* started to be evaluated in critical terms by the modern-educated elite. In 1903, for example, Muhammad Hilmi Zain al-Din published a book entitled *Madarr al-zar* ('The Negative Effects of the Zar'). Another, even more critical title, *Kitab bida' al-fujjar fi haflat al-zar* ('The Book of the Debauchees' Heresies in the Zar Celebrations'), appeared in 1911 (Littmann 1950, v). Following such disapproving judgments, the authorities in Cairo made it compulsory in 1964 to license *zar* celebrations (de Jong 1984, 495).

In accordance with these developments, Egyptian cinema has (to the present day) mocked and denounced the *zar* as either foolishness or fraud. Such negative representations have surfaced in numerous works. Stereotypical characters have been made to embody the practices in question, such as the madman in *Alley of Fools/Darb al-mahabil* (1955), who dresses up like a traditional shaman and lives by annoying shop owners and people on the streets. He is explicitly depicted as an imbecile. In Salah Abu Seif's *Raya and Sakina* (1953), an early Egyptian thriller, two women and their gang perform *zar*-like celebrations as a means of duping well-to-do women, killing them, and stealing their jewelry. A similar depiction is given in *Women's Magician/Sahir al-nisa'* (1958) by Fatin 'Abd al-Wahab, where Farid Shawqi represents a criminal who dupes prosperous women with the aid of traditional magic. In *The Imbecile/al-Halfut* (1985) by Samir Saif, the comedian 'Adil Imam dresses up as a woman and sneaks into a *zar* celebration in order to watch women while they are at ease.

No wonder then that the same practice surfaced in *The Ladies' Threshold* as an embodiment of fraud and indecency. This applies also to *The Amulet/al-Ta'wiza* (1987), a 1980s horror film. Here the *zar* is not even represented as an exclusively female space but is organized by a male *shaykh* in the company of a lot of dubious-looking men. The same applies to *The Ladies' Threshold*. The ritual here has been recoded as an opportunity for a form of indecent gender-mixing instead of what it originally was: a secluded space where women could meet and cope with their problems and, as argued by Janice Boddy, who investigated this practice in Sudan, find a place in their community despite a number of restrictive and oppressive factors—including marriage—that commonly set women at odds with society (Boddy 1989, 166).

It is apparent that popular demonology has been negatively inscribed within the Egyptian discourse of modernism, a discourse which holds up the binary concept of enlightenment and objective science (as introduced by the Occident) as the key to progress and modernity, in opposition to local ignorance and superstition. Thus, even recent Egyptian horror films, such as *The Amulet* by Muhammad Shebl, and Muhammad Radi's *Humans and Demons/al-Ins wa-l-jinn* (1985), whose core is the idea of supernaturalism, have paradoxically worked to uphold the negative juxtaposition of women and *zar*-magic.

It is women who offer the demon easy access to the human world, be it Rawya in *The Amulet* who is the most haunted of her family, or Dr. Fatima in *Humans and Demons*, as we will see later. They are all too easy to impress, and quicker than men in resorting to the popular *dajjal* (humbug). They prove indeed to be *naqisat 'aql wa din* ('lacking in mind and religion') as a popular saying describes women.[18] Mothers in particular seem to be "deemed 'ignorant'" to use Omnia Shakry's words (Shakry 1998, 157), as it is always they who are the first to suggest that their daughters ask for the shaman's intervention.

This is evident in *The Amulet*, which presents Mahmud and his wife Rawya as victims of the general housing crisis in Egypt, forced to share an old house with Mahmud's mother and siblings. A broker tries to lure them into selling it with a large sum of money and the offer of a new, modern apartment. When Mahmud refuses to let his father's house go, the broker resorts to spells. A demon takes possession of the house, moves furniture, destroys possessions, and sets it on fire. Eventually, Mahmud's younger sister has a nervous breakdown while the rest of the family struggles to cope with the problem.

Released in 1987, the film, with its implicit criticism of Sadat's Open Door economic policy, was as much concerned with the social order of its time as with modernity, notably the complex relationship between metaphysics and rational thinking. This is expressed through the conflicting strategies adopted by the different characters to counter the demonic invasion of their home. Mahmud, the male head of the family, launches then a criminal investigation and receives support from his future brother-in-law, a sympathetic police officer. Mahmud's mother, in contrast, secretly proposes to her daughter-in-law Rawya that they visit a shaman who is known to have the power to break spells. After a frightening visit, the two women invite him to hold a *zar* celebration. However, the ritual gets violently interrupted by Mahmud and the officer. The latter denounces the shaman and his companions as crooks and threatens them with further procedings. With the evil persisting, Mahmud's mother tries a final strategy, asking a Muslim *shaykh* to come and see her.

He asks Rawya, who has just been overwhelmed by the vision of being showered in blood, to show strong faith, and provides comfort by repeating the line, *ma 'afrit illa bani Adam* ('the only evil spirits are human beings'). Quoting holy scripture eventually proves to be the proper cure for the malediction. While Rawya and her mother-in-law incessantly recite the Qur'an, the soundtrack reinforces their recitation with a loud call to prayer. Meanwhile, the monstrous features of the broker who had pressured the family to sell their house are revealed: he is transformed into a huge billy-goat with long horns, with which he gores his human assistant. The film ends with a prayer recital and a low-angled shot of an imposing mosque.

Just like *The Amulet, Humans and Demons,* directed by mainstream filmmaker Muhammad Radi and starring the Egyptian king of comedy 'Adil Imam as the demon, reserves exclusive rights for orthodox scriptural belief while simultaneously focusing on the labile female psyche. Along such lines it sketches out an ideal of a modern bourgeois religiosity and sexual morality. Dr. Fatima (Yusra), a highly successful specialist, returns from a mission abroad to join her mother and sister in Egypt. Her professor and colleague, Dr. Usama, awaits at her former research institute to propose not only a job but marriage. However, Fatima is haunted by a demon called Galal, in remembrance of her first fiancé who was killed in a car accident.

Initially seeking psychological treatment, Fatima becomes more and more convinced that she is dealing with a very powerful genie who wishes to marry her. Her mother asks a shaman for help, and after several unpleasant procedures (such as stepping over corpses in a graveyard at night), Fatima experiences a nervous breakdown. Eventually, Dr. Usama confronts the demon in order to win the hand of his beloved. His final and most powerful weapon is to recite the Qur'an. On this occasion, the film characters express their firm belief in the existence of demons and state that they are mentioned in the holy scriptures. Thus, orthodox belief is again presented as the sole means of combating the *jinn.*

It is no accident that Dr. Usama and Dr. Fatima are both depicted as highly-educated scientists, affirming the compatibility of Muslim faith with modern knowledge and science on the one hand, while at the same time scapegoating popular quasi-religious practices. This policy of excluding aspects of popular tradition is fundamental in the repackaging of cultural values, which serves to cement the image of a unified and exclusive scriptural (and modernist) Islam and—more important for our investigation—to reposition knowledge along gender lines.

Dr. Fatima, equipped with sufficiently contradictory traits of character, is suspected by the psychoanalyst of suffering from a guilt complex after the loss of her first fiancé, which is why she believes that the demon Galal desires to marry her. Cohabitation with a *jinn* is a common though not exclusive motif in popular belief, in which case a woman is said to be possessed by a male demon. In fact, the whole history of the *zar* is based on this particular motif, as Enno Littmann argues. As legend tells it, the sultan of the *jinn*, or demon king, entered the body of a princess after her father, the pharaoh, refused to let him marry her. It took a magician–priestess named Zara to appease him, by organizing a celebration in line with his wishes.

Yusra, Na'ima al-Sa
and Tahiyya Carioc
The Amulet, 1987

The symptoms Dr. Fatima develops after several encounters with the increasingly possessive demon are clearly hysterical, and result in illness followed by hospitalization. In all of this the allusion to repressed female sexuality seems quite clear; even her prospective bridegroom suggests that immediate marriage would be the best cure. Thus, Dr. Fatima is portrayed as a woman with a scientific education who refuses to be dominated by a man for the sake of her career. The way she is approached by her male colleague is highly rational, reminiscent of two contractors or business associates. They never flirt or touch; instead he declares his respect for her professional achievements. He visits her at home only once, in an emergency, whereas the demon sneaks into Fatima's bedroom at will—usually at night when she is in bed.

In contrast to the legend the film, as noted above, achieves final appeasement via submission to the law of orthodox religion, and to the concept of a bourgeois, strongly rational and desexualized marital relation. The indirect message conveyed by the film's narrative and characters is, in spite of its approval of women's education, that a woman's career may conflict with her emotional life. Moreover, formerly female-dominated forms of healing are rejected as inappropriate and backward, thus doing away with their transgressive potential.

All this conflicts sharply with what *zar* studies suggest, namely that the practice in reality was meant to enable women's transgressiveness. Repressed female sexuality was part of the equation, but the *zar*, including the possession by male *jinn*, was a means for resisting it. "They move her from a monological (monolithic) world where other voices—alien cultures, feminine perspectives—are disclaimed, exist only 'in absentia,' to a polyphonous world where others may speak . . . . Here the *zar* as an aesthetic genre resembles the novel as described by Bakhtin . . . , where social heteroglossia, the existence of multiple expressive worlds, is not muted but incorporated into the 'text' itself, effectively de-centering hegemonic truth" (Boddy 1989, 309).

This possibility of 'heteroglossia' however has been completely denied by the Egyptian cinematic representation of the *zar*. It has instead aired the obvious discomfort with which modernist discourse meets popular religion and syncretistic transgressive and female-oriented practices. What the recurrent and stereotypical depiction of the *zar* has worked to conceal, therefore, is that in modern (cinematic) representation the so-called negative tradition is not that much more than an ideological construction.

Inside the Bourgeois Home

During the 1950s the motif of the troubled quasi-secluded woman in her haunted home made its appearance in the work of one director, Kamal El-Cheikh, who has been considered a sort of godfather to the Egyptian thriller. The Egyptian film critic 'Ali Abu Shadi stated that crime appeared in Egyptian movies from as early as the 1930s and 1940s, yet he attributed the first true thriller to the director (Abu-Shadi 1986, 125). El-Cheikh, who was trained as an editor at Studio Misr, made his successful debut with *House Number 13/al-Manzil raqam 13* in 1952 and realized in the following a number of well-executed gangster films and thrillers.

Interestingly, during the 1950s and 1960s the Egyptian thriller did not make any references to the supernatural but could rather be described as a rational 'psychological drama' that centered on bourgeois 'modern' men and women in which gender relations, including marriage, presented one of the sources of endangerment for women, coded largely in spatial terms. The attempt to distinguish between horror film and thriller is certainly problematic—not least because of the fluidity and constant shifts in meaning discussed by Rick Altman (Altman 1999, 62). Nonetheless it seems tempting to employ Robin Wood's handy characterization of the horror film as normality threatened by monsters (Wood 1985, 204). There is no doubt that it is precisely imperiled normality that lies at the meeting point of horror film and thriller, but if the latter relies on quasi-natural and objective causes in order to incite fear, the former draws primarily upon the animalistic, monstrous, supernatural, or quasi-religious to create its sensational effects (cf. Carroll 1990, 145, 189).

At this point it seems interesting to ask what kind of Egyptian normality is it that encounters the supernatural. Whereas in the 1960s thriller, the individual's imperilment was designed more on the gendered and psychological level, in the case of the two 1980s horror films discussed above, women were quite clearly portrayed as the gateway to the supernatural. This is not to say that magic and ghosts did not make any earlier appearances, but they were embedded in a completely harmless and mostly profoundly comic realization, as in *The Vanishing Cap/Taqiyat al-ikhfa'* (1944), *Lady Ghost/'Afrita Hanim* (1949), and *Isma'il Yasin's Ghost* (1954), as well as in some horror parodies drawing on Western models, such as *Ghost House/Bayt al-ashbah* (1951) and the mummy-story *Isma'il Yasin meets Frankenstein/Haram 'alayk* (1953), all of which (except for *The Vanishing Cap*) starred the comedian Isma'il Yasin.

In a generally comic context, and lacking the latest in sensational special effects, the *'afrit* or ghost in these films spread fear and confusion more among the characters than the audience. In *Isma'il Yasin's Ghost*, for example, the ghost of a murdered belly dancer haunts the comedian until he finds the culprit responsible for her death. The more irrational, supernaturalistic

'Imad Hamdi in *House Number 13*, 1952

approach, including the corresponding *mise-en-scène,* was saved for the 1980s, for Shebl and Radi made a serious attempt to apply not only the motifs, but the familiar technical and visual repertory of the genre in a consistent manner (such as low- and wide-angled shots, dark lighting, mobile camerawork from the point of view of the unseen monster, and other typical special effects, including fire, smoke, and moving objects), thus providing a less parodic and stronger 'realistic' presentation of the horror.

So-called *real*-ization was also a characteristic of the (partly psychological) 1950s and 1960s thrillers directed by Kamal El-Cheikh, all of which centered on women, such as *Death Traders/Tujjar al-mawt* (1957), *The Lady of the Palace/Sayyidat al-qasr* (1958), and *The Last Night/al-Layla al-akhira* (1963). Contrary to many police films largely dealing with criminal gangs or thug films, these films were explicitly situated in a middle- to upper-class bourgeois environment. *House Number 13,* for example, tells a *Dr. Caligari*-type tale in which hypnosis is used to incite a successful young architect to commit murder on behalf of his doctor. This went along with the introduction of a sophisticated and effective *mise-en-scène,* particularly in lighting and set design, and a suspense-oriented editing style.

Crucial to this kind of thriller was the preoccupation with crime and the evil nature of humans (but not any occult, demonic, or extra-natural forces); in other words it presented a kind of rational horror, at its most characteristic in El-Cheikh's *The Last Night.* This film relied heavily on a recurrent thriller motif, namely lost identity, enacted through a highly claustrophobic marital drama. The phobic effect was not only produced by the narrative structure but also by a set design that used a suffocating but fashionable interior accentuated by expressive black-and-white photography and low-key lighting. Set almost entirely at night, it grows increasingly dark in the second half as it moves toward the final showdown: the attack on the heroine's life, where she is chased mercilessly by her husband through their home.

Fatin Hamama, the petite actress who often played sensitive but cheerful young girls in melodrama, features in this work as a woman who wakes up one morning to discover herself a wife and the mother of a grown-up

daughter. Yet all she can remember of her past is her preparations for marriage to a totally different man. In the course of the film, she tries to regain
her memory of how this mysterious change occurred. Meanwhile, her strict
and unfriendly husband observes her suspiciously. Gradually she grasps her
true identity and discovers that her husband is an imposter. In response, he
attempts to murder her, but her sympathetic doctor is able to save her life at
the last minute. What she learns is that she lost her memory on the eve of her
wedding, when an air raid on Port Said killed her entire family, including her
married sister. Her brother-in-law, thus widowed, simply declared her his
wife and moved with her and his little daughter to another town.

El-Cheikh's narrative presents itself as a typical tale of familiar horror,
or in the Freudian sense as a manifestation of the uncanny, literally the
unhomely, unfamiliar *(das Unheimliche)* that emanates from the familiar *(das
Heimliche)* (cf. Schneider 2000, 171). In fact, our heroine encounters the
deadliest threats in the shelter of what is supposed to be the most intimate
relationship possible. The horror of her marriage, however, is not simply that
of physical violence or male domination (which may be experienced in any
marriage); rather, what is at stake here is male manipulation and domination
of *female identity*. The heroine is not only deprived of her original love and
twenty years of her youth, but is also deceived into entering a false marriage
and forced to lead the life of another person — which are indeed the legitimate
complaints of any woman who gets pushed into an (arranged) marriage.

The implicit concept that enables this drama to unfold is the conflict
between individual desire and the constraints of the nuclear bourgeois family.
In contrast to the traditional extended (but partly segregated) family, the
nuclear bourgeois type is considered, contrary to common Western perceptions, to be responsible for depriving women of the shelter of female
solidarity, diminishing their power in the home, and thus reinforcing male
dominance (Abu-Lughod 1998, 12). It is precisely this focus on the dynamics of modern nuclear family life that brings the narrative close to Freudian
psychological drama. The husband's control — not only over his wife's body,
but over her very soul — is what destabilizes her, and this translates into a

psychic problem as well. Yet unlike Alfred Hitchcock's *Psycho* (1960) for example, where horror is triggered by insanity, *The Last Night* makes a sincere effort to present psychic aberration as fake. Whereas *Psycho*'s finale offers an ironic and quite evident anti-climax in which the psychologist explains in retrospect the main character's abnormal development, in *The Last Night* a comparable role is played by the doctor, who realizes in contrast that she/his patient is *not* sick and who helps her to look for the true, social reasons for her uneasiness.

One of the fundamental qualities that place this psychological drama very much in the bourgeois sphere—apart from its focus on the nuclear family—is situated on a very visual and direct level, namely the cinematic set. The couple's home is a spacious modern villa, luxuriously furnished, set in an affluent neighborhood with gardens and empty streets very different from the lower-class alley common in films. All this strongly underlines the heroine's solitude and her state of being abandoned to the hostile male.

Gender Spatiality

In her classic study on melodrama Laura Mulvey identified some of the implications gender has on the representation of cinematic space, namely the way film associates gender with space and action. While the Western or adventure film presents male heroes who roam through the space outside, melodrama (and the female-oriented thriller) tends to evolve around female characters bound to the inside of home and family. "Problems of class difference and sexual difference are translated into mythology through a series of spatial metaphors: interior/exterior, inside/outside, inclusion/exclusion. . . . [The] private sphere, the domestic, is an essential adjunct to bourgeois marriage and is thus associated with woman, not simply as a female, but as a wife and mother. It is the mother who guarantees the privacy of the home by maintaining its respectability" (Mulvey 1989, 69); hence "[i]n contrast to woman as icon, the active male figure . . . demands a three-dimensional space . . . He is a figure in a landscape" (Mulvey 1989, 20).

Ironically, in a Middle Eastern context Mulvey's findings about the divided 'segregated' space would invite an orientalist interpretation in the light of regional cultural practices, rather than as a by-product of 'bourgeois' social formation, which in fact is more likely to be its source for the films in question. This is not to say that gender segregation did not play a role in ideas negotiated through cinema. Seclusion, or the invisibility of women in public space, has been at times transposed to the screen. Taking Algerian cinema as an example, Ratiba Hadj-Moussa showed the existence of a clear spatial dichotomy in describing the problematic admission of women to the public (film) space.

In a further instance, Algerian cinema, which has hardly ever presented any love stories, transferred male longing onto objects that at the utmost symbolized the absent woman as an ultimate incorporation of the veiled female body. As can be seen in *Omar Gatlato* (1976) by Merzaq Allouache and *The South Wind/Rih al-janub* (1975) by Mohamed Slim Riad, voices and windows became avenues of desire, excluding the contact with the real body, the real woman. In both films, male curiosity to approach women is aroused by glimpses through windows (Hadj-Moussa 1994, 238). Objects in this context are emotionally charged, functioning as quasi-fetishes for the woman, herewith representing suppressed desire in a strategy similar to that of melodrama.

Unlike the cited Algerian examples, many popular Egyptian films are highly ambiguous and contradictory in their spatial categorization, due to their submission to generic rules. It is true that melodrama tends to associate women (but also men) with home and family, relying on emotional sublimation in object-use and gesture, as will be explained later. The example of the white rose and the pearl necklace in *The White Rose* has been sufficiently described and seems typical enough (Shafik 1998, 61). However, while Algerian films hardly ever told any love stories, Egyptian cinema introduced the amorous couple right from the beginning as a man and a woman occupying the same space at once, a move that can certainly be considered part of the modernist agenda. It is true that sexual difference has been to some extent coded spatially, yet not in as distinct and clear a manner as is the case in Algeria. If women tended to be relegated to the home, that is, the familiar space, and men to the public, this very codification has been negotiated constantly and in different ways over time.

Furthermore, some films drew from both sources in their negotiations: 'traditional' concepts as well as modern bourgeois ideals. One film that used space overtly for negotiating gender roles and relations was Fatin 'Abd al-Wahab's comedy *Miss Hanafi/al-Anisa Hanafi* (1954). Here, the window of the family's home represents a point of major controversy between Hanafi and his stepsister Nawa'im throughout the film. Starring Isma'il Yasin in the role of Hanafi, the film may be classified as farce rather than comedy, with all its carnivalesque and transgressive qualities. One of the most stunning aspects of this particular work was moreover its inclusion of an irrevocable sexual transgression (cf. Menicucci 1998 on the issue of homo- and transsexuality in Egyptian cinema).

Yasin, who stars as a young man of little education with no clear professional affiliation, is urged by his father and stepmother to marry his stepmother's daughter by a previous marriage. Both young people hate the idea: Nawa'im is in love with a handsome neighbor who is about to graduate as a veterinarian, while he is simply unable to imagine marrying his 'sister.' Eventually, they bow to their respective parents' pressure and marry, but the same night, before consummating the marriage, Hanafi falls ill, is taken to the hospital—and returns home as a girl! Everyone is happy now, except for the parents who have to search for a suitable match for two daughters. After several failed attempts to arrange a marriage for Hanafi, by now a buxom girl with a loose tongue, he disappears. When he returns she is nine months' pregnant and married to her former friend, the butcher. Eventually her sister, too, is allowed to marry her beloved veterinarian and the film closes with a lot of embracing couples.

Everything revolves in this film around young people finding their proper match. Yet in one scene, Nawa'im addresses her now-female brother who formerly tried to seclude her at home: "Do you see now that we should be educated to be able to raise your children properly?" This line seems quite out of context, as Hanafi shows no interest in education at all, but spends all his efforts in dressing up and flirting with the butcher. There is no question about female labor. The only allusion to it is to confirm the difference in gender roles; Hanafi complains about the unpleasant kind of work, such as washing, that he is now expected to do as a woman. Male and female realms and roles remain, in spite of the change of sex, stable and distinct. Hanafi's switch confirms the difference instead of denying or at least questioning it. Education, as the stepsister's quoted line suggests, is a quite superimposed message, still in negotiation, so to speak, with the concept of woman as object of male admiration and as housewife.

Yet the window issue crystallizes the film's main transgressions and negotiations, which, interestingly, do not refer very much to the modernist agenda. Still a man, Hanafi is annoyed by his sister's peeping out of the window. In an attempt to safeguard the family's reputation he closes the shutter definitively, by nailing it to the window frame. Turned into a woman, Hanafi is now himself interested in peeping at his old friends in the alley. He opens the window but is caught by Nawa'im, who insists now, in her turn, that the window should remain shut. She appeals to her stepfather,

Zinat Sidqi, Magda, and Isma'il Yasin in *Miss Hanafi*, 1954

who decides that Hanafi, now a woman, must submit to the same rules as the other women. Of course Hanafi still finds ways to meet his admirer on the staircase, which (just like the roof, where Nawa'im used to encounter her lover) is a space in-between, where inside and outside merge and can be transgressed for a while.

The stairs, the roof, or the balcony as an intermediate place, a meeting point situated on the verge of inside and outside, though often filled with the danger of discovery for the couple in love, still recur in recent films, to name only the fiction short *The Kite/Tiri ya tayara* (1996) or the full-length *Girls' Secrets/Asrar al-banat* (2001). It happens when the narration is centered on segregation, female moral reputation, and family honor to be defended. A less dubious location, even romantic, but highly stereotypical for cross-gender encounters, is the park and the café on the Nile. This is where lovers meet and socialize, in film and in reality, openly or clandestinely.

At the same time, the street has carried a much less exclusive connotation than in Algeria. For women it may be the site of cross-sexual encounters, of seduction even, but also a place for regular activity including virtuous work—particularly since the 1950s, if we just think of the soft-drink seller (Hind Rustum) in *Cairo Main Station* (1958) or more recently the snack-booth owner (Layla 'Ilwi) in *Smile for the Picture/Idhak al-sura titla' hilwa* (1998). In fact, before 1952 there was not much space for women on the street, in as much as there was not much work for middle- and upper-class women to do outside the home, except for the basic female occupations: servants, nurses, entertainers. But this changed drastically, if not on a quantitative at least in a qualitative manner. Particularly in realist-oriented films, women have been represented working on the street in honorable professions.

One of the most unforgettable 'lower-class' characters was the powerful and witty *mu'allima* (literally 'master,' a professional or independent small-scale entrepreneur) in Salah Abu Seif's *The Thug*. Tahiyya Carioca, playing the role of a female produce-vender in a market with abounding charm, gave the hero, at first naive after his arrival from the countryside, the initial support that enabled him eventually to survive and succeed as a market trader. The *mu'allima* in general signifies a working-class businesswoman with little or no formal education who runs a small enterprise, such as a café or a workshop. Usually this type is characterized as an honorable *bint al-balad* (literally 'girl of the country'). *Banat* (girls) *al-balad* enjoy a good reputation: they are experienced, witty, brave, hospitable, show solidarity, and care about their neighbors. They are, moreover, economically independent and "combine coquetry and glamorous attire with a concern for reserve and modesty in dressing" (van Nieuwkerk 1995, 112).

This is exactly what Tahiyya Carioca represents in *The Thug*. A real *mu'allima*, she has no problem in mingling with men and backing the film's hero Haridi in his fight against the criminal monopolists of the markets. A transformation of her personality in the film takes place, however only after she gets married to Haridi and stays at home. She increasingly loses influence over her husband and is finally disillusioned on discovering that he himself has mutated into an evil and egocentric monopolist. It is thus that the initially independent and bold *mu'allima* character experiences a frustrating setback through succumbing to the model of the sheltered and protected housewife. The questionable outcome of the heroine's marriage and submission to male dominance could be read as a negative comment on the confinement of an independent woman to the home. It has to be admitted, though, that this specific reading was probably not of major importance to writer and filmmaker, but was a means through which to emphasize the husband's drastic about-turn and betrayal of his most loyal supporters.

Spatial cinematic associations have not only social but also moral implications. Although melodrama and to some extent thrillers insisted on the home as the locus of female drama, it is also likely to be the place of virtue, in contrast to public places, such as streets and landscapes. The most recurrent and also most problematic of all public spaces is the nightclub, a location with which Egyptian cinema became frantically obsessed. The nightclub is linked almost per se to the character of the belly dancer. As

Farid Shawqi and Tahiyya Carioca in *The Thug,* 1957

Mona Hadidi has pointed out in her study, this profession enjoyed a disproportionately high representation among the 1962 to 1972 film samples she
examined (9.5 percent of the leading female characters were belly dancers).
The association of the dancer with crime was again disproportionately high
(Hadidi 1977, 301).

Other narratives associated the very space of the nightclub with seduction and sexual aberration. The most prominent example is Tahiyya
Carioca's nightmare in *Take Care of Zuzu/Khalli balak min Zuzu* (1972),
imagining her student daughter's descent from dancing in a nightclub into
prostitution. Hence, the location is pretty much reminiscent of the representation of the city in nineteenth-century melodrama, according to Laura
Mulvey "an outside to the rule of order. To the individual swallowed up in
the crowd, to the law in search of a criminal, to morality faced with a pro-
fusion of bars and prostitutes, the city at night epitomises chaos and
uncertainty" (Mulvey 1989, 70). The dubious character of this locale in
Egyptian cinema has been cemented by an endless number of film scenes set
there for the mere sake of including musical elements or providing erotic tit-
illation in narrative films, a strategy recognized by the audiences for what it
was, a form of sensationalism.

However, it is noteworthy that the nightclub displayed at times a lighter side, alternating with its role as the ultimate hotbed of vice. In the first case it represented the locus of an almost infantile longing for social ascent and professional success. Numerous narratives starring the dancers Samya Gamal and Na'ima 'Akif evolved since the 1940s around young, talented but penniless girls whose biggest dream came true when they achieved fame by dancing in a renowned nightclub or theater. This may be read in the context of a temporary reevaluation of the oriental dance first initiated by original performers and dancers such as Syrian-born Badi'a Masabni, who began her career in Egypt in the 1920s as a nightclub owner introducing other talented dancers. Such themes were also inspired by Western fantasies of oriental dance that became highly fashionable at the turn of the century in the West (Buonaventura 1994, 117). Real coming-to-fame stories (for instance those of Tahiyya Carioca and Samya Gamal, who were trained at Masabni's clubs, advancing eventually to become top stars), along with the high standard and originality of these performers, may have added to the temporary positive evaluation of their profession, at least in some film narratives. In the 1970s, with the spreading of a new Gulf-inspired morality, this development was reversed, and the nightclub as the major site of professional belly dancing was increasingly dismissed as a place equated entirely with crime, prostitution, and immorality.

Woman and the Gaze

One of the major functions of belly-dance and nightclub scenes in Egyptian cinema has doubtless been to permit male voyeurism: to offer the opportunity to watch a woman's body isolated through *mise-en-scène* and editing into close-ups featuring the breasts, the legs, or the belly. This kind of visual cinematic discontinuity has fostered the ultimate objectification of woman, according to Laura Mulvey: "One part of a fragmented body destroys the Renaissance space, the illusion of depth demanded by the narrative; it gives flatness, the quality of a cut-out or icon" (Mulvey 1989, 20). Examples of this strategy abound: The opening scene of *A Woman Bound to Fall/Imra'a 'ayyila li-l-suqut* (1992), for instance, is structured exactly in that sense. Ahlam (Yusra) is seen to present a belly dance. The camera focuses on her face and the different parts of her body covered by a glittery, cheap-looking costume. The interior and the guests who watch her are clearly depicted as a brothel and its customers.

Hence the female entertainer in particular, be she singer, dancer, or performer has been charged with the most vivid and likewise dramatic fantasies in Egyptian cinema and situated, not only in a metaphoric sense but also through the point-of-view editing, in such a way as to be 'looked at.' In *The Red Lipstick/Ahmar shafayif* (1946) by Wali al-Din Samih it is the belly dancing scene that is situated at the dramatic turning point in the fate of the male hero (performed by comedian Nagib al-Rihani in one of his least comic films). Dancer Samya Gamal appears in this film as a leading player for the first time, in the role of a seductive maid. In a pivotal scene she entertains her employers and their guests with her belly dancing. The sequence is structured through her dancing body crosscut with images of the others looking at her and commenting on her capabilities. Most expressive are the hero's (Nagib al-Rihani) and his wife's faces: he is full of admiration, unable to take his eyes from the dancer, while his wife suspiciously monitors him and the dancer alternately. The dancer in contrast does not direct her look at anyone. Subsequently the wife's jealousy and the servant/dancer's seductive comportment result in her being cast out and the husband leaving the house to return only at the very happy ending.

The belly dancer is the spectacular female body per se that functions only through its isolation in terms of film editing, but in fact it is also 'cut-out' in terms of choreography. As Marjorie Franken demonstrated in the case of Farida Fahmi and the post-independence Rida Dance Group, Fahmi was—unlike other dancers of her time—able to incorporate the virtuous *bint al-balad* character successfully in her performance by referring, through costumes and choreography, to national 'traditional' culture rather than vaudeville and nightclub entertainment. Although technically her body movements did not differ much from that of regular 'oriental dance,' she was able to evoke these positive connotations, mainly because she performed within a dance company characterized as folkloric (Franken 1998, 267). Fahmi could not therefore be isolated as a single dancer and was consequently less subjected to gazing.

The woman-as-icon structure runs not only through dance scenes but also through other occasions. Cut-out editing is applied for instance in *Terrorism and Kebab* (1992) by Sharif 'Arafa, when Yusra, featuring as a fugitive prostitute, suddenly appears on the stairs above the hostages. They are cowering on the floor, guarded by the armed 'Adil Imam. Accompanied by a soft rocking music her disembodied legs appear, and then the rest of her, swaying down the stairs. There follows a close-up of her breast, covered in a glittery amber material, showing a hand removing a comb from her cleavage. She arranges her hair first, takes off her jacket, and jumps out onto the stairs landing, as though appearing on a stage. Her performance is watched breathlessly by the hostages, including one bearded Islamist and his female colleague, a veiled elderly employee (An'am Salusa). The fact of them both staring at her in particular underscores even more the iconic spectacularity of glamorous Yusra's appearance.

Western film theory has spent much time in assessing the importance of the gaze to a gendered process of looking. It drew primarily on Freudian psychoanalysis and its distinction between active 'aggressive' male and passive 'masochistic' female sexuality. A concept that has in Mulvey's opinion decisive repercussions on the positioning of the female spectator: "The correct road, *femininity*, leads to increasing repression of 'the active' (the 'phallic phase' in Freud's terms). In this sense Hollywood genre films structured around masculine pleasure, offering the identification with the *active* point of view, allow a woman spectator to rediscover that lost aspect of her sexual identity, the never fully repressed bed-rock of feminine neurosis" (Mulvey 1989, 31). This view was partly adopted by other theorists of her time, such as Annette Kuhn and Ann Kaplan.

Mulvey did not necessarily associate this concept, namely the repression of the active, with nature as Freud did, but left it open to the probability

Yusra and 'Adil Imam in
Terrorism and Kebab, 1992

of being a product of culture instead of nature (see the Freud critique of French feminist Luce Irigaray, 1990). Generally Mulvey's notions have been qualified not only through subsequent generations of feminist film theorists informed by ideas of multiculturalism, but also by non-Western cultural critics and sociologists, most notably the Moroccan Fatima Mernissi, who finds Freud's binarist gender concept strongly problematic. In her view, the way Sigmund Freud interpreted and universalized sexual difference according to cultural as well as biological ideas was deeply rooted in his time and social formation. For example, he described the female egg as passive, in contrast to the active male sperm. More problematic, however, was his description of the procreative act in terms like chase, attack, and penetration—reminding Mernissi of a battlefield rather than a "garden of desire" (Mernissi 1987, 20). In contrast, earlier Muslim thinking, represented among others by Imam al-Ghazali's texts from the tenth century, conceived male and female sexuality as one and the same force, thereby permitting an equally active sexuality to women (Mernissi 1987, 21). This, however, had serious repercussions on woman's position, as it seemed even more necessary to conceal and seclude her in order to protect men from her 'power' to lure simply by virtue of being visible.

In Abdelwahab Bouhdiba's words, "the look, the last entrenchment of the frontier of the sexes was to become the object of strict religious recommendations" transforming the sexual partner into an "être-regard" or "being as a look" (Bouhdiba 1998, 37). As a saying of the Prophet goes: 'The look is an arrow of Iblis' (Bouhdiba 1998, 39), and the Qur'an has asked the believers in general to cast down their eyes and to guard their private parts. Women were requested not to reveal their adornment and to cast their veils over their bosoms (Bouhdiba 1998, 36). This command was adopted by the misogynist traditions of Mesopotamian, Greco-Roman, and Byzantine culture and developed further into the kind of veiling prevalent in Arab-Muslim society (Ahmed 1992, 55).

The concept of intimacy produced by veiling was negatively connoted with the term *'awra*. Men's private parts and the woman's body, and even her voice, were considered *'awra*. The linguistic root of the word *'awra* is *'awr* and signifies the loss of the eye. Hence, the sight of what is prohibited is connoted as blinding. This traditional Muslim concept appears strongly distinct from Freud's 'castrating,' 'penetrating' gaze, for the 'blinding' effect or in other words the threat of castration comes here from women and not from men. Even though issued from a completely different position, a criticism uttered by film scholar Richard Dyer goes in the same direction. He wondered why women should be afraid of castration or penetration, leading back to this 'Freudian' fear instead to the threat of homo-eroticism: "It is clear that castration can only be a threat to men, and more probable that it is the taboo of male anal eroticism that causes masculine-defined men to construct penetration as frightening . . . an act of violence" (Dyer 2002, 128).

Going back to the Muslim conception, it has to be stated that the notion of *'awra* had very practical repercussions on Muslim women. Although the Qur'an enjoins men also to "guard their private parts," in practice woman's body has been much more governed by the necessity to hide. Because of the effect the sight of a woman's body can have on men it was believed to provoke *fitna* or chaos. As a result, her whole sexuality was conceived as problematic, for woman could be associated with "a conceptual universe where her body represents a threat, a source of fear" (Malti-Douglas 1992, 43). With this understanding of the gaze and its role in engendering a stereo-typical understanding of woman, it is comprehensible to what extent the emphasis on a woman's erotic body on the screen may be perceived as a violation of religion, tradition and morals.

No wonder then, that the issue of the gaze played a pivotal role in restructuring postrevolutionary Islamic cinema in Iran. As Hamid Naficy demonstrated, the Muslim-oriented reading of the gaze had far-reaching implications for the positioning of women within Iranian narratives, resulting in the creation of what he called the "averted" or "veiled look." In his view, men are considered to be the most affected by their own direct look: "Instead of controlling women through their gaze, men are lured and captured by the sight of women and . . . they are thereby 'humiliated' and made 'abject' by women" (Naficy 1991, 35). This "masochistic effect" indirectly implies two recurrent assumptions, first that of a basically seductive female body and second an unmediated "link between vision and corruption" (Naficy 1991, 35). In recent 'purified' Iranian cinema this led directors to avoid close-ups and to stay away from the system of 'suture,' or in other words, from shot/point-of-view shot editing and to use averted ways of looking in the art of performance, thereby producing the 'veiled look.'

Egyptian cinema, however, did not undergo the same process of Islamization as Iranian cinema, but has remained on the 'dark' side of moral binarism. In particular the retreat and veiling of actresses during the early 1990s was able to confirm cinematic practices as being opposed to Islamist-defined piety. The representation of the female body as cut-out icon in combination with the invitation to direct gazing seem crucial in upholding this opposition. What can be confirmed is that Egyptian film has done a great deal to support unilateral male gazing. Translated into the typical realization of a romantic scene, this has meant that the male protagonist looks first at his female opposite, while she either timidly responds or casts her eyes downward. In contrast, a look that comes first from the woman is likely to be read as an invitation or a transgression of morals by the woman. Thus the editing scheme used in these kinds of scenes is bound into the phallic Freudian theory confirming male penetrating power and female vulnerability.

No wonder that the resistance of women directors (most notably Inas al-Dighidi, who made her first film in 1985) to male domination showed itself primarily in trying to reverse the 'Freudian model' (that is, gaze equal to aggression) although without necessarily transgressing it. One central scene in *Cheap Flesh/Lahm rakhis* (1995) by Inas al-Dighidi may serve as an example. The film as a whole deals with three peasant girls who search for a way out of their deprivation by looking for jobs, only to end up in unhappy marriages, a fate from which only Nagafa, the most self-defined and successful of the three (played by Ilham Shahin) is able to escape. The scene in question shows how the trafficker presents Nagafa's friend Ikhlas to an affluent customer who has come to the Egyptian countryside in search of a wife. While Nagafa exposes the men's dealings, insults them, and leaves, Ikhlas remains and submits to being examined thoroughly by the affluent groom. The man stares (point-of-view shots) literally at every part of her body, including her buttocks, while she shyly lowers her eyes trying to get a glimpse of him from beneath her eyelashes, as an ultimate passive succumbing to male desire.

Female activity is translated later in the film into a sequence of point-of-view-shot editing confirming the woman's personal independence. After Nagafa has successfully established her workshop, she encounters a sympathetic man in an elevator. While they stand facing each other, she is the one to direct her look at him first. The heroine's overt gaze at a strange man signifies clearly her individual initiative and insistence on making an active choice. That it was not an immoral invitation is subsequently underlined with the couple's marriage.

Director al-Dighidi's awareness of the power of gazing is made obvious in many other instances. Her *Night Talk/Kalam al-layl* (1999) opens with a thoroughly voyeuristic scene: Gala Fahmi in the role of the courtesan

Cookie is watched through a video camera while she stretches seductively on her bed. As the different parts of her body are emphasized through the editing, her slow movements are well calculated to support the seductive effect, as is the extremely low-key lighting. While the room is cast in deep blue, different parts of her body are picked out by the warm, bright, and yellowish key light. This woman is overtly on display and expecting to be watched. However, what comes as a surprise is that the camera operator turns out to be a woman, who is moreover giving her directions on how to perform. Amina (Yusra), who holds the camera, seems to be the impressario, the one in power. This impression is again reversed in the course of the action, which subsequently reveals that Cookie is actually Amina's employer. When Amina at one point tries to quit, Cookie prevents her by every means, including blackmail, because she fears Amina may reveal some of the compromising information she has acquired about her employer's highly placed clients.

The relationship of the two women is clearly defined in terms of economic and social power. While Cookie is linked to powerful men and enjoys enormous privileges, Amina suffers from material but also emotional deprivation that forces her to accept her employer's humiliating treatment. At the same time she is watched suspiciously—and also haunted—because of her knowledge of what she has seen. Hence, the opening sequence underlines that the only power the underprivileged woman possesses in this narrative is her gaze. It is this gaze that brings about the most existential dangers she is exposed to throughout the film, but it also represents the most crucial statement in the narrative context. For it openly negates the uncomplicated linkage between power and gaze by re-coding gazing as an imminent threat. The look at the female body reflects back on its owner, the voyeur. This threat is not directed only at Amina (who functions rather as mediator of the male look) but at the end it most strongly affects the men who are involved with Cookie, for their involvement is eventually what causes the scandal and terminates their careers. At this particular level, the male spectator or voyeur gets punished for his gaze.

Female Bonding

Another crucial aspect of *Night Talk* is the involvement of two women in the issue of gazing. While one deliberately takes it upon herself to become the object of male gazing and desire in order to participate in the realm of power, the other woman operates outside that field. Instead, she oscillates between power (of the gaze) and powerlessness (of a socially deprived human). This is how the film succeeds in introducing ambiguity into the conventional binary concept of femininity equals subject of gaze equals gentle sex equals victim. In fact, this ambiguity is a recurrent structuring element in director Inas al-Dighidi's work, introducing an element of feminine dualism that may amount to conflicting and controversial 'femininities.'

The fiercest opponent of Raga', the title role in *The Murderess/al-Qatila* (1992) by al-Dighidi, is actually a woman. The prominent wife of one of the heroine's victims uses all the means provided by her social position to get Raga' convicted and sentenced to death. The mercilessness of this influential woman seems in a way to heighten the protagonist's vulnerability and victimized position. It appears as the dark side of the feminine, but also of the social system, as both women are clearly opposites in terms of class. Not so in *Lace/Dantilla* (1998) by the same director, where the two heroines are differentiated by virtue of type and character traits. Best friends, one is timid and shy, the other extravagant and assertive; they are divided and reunited over one and the same man.

In the opening scenes of *Lace* in particular, the different personalities of the two women are coded through body language and gazing. Maryam, performed by Ilham Shahin, is a lawyer, a reserved personality, always modestly dressed. She tends to hold back and cast her eyes down when approached by a man. Not so for Sahar (Yusra), who works as an entertainer. She appears aggressive and fully aware of her female attractiveness, as in her first encounter with the police officer Husam. Dressed in a striking, colorful manner, she leans over his desk and looks straight into his eyes while talking to him. Later he spends a lot of time deciding whether he prefers the active or passive female type, allegorically embodied in the two competing versions of femininity. In the course of the film it turns out that the narrative too has difficulty making up its mind. It conflates both women into the sexually omnipotent type, as long as (married to the same man) they are competing for his attention. But the storyline separates their character traits again when they desert their husband and unite in friendship at the end.

Woman director Inas al-Dighidi has sometimes been engaged in reproducing a binary image of woman but has also often alluded to more polyphone and multiple identities. If the three friends in *Cheap Flesh* are split in terms of strength and persistence, they nonetheless demonstrate the dispensability of the male in their strategies of survival, which is first of all made possible because they operate as a group and not as isolated individuals. The same applies to *Lace*, where the two friends indulge for a while in exaggerated jealousy, expressed in endless fights, after deciding to marry the same man. However, it is not they who are exposed at the end of the film, but their common husband, who starts neglecting his job as a police officer because of his two wives' ruses. Eventually, his boss has him dragged to the police station—in glaring red underpants, the ultimate parody of his cock-of-the-walk existence.

An emerging deconstructive polyphony regarding feminity is not confined to al-Dighidi's work. With more middle-class women having carved out a measure of economic independence through education and labor, male anxieties and the binary view of women could not be maintained consistently, as may be illustrated in some film examples realized by male directors in the 1980s and 1990s, which in parts opened up to be polysemic, that is, to take a more inclusive and less binary and 'miserable' view of gender. With this, female bonding and motherhood attained a positive depiction and centrality hitherto unknown. The New Realist *Dreams of Hind and Camelia/Ahlam Hind wa Kamilya* (1988) by Mohamed Khan, for instance, relied on the motif of female solidarity as a response to female economic and sexual exploitation. It was echoed later in a series of other feature films focusing on women friends, such as *Cheap Flesh* (1995) and *My Life, My Passion/Ya dunya ya gharami* (1996).

Yusra, Mahmud Himida, and Ilham Shahin in *Lace*, 1998

Dreams of Hind and Camelia presented two Cairene maids struggling against oppressive circumstances that are caused by their employers or their own male family members. The symbiotic relationship of the two develops out of their problems, but also because they are so different. Hind ('Aida Riyad) is characterized as more sentimental and easy to impress, which makes her fall in love with the kind but unreliable pickpocket 'Id (Ahmad Zaki). By contrast, Camelia (Nagla' Fathi) seems rather tough and prag-matic. Although this does not save her from the annoyances of her brother, who makes her feel that she is a burden to the extent that she rushes into an unpleasant temporary marriage, she is able to counter 'Id for Hind's sake. She pressures him to marry her friend after the latter turns out to be preg-nant. However, 'Id gets involved in a smuggling affair, is arrested, and leaves Hind (and his illegally earned money) in Camelia's care. She helps Hind to give birth to her child, Ahlam. Later they travel to the seaside together, and on the way they are attacked and robbed. Nonetheless the film ends with all three enjoying the beach.

In a way Mohamed Khan, who also wrote the script, outbalances the social victimization of its heroines through their solidarity, which serves as a source of strength and resistance. The motif of solidarity, particularly in communities, appeared often in realist films, such as *Determination/al-'Azima* (1939), *The Thug* (1957), or *The Earth/al-Ard* (1970). Yet in *Dreams of Hind and Camelia* it is reinterpreted in a completely gendered way, being confined to the female protagonists. More than that, the male hero, though agreeable, is apparently incapable of coping with his life and eventually is made dispensable—even in the most fundamental way; for although it is he who has fathered Hind's child biologically, it is Camelia who replaces him socially by taking over the role of the protector of mother and child. In fact, the very title of the film is meant to allude to this symbiotic female relationship. For Hind's child is named Ahlam or 'dreams.' The Arabic title may thus be read in two ways, either as a series of names: *Ahlam, Hind, and Camelia* or, as it has been translated into English, *Dreams of Hind and Camelia*. The second version turns *ahlam* (dreams) into something related and created solely by Hind and Camelia.

If *Dreams of Hind and Camelia* had been made by a woman, the film would have been much easier to appropriate for a lesbian reading. In Egypt, lesbians, just like gay men, are not permitted to mobilize in public as a group or to interact with the media in a distinct collective way because of various social pressures. The successful distribution of this film in the West, in contrast to many other Egyptian works (or even equally well-made films by the same director) is an indicator of its potential pro-feminist and even lesbian reading. However, in the Egyptian context other readings suggest themselves as well. First, the realist reading, that is, the quasi-truthful description of lower-class conditions, where the obstacles and pressures placed on men are so burdensome that they fail to meet male ideals of honor, protection, economic success, etc. Compared to the innumerable 'success stories' of popular Egyptian film, which describe how men (and also women) overcome their poverty and achieve social ascent, this film seems rather pragmatic in its rejection of such a narrative. Its pragmatism is certainly part of its realist strategy.

The film's most crucial message, however, is its rejection of melo-drama's binary view, which makes class division run along gender lines. Instead the character traits refuse to polarize the protagonists, but create a variety of shifting roles. Not only is the notion of masculinity questioned and dissected, but femininity too is reconstructed to embody a variety of contra-dictory and opposed elements, even notions of power and powerlessness at the same time. It certainly emphasizes motherhood as a creative process ('dreams')—but it also underlines a range of femininities worked out in the character traits of its heroines. If Hind is sentimental, she is also capable of forgiving and supporting (a stranded man and a child). If Camelia is cor-nered by her brother and eventually forced into an unpleasant marriage, she is nonetheless capable of earning money, finding shelter, and supporting Hind and her daughter.

Female solidarity has been also quintessential to Inas al-Dighidi's previ-ously discussed *Cheap Flesh* (1995), even if her take on motherhood is not as positive as Khan's. Less realist in its *mise-en-scène* and aspirations, the plot isolates a man, the trafficker, and a woman, Nagafa, as the major antag-onists, whose encounter dictates certain key moments of the film. Nagafa and her two girlfriends resort to the services of a trafficker, who claims to be able to provide them jobs. In fact he persuades two of the girls into mar-riages with affluent Arabs. Only Nagafa accepts a job as a servant. Cleverly, she profits from her industriousness, saves money and improves her posi-tion. Her friends fare much worse. The first leaves with her aged husband to a Gulf country, only to find that she has been chosen to serve the man's other wives and, furthermore, is forced to accept 'unnatural' sexual practices (alluded to in the film as anal intercourse). The second is duped into a mar-riage with an (unspecified) Arab, and discovers only after becoming pregnant that her marriage contract was forged. In desperation she abandons her newborn child. The two women appeal repeatedly to the trafficker but in vain: the only one capable of offering any support is their friend Nagafa. She has succeeded in opening a small factory and confronts the trafficker for the women's sake. He takes revenge by filing a complaint with the police,

'Aida Riyad and Nagla' Fathi in *Dreams of Hind and Camelia*, 1988

causing a raid on Nagafa's. Nonetheless the film closes with the main protagonist having achieved considerable economic success—and found a
likeable and supportive man to marry.

Success and social ascent are constitutive elements in *Cheap Flesh*. As
such it represents a different ideological stance from *Dreams of Hind and
Camelia*. It is not only their gender and misery but also the girls' aspirations
for a better life that make them vulnerable. Decisive, however, is that the
struggle for social ascent which drives many male-oriented narratives is told
here as a female story. Also, the heroines are very much poles apart in terms
of cleverness, efficiency, and strength. Yet the weaker and more abused
women are not discarded from the story but drawn into the domain of the successful woman. Some of her power spreads to her friends and keeps them
alive. Motherhood, however, is presented as burden and a constraint, a source
of ordeal particularly in the case of Tawhida who eventually abandons her
child. Unlike *Dreams of Hind and Camelia,* al-Dighidi's interpretation of
female bonding, despite being offered by a woman, is much less polysemic in
terms of variety and sexual difference, yet it is at least negotiated as one possibility for women to display their strength.

Women in Action

Apart from female-bonding films, numerous other cinematic representations have been shaped around negotiations along the active-passive gender dichotomy. Recent feminist film theory, for example, has devoted much attention to the shifting roles of women in relation to violent action and space as experienced in the last two decades of Hollywood film. The emergence of female action heroines as well as the rape-revenge cycle has been investigated and interpreted as, among other things, a negotiation and mainstreaming of feminist ideas (Read 2000, 198). In Egypt, too, the female avenger and later the rape-revenge cycle appeared, largely in the context of action cinema. To explain this as mere plagiarism would be to throw out the baby with the bath water.

For, in spite of its popularity with audiences, the action film as a genre has been neither quickly nor easily adopted by the Egyptian film industry. I would even argue that the recurrent technical deficiencies of this genre when produced locally are symptomatic. For in fact, it does not only seem to reflect difficulties in accommodating high technology as embodied by the "manufactured" body builder's "spectacular body" (Tasker 1993, 78) and by "musculinity" (namely sexual identity as signified through the muscular body) (Tasker 1993, 149) but also reenacts a certain type of parodic musculinity, as we will see later in the case of comic star 'Adil Imam, that is nonetheless based on the idea that physical strength equals the male body (equals virility).

The extent to which physical force is likely to be linked to the prevalent concept of masculinity, may be clarified through the few exceptional physically 'strong' female characters that have appeared on screen. As a rule, the muscular or sportive woman is likely to be presented as ridiculous and ugly in features, dress and body language because she is quasi-masculine. B-actress Samah Anwar, for instance, built up her persona during the 1980s as a tough and sporty young woman capable even of using karate. When she appeared in more prestigious productions she was usually typecast in supporting roles as a tough little attractive or intellectual young woman, usually dressed in trousers or sports clothes, as in Inas al-Dighidi's *One Woman is Not Enough/Imra'a wahida la takfi* (1990), in which she featured as one object of the hero's many amorous entanglements.

The association of women with physical force served mainly as spectacle or gag, as demonstrated in *Crabs* (1990) by Khairy Beshara. In this work the comic exceptionality of the muscular woman is perfectly exemplified. The protagonists are a group of young sporty lower-class men who work for an upper-class couple as entertainers by organizing boxing matches, among other things. Eventually they realize that their employers have started to get bored, so they hire a group of female wrestlers. The women's parodic masculinity is expressed in checked shirts, shapeless trousers, ugly faces, and plump features. Their spectacular and slightly comic appearance and performance save the day for the male heroes.

Thus, the cinematic use of muscular women is first of all supposed to result in a comic catharsis. It reinforces the basic gendered binarism of soft/hard and fat/muscular that governs the concept of wo/men's physical constitution. This binarism was strongly underlined in the striking corpulence of some popular female Egyptian film stars of the 1980s and early 1990s, and is a phenomenon that has been reversed only toward the end of that decade. Some cineastes suspected that it was the result of the simultaneous shift of the Egyptian export market toward the Arabian Peninsula. An additional factor may also be the increased post-*infitah* social mobility, assisted by labor migration to the Gulf, which allowed traditional lower-class taste for female corpulence to come to the fore. Thus, while leading actresses of the 1930s to 1960s were either petite or curvaceous the players of the 1980s and 1990s showed an increasing tendency to be overtly plump to name just Layla 'Ilwi, Nabila 'Ubaid, Ilham Shahin, and Ma'ali Zayid. Even Yusra, who was rather slim at first, started to put on weight in the late 1980s. Only Nadia al-Gindi kept her figure despite increasing age.

It is important to see that al-Gindi, the self-styled diva of Egyptian action films of the 1980s and 1990s, did not adopt 'male body characteristics' even though she specialized in this male-dominated genre. She has commonly

Samah Anwar (left) and Fifi 'Abdu in *One Woman is Not Enough*, 1990

prefered to represent tough women *despite* her feminine outlook and her seeming adoration of the 'gentle sex' concept that was underlined again and again in overt or metaphoric sexual abuse or seduction scenes, as in *The Spy Hikmat Fahmi* (1994), *Mission in Tel Aviv* (1992), and *48 Hours in Israel/48 sa'a fi Isra'il* (1998). At the same time Nadia al-Gindi emphasized her sex appeal through dress, make up, and body language, as well as her partly real and partly suggested undressing, which she used to trick her adversaries.

Since it is primarily because of her gender that al-Gindi's spies are able to vanquish their male opponents, her femininity comes close to masquerade. The runaway heroine in *The Samya Sha'rawi File/Malaff Samya Sha'rawi* (1988), for example, enters a shop where she changes her clothes in order to dupe and escape her persecutors. Other even more striking metamorphoses of her characters occur during the recurrent scenes of torture by male opponents, the only scenes al-Gindi performs without any make up. Despite the strongly masochistic impression of those scenes, they still allow for other readings, as the moment of her characters' strongest vulnerability and weakness is at the same time the moment she removes her most 'feminizing' ornament, to leave only blank resistance.

What is also striking about al-Gindi's action persona is that she has rarely represented a female avenger. Lately she has prefered pragmatic individuals in search of personal advantage. Apart from that, she signals the quite unprecedented advent of women as central figures in action-oriented narratives. In fact, women have rarely been central to Egyptian gangster movies or action films. Only occasionally, as in *Raya and Sakina* (1953) and *A Crime in the Calm Neighborhood* (1967), had they featured as dangerous gang leaders. Armed women appeared only occasionally and in varied generic contexts. One harmless example is *The Women's Police/al-Bulis al-nisa'i* (1988) by 'Abd al-'Alim starring Ilham Shahin as a young police officer who—supported by her male colleagues—is capable of solving difficult cases. Much more brutal were two New Realist 'action' films, *The Cell/al-Takhshiba* (1984) and *The Execution Squad/Katibat al-i'dam* (1989), both by 'Atef El-Tayeb, which were echoed subsequently during the 1990s with films like *Disco Disco/Disku disku* (1994), *The Murderess*, and *The Woman and the Cleaver*.

The Cell presented Nabila 'Ubaid in the role of a victim who is gradually transformed into an avenger. While filing a complaint at the police station she instead gets deliberately arrested, humiliated, and falsely accused of a crime. After a long, psychologically subtle struggle with the police officer in charge, she finally chases and kills him. Typical of this realist narrative is that the woman does not so much avenge a sexual assault—as would be the case in a rape-revenge story—but fights back because of a more general and gender-unspecific social abuse. The same applies to *The Execution Squad* in which Ma'ali Zayid decides to take up arms in order to hunt the corrupt businessman who was responsible for her father's death.

None of these female avengers, including Nadia al-Gindi's action heroines, use their muscles. They rely either on their brain or on weapons. Early feminist film theory has tended to view the woman with the gun as the phallic woman (Kaplan 1983, 59). This is again a psychoanalytical interpretation that is based on a male perspective, that is, the armed woman perceived as a masculinized castrating threat. Yacinda Read has proposed, particularly in combination with the revenge motif a different understanding, for she observed a stronger 'femininization' in dress and make up of the avenger from the moment she decides to take revenge (Read 2001, 50). Hence Read perceived this figure rather as a negotiation between feminism and femininity, or to be more precise, an attempt to imagine a tough, though feminine woman. This interpretation allows a reading of the weapon less in Freudian terms, neither as male fetishism nor as a female lack (of penis), but rather as a mainstreaming of feminism meant to bring new notions of female activity and agency in line with traditional concepts of a feminine appearance, something that certainly also holds true for Egyptian action heroines.

Female revenge is not a recent motif. In *The Call of the Curlew* (1959) Amna (Fatin Hamama) decides to revenge her sister's seduction and death. Her means, however, are merely psychological: she plans to lure the seducer into a relationship that may empower her to torture him emotionally. She does not take up arms. However, she almost falls prey to her own avenge on the emotional level. This applies also to another film from the same period, the crime-of-honor drama *Blood on the Nile/Dima' 'ala al-Nil* (1961) by Niazi Mustafa starring Hind Rustum. Ironically in this case, the turning point that throws the raging avenger back into her 'femininity' comes at the moment at which she takes up arms. After having shot and injured her husband's murderer, a man from a neighboring village, she has a change of heart and nurses her enemy's wound, not only then falling in love with him, but learning that she had earlier been betrayed by the very husband whom she was trying to avenge.

The motif of the armed female avenger trapped by her emotional vulnerability was subsequently reenacted by Nadia al-Gindi in the melodrama *al-Batniya/al-Batniya* (1980). Challenging the leader of a clan in order to avenge her own seduction and humiliation, she unknowingly kills her own son. Thus the melodramatic twist disempowers her at the very moment when she becomes powerful enough to take effective action. This is reminiscent of Amna, punished by her own plan of revenge. These typical melodramatic devices gradually ceased, giving way to the possibility of real, unpunished revenge—particularly social revenge.

Ma'ali Zayid as the female avenger in *The Execution Squad*, 1989

Thus, recent female avengers fall loosely into two distinct categories: the 'political' and the 'sexual' avenger. The political avenger is a cross-gender category, as the sex of the avenger is secondary. The headmistress in *Disco Disco* (1994) who kills the drug-dealer in order to save her pupils could be easily exchanged for a man. Not so the florist in *The Murderess* or the wife in *The Woman and the Cleaver/al-Mar'a wa-l-satur* (1997), as will be discussed shortly. The reason for the revenge in the first is a social one, not sexually defined as in the other two, which may be considered the major rape-revenge narratives of the 1990s.

The Woman and the Cleaver by Sa'id Marzuq took up a real crime that happened in Alexandria involving a woman who had killed and cut her husband into pieces. The film reenacts the crime as a flashback, starting with the discovery of the body parts and the investigation. It is centered on the female protagonist, an affluent widow and mother of an adolescent daughter who is approached by an elderly and seemingly respectable official. After their marriage he manages to take over her property. When she discovers his real character it is already too late. However, she decides not to leave him, hoping to retrieve some of her belongings, but after her daughter is sexually molested by her stepfather and she herself is abused and raped by him, she eventually decides to kill and dismember him.

The plot constructs the wife clearly as a victim. This is underlined by director Saʻid Marzuq's *mise-en-scène*. In a strikingly visual film language he choses several unusual locations at the seaside and special times of day, such as foggy dawns and deep dark nights, to create a hopeless and desperate atmosphere. He also underlines the woman's 'object' position through a series of distinctive and contrasting low- and high-angle camera perspectives applied particularly in the abuse, rape, and killing scenes. Nabila ʻUbaid's body language, always apt to elicit sympathy, is also calculated to reassert her vulnerability. Even more importantly, the film's structure shows the woman as trapped in an action-reaction structure where her enemy is always a step ahead. Even the murder is represented as a reaction, not a premeditated choice. Thus, the heroine is constructed along the lines of passivity.

Not so a film by female director Inas al-Dighidi, though she also adduces rape and male abuse as a reason for her heroine's crimes in *The Murderess*. Even though the action-reaction pattern is not completely absent from the plot, it does not govern the succession of scenes as much as in *The Woman and the Cleaver*. Instead, the reason for the woman's action is only induced into the action twice: once in the prologue where the heroine (performed by belly dancer Fifi ʻAbdu), then a little schoolgirl, is raped in a park; and then as a flashback showing the abuses of the adult woman by her husband and how she responds by killing him. The rest of the plot is divided into alternating sections, in accordance with the heroine's schizophrenia. By day, Raga' is known as a silent, gentle florist, whereas at night she dresses up, accompanies men to their homes—and leaves them dead.

Crucial to the *mise-en-scène* of this part is not only the nocturnal settings in the nightclub but also the woman's 'vamp' outfit of tight, short black dress and high heels. Contrary to *The Woman and the Cleaver*, where the portrayal of the heroine remains in a way dull and flat, as she uniformly represents weakness and vulnerability, al-Dighidi's heroine sparkles with contradictions. It is her constant transformation, her binary construction, that shapes the film's ebb and flow. No wonder it ends as violently as it starts: a completely disintegrated woman is taken to the gallows, dragged half unconscious through the prison corridors, urinating on the floor out of fear. This final scene is conceived as an outcome of the prelude, creating sympathy for the murderess and marking the completion of the circle of injustice. As much as it represents the ultimate punishment of the 'dark' side of the heroine, it does not completely undermine the force of the killing scenes, as neither her surroundings nor the law have proven able to deal with or take into account her 'good' side.

Feminism as a Problem: The Case of Inas al-Dighidi

As we saw in the case of Inas al-Dighidi, women directors have not necessarily transcended the victim discourse in favor of a stronger enpowerment of their female characters, at least during the 1980s, even though critics started praising 'women's cinema' *(sinima al-mar'a)* as a new film category. Yet with the appearance of a larger number of women directors in the mid-1980s the question rose as to whether these woman directors were really able to enforce a new agenda, artistically and intellectually, in the form of a women's cinema, or if they even produced a feminist counter-cinema that deviates markedly from mainstream representations.

In the first place it has to be stated that this question starts from a false assumption, in portraying mainstream cinema as univocal and conservative by nature. Some of the major concepts of Western second-wave feminist film theory formulated two decades ago by scholars such as Laura Mulvey, Pam Cook, and Claire Johnson regarded film industry as a feature of the patriarchal system in so far as its products were designed primarily for male desire. To them woman's image was not simply distorted but conceived as an overall ideological construction based to a large extent on language and psychology (cf. Penley 1988, 1–24). Largely in accordance with the Freudian model these theorists considered the manner of women's representation on the screen (as well as the assumed psychoanalytic disposition of the female spectator) responsible for woman being relegated to the realm of the object who could by no means acquire the status of a subject of desire (Mulvey 1989, 31).

However, this concept was strongly class-biased. While the average female spectator was believed to have been 'duped' by popular cinema, the educated academic female critic was assumed to be more informed and enjoying larger awareness. Consequently, only feminist avant-garde cinema or 'counter-cinema' was regarded as capable of revolutionizing women's position in patriarchal society (Johnston 1988, 40). However, the psychological as well as ideological implications of these early key theories were later qualified by Tina Modleski and Jackie Stacey as monolithic, static, and ahistorical, but also as a false generalization of the female spectator that disregards actual differences in class, race, and sexual orientation.

Fifi 'Abdu in *The Murderess*, 1992

Although this controversial debate did not make its way into Egyptian film criticism, the arguments raised by it resemble, not so much in detail but in overall orientation, the criticism uttered by Latin American representatives and third worldist cinema against mainstream film and whose views began to gain currency in the Arab world, too (Shafik 1998, 29). The discursive schism that 'progressive' film critics set up, differentiating between mainstream and 'counter-cinema,' in the first place perpetuated the uncomprehending evaluation of popular 'lowbrow' cinema such as melodrama or later the action film. What was also profoundly problematic in the case of Egypt, was that critics failed to acknowledge the misconception that addressing gender inequality is not necessarily equal to defending a culturally alternative or counter position and that in fact many of these so-called feminist works were by no means more liberating, and no less a site of a discursive 'struggle,' than any other commercial films.

One case in point is the work of director Inas al-Dighidi, the first Egyptian woman who succeeded as a really popular, commercially successful, mainstream director with fifteen full-length feature films in fourteen years (Hillauer 2005, 61). Nevertheless her 'persona' and work do exemplify certain problematic aspects of gender relations in Egyptian society: on the one hand, negotiating sexual identity quite openly; on the other, by creating an ambiguous polyphony of male and female voices. It is precisely because of her partly fierce, partly ironic depictions of male and female deficiencies, that her work does not lend itself to a coherent feminist perspective. The inclusion of contradictory competitive discursive items leaves in some of her works enough space, if not to challenge, at least to undermine the most dominant discourses related to women, even though in the press al-Dighidi has denied vigorously any affiliation to feminism or the so-called women's film *(sinima al-mar'a)*. Yet it seems that this denial is most symptomatic of her defensive self-assertion as a woman in a man's world, in particular, and of the problematic situation of women directors in the Egyptian film industry in general. This is what al-Dighidi's biography and films suggest; but it is also rooted in the historically discontinuous female presence in leading film professions.

Inas al-Dighidi was born in Cairo in 1954. She graduated in 1975 from the Higher Film Institute. A former assistant of Henri Barakat, Hasan al-Imam, and Salah Abu Seif among others, she managed after ten years of training to become one of the most prominent directors in mainstream cinema, combining largely female-oriented topics with relatively spectacular plots and a polished *mise-en-scène*. Her popular approach has permitted her (unlike committed New Realist directors, among others Khairy Beshara, Daoud 'Abd El-Sayed, Mohamed Khan, and the art film director Yousry Nasrallah), to release one or two films a year. What has added to her 'popular' outlook is that she has always felt at ease with what passes in Egypt as sex scenes. At the same time, she has often ignored sophisticated depictions of realistic characters and environments. The most striking feature of her work, however, has been its adoption of contradictory cross-sexual oriented strategies.

Women Directors

Al-Dighidi's exceptional success raises the question about the circumstances that may have allowed her and prevented others from rising to the top of the film industry at that particular time. This is an even more interesting question considering the fact that several women played a major role in establishing national cinema in Egypt. Numerous artists and actresses, starting with 'Aziza Amir, Assia Daghir, Fatima Rushdi, and Bahiga Hafiz worked in the late 1920s and 1930s as producers, scriptwriters, and directors. The first full-length feature to be considered entirely Egyptian, *Layla*, was codirected in 1927 by theater actress 'Aziza Amir, who also produced and starred in the film. Amir had been trained in Yusuf Wahbi's theater troupe Ramsis. In 1933 she directed her second and last film, *Atone for your Sin/Kaffari 'an khati'atik*. In 1929 *The Lady from the Desert* starred the Lebanese actress Assia Daghir who had also produced the film. Subsequently, Daghir not only performed in many films but remained one of Egypt's important producers until the 1980s.

In 1933 the popular actress Fatima Rushdi directed her only film, *The Marriage/al-Zawaj*. Even more important was the highly gifted Bahiga Hafiz, also a musical composer. In 1932 she produced, composed the soundtrack for, and starred in *The Victims/al-Dahaya* by Badr Lama, and in 1937 she directed the lavish costume drama, *Layla, the Bedouin*. Furthermore, the actress and belly dancer Amina Muhammad similarly acted in, produced, and directed her first and only film, *Tita Wong* (1937). This was the last Egyptian feature film directed by a woman until 1966, when actress Magda al-Sabbahi made the poorly received *Whom I Love/Man uhibb*. Sabbahi had started acting in 1949, largely in the roles of naive, spoilt girls. Her most interesting role was as a *mujahida* (resistance fighter) in Youssef Chahine's *Jamila the Algerian/Jamila al-jaza'iriya* (1958). She was still working as a producer in the late 1990s.

For a long interregnum, which ended in 1984 with the appearance of Nadia Hamza's *Sea of Illusions/Bahr al-awham*, no woman succeeded in directing a full-length feature film. Some of the main reasons for this silence may have been the economic consolidation but also the industrialization of film production that took place in the late 1930s. A good deal of the early cineastes, men and women, were members of prosperous families or had acquired property and fame through their previous artistic work, something that facilitated their investment in the new medium. Elite women had anyway, since the late nineteenth century, formed the vanguard of feminist consciousness challenging some of the traditional gender biases of their own class. For a director like Bahiga Hafiz, who came from an affluent family, had studied music in Paris, and whose activity in cinema was explicitly rooted in a feminist understanding, the step into the thriving seventh art was still thorny enough.

"Many have criticized me for having chosen this profession, calling it a great scandal! But have they ever considered the difficulties of all kinds thrown in the way of a woman alone, who is without resources but wishes to remain independent? What pushed me toward the cinema therefore was not mere whim nor a simple wish to appear before the public but my need to create a condition that would guarantee my freedom" (quoted in Badran 1996, 191).

Bahiga Hafiz's boldness cost her dearly: she not only lost the support of her family, but ruined herself financially so that she is said to have passed away in 1982 alone and impoverished ('Abd al-Rahman 2002, 47). Other women from a less privileged background, to name only 'Aziza Amir, or the dancer Amina Muhammad, were also brave enough to venture their own money in the production of films. But this was nonetheless a rather experimental enterprise, not least because most of these women did not find the means or the opportunity to direct a second film. Doubtless in today's perspective they may be considered 'independent cinema' producers who used only the most rudimentary division of labor, a form of production that could hardly survive, given the rising competition of large and financially potent enterprises such as Studio Misr.

Despite the existence and important contribution of those women pioneers, moral objections to women's participation in entertainment persisted for a long time, even though the general conditions hostile to women's education had changed by the second half of the twentieth century. After the foundation of the national Higher Film Institute in 1959, education and training in film-related professions was available for everyone and offered moreover the opportunity to receive academic degrees. Many girls joined the Institute, were trained in different fields ranging from editing, through set design to script writing and directing, and even became professors at the Institute. Yet families were not always supportive, as Sandra Nash'at, the director of half a dozen full-length films (among them two television films) affirmed (Hillauer 2001, 91). Inas al-Dighidi, too, reported how strongly her family resisted her decision to study cinema and how long it took them to accept her work as worthwhile (Ihab 1993, 23).

It may be true that prejudices and restrictive morals are the reason why it took women such a long time to reappear in the ranks of film directors. However, this is not the only reason, as it is telling to compare the presence of women in secondary film branches and professions to their feature film directing. Female filmmakers have succeeded in entering in larger numbers the less expensive and more marginal field of the short film and documentary. One of the first women to direct documentaries for television was Sa'diyya Ghunim in 1961. Others followed in directing films for the

National Film Center, such as Farida 'Arman, Mona Migahid, Firyal Kamil and Nabiha Lutfi. Documentary filmmaker Ateyyat El Abnoudy has made a name for herself abroad since 1971. Apart from that, numerous women have worked as scriptwriters for television. It must be suspected that the true reason for the shortage of female directors of full-length feature film is that women are not easily admitted to the film industry. They may have difficulties exploiting the so far male-dominated professional networks. Possibly also producers have been reluctant to entrust high budgets to female directors, as mentioned by Inas al-Dighidi for instance ('Ali 1985, 47).

Notwithstanding, the year 1985 represented a kind of turning point. A total of three films by three different women were released: Nadia Salim's unsuccessful comedy *The Doorkeeper Manages the Building/Sahib al-idara bawwab al-'imara*, Nadia Hamza's *The Women/al-Nisa'*, and Inas al-Dighidi's *Pardon Me, Law!* Asma' al-Bakri's first film, *Beggars and Noblemen/Shahadhun wa nubala'* (1991), adapted from an existentialist novel by Albert Cossery (Qusairi), was most appreciated abroad. The most prolific directors so far have been Nadia Hamza and Inas al-Dighidi, followed more recently by Sandra Nash'at and Kamla Abu Zikri.

Most of the new women directors were trained at the Higher Film Institute and work according to the conditions in the film industry, or in the case of An'am Muhammad 'Ali, 'Ilwiya Zaki, and Sandra Nash'at (at first), in television. They have dealt with a variety of topics and do not necessarily focus on women's issues. 'Ali for example directed the spectacular male-dominated war film, *The Way to Eilat/al-Tariq ila Eilat* (1995) but also the highly successful television serial *Umm Kulthum* (1999). Ironically, it is mainly Inas al-Dighidi who, despite her denials and preference for genre cinema, ranging from crime to comedy, has constantly addressed gender relations, including inequality and abuse, in films such as *The Murderess, Cheap Flesh, Lobster/Istakuza* (1996), and *Lace*.

Woman-Director Against Her Sex?

Doubtless, Inas al-Dighidi's career was possible because of the increasing admission of women to the whole audiovisual field, despite the fact that in feature film production she remained a pretty exceptional case throughout the 1990s. In press accounts she has herself framed her success in quite a gendered way. She was the only girl among several brothers who she felt had received, unlike her, a "first class citizen treatment" (Ihab 1993, 23). This fired her ambition to succeed in a male domain (Ihab 1993, 24). In the press Inas al-Dighidi (like actress Nadia al-Gindi, as we will see later) was often placed in a defensive position, morally and ideologically. Already in 1985 she was accused of going too far in her presentation of "sex-scenes" and of being "blindly biased for the daughters of her sex" ('Ali 1985, 46). From the start, al-Dighidi granted that she had a feeling for women's issues, but did not want to be reduced to them. In 1990 she was quoted as insisting, "I am not specialized in women's film" ('Ayad 1990). Also al-Gumhuriya newspaper wrote that she "refuses her name to be linked to films that discuss women's issues only. She rather directs realist films that concern everybody" ('Afifi 1990). At the same time magazines began to print pictures of the director with her children.

Two points seem pivotal in the director's self defense: first, the refusal to be associated with women's film as a special category; second, the view that women's issues are considered secondary or marginal per se, as indicated by the qualifier 'only.' Al-Dighidi's refusal to let her sex play any role in the evaluation of her work shows an attempt to escape from the stigma and the marginalization that those categories evidently produce. The director seems to have found herself in the odd position of being forced to dissociate herself, at least verbally, from any particularly feminist perspective, whereby she has been caught in a futile attempt to divert attention from her sex. The futility of this is signaled also by the way the press has constructed the director's persona, similar to that of a film star, by stressing her personal status, her marriage, her children, and so on, which is not done in the case of male directors.

How challenging the question of 'women's film' is to the director's eval-uation was clarified in Gene al-Muqadasi's study *Feminist Cinema? The Films of Inas al-Dighidi and Nadia Hamza.* Posing this question al-Muqadasi quoted the critic and scriptwriter Rafiq al-Sabban, who holds al-Dighidi's work as a good example of women's film, and one of my own statements that al-Dighidi does not represent such a cinema (al-Muqadasi 2000, 381). While al-Muqadasi admits that whether or not these films may be considered feminine or even feminist is a complicated question, she nonetheless argues that these films have a feminist dimension, as they seek to improve women's condition in society, without further defining and work-ing out the film-history implications of the terminology she applies.

From the 1970s Western feminist film theory endeavored to envision a new feminist cinema that was thought to exist in opposition to mainstream and patriarchal production. Kaplan, for instance, praised the counter-cin-ema and avant-garde fictions by Marguerite Duras, Margarethe von Trotta, and Yvonne Rainer because they refused to construct "the masochistic female spectator," refrained from offering an idealized image of woman (Kaplan 1983, 104) and held back pleasures linked to sub-conscious expe-riences. Moreover, Kaplan cited a number of feminist experimental and documentary productions that worked on expressing female subjectivity, attempted to deconstruct "classical patriarchal texts" through which women "are spoken," and, last but not least, reflected women's history "and the whole problem of writing history" (Kaplan 1983, 138).

On the other hand, out of the sensibility created through feminist analy-ses, film theorists in general began developing the notion of 'women's film' as a genre description of melodrama and 'weepies' as a way to comprehend women's special role in them, be it as agent or addressee (Altman 1998, 27). It is evident that al-Dighidi's work does not fit into either classification: counter-cinema or popular women's film. Moreover, it is questionable how useful such categories are in our attempt to comprehend what a woman director has to say about her gender and what issues she negotiates implic-itly. In fact, I think they are detrimental to real analysis. For they gloss over the ideological and discursive fissures and negotiations that take place in the cinematic work, irrespective of any gender affiliation.

Al-Dighidi's oeuvre, just like that of male directors, is filled with contradictions and negotiations regarding women's position in real and imaginary societies. Moreover, her films do not lend themselves to quick definitions of either the feminine or the feminist, even if they show a tendency to subvert current gender concepts, as becomes clear, too, when we review the director's development. For al-Dighidi's filmography itself is divided into two slightly different periods: the first is dominated by vulnerable women and strong, violent male father figures, while the second is characterized by same-level heterosexual confrontations.

Her first film *Pardon Me, Law!* (1985) dealt overtly with gender inequality by pointing out how the law differentiates between man and woman in the case of the same crime. This melodramatic stance was further underlined in her two consecutive films *Time of the Prohibited/Zaman al-mamnu'* (1988) and *The Challenge.* The latter continued the story of *Pardon Me, Law!* presenting the protagonist struggling in vain against her dominant former father-in-law to retrieve the custody of her son. Subsequently, al-Dighidi's narratives included more and more aggressive female characters, along with the defensive type. This multiplication of the feminine aspect is particularly apparent in a film like *Cheap Flesh* with its three heroines. This trio was preceded earlier by another in *One Woman is Not Enough.* Although this particular film suggested, like *Lace*, a cock-of-the-walk theme, it underlined the variety of the three heroines affiliated to the hero (Ahmad Zaki). His indecisiveness in view of their very different personalities is constructed less around his virility than it is around the three women's differences.

The notion of intra-feminine difference was also emphasized through the constant pairings that occasionally amounted to schizophrenia. In *Lace* the two girlfriends are confronted with male paralysis, as the main character is not able to decide which of the two women he loves more. What seems at first sight to be an ironic comment on polygamous practices is at second glance the worship of female irresistibility, for these powerful sirens are not far from the traditional concept that equates woman with sexuality. While in this particular film the difference between the two heroines was eradicated the moment they came to possess the same man sexually, other works were more insistent in their assertion of intra-sexual disparity, even in alienating a woman from her own sexuality, such as the heroines of *The Murderess* and *Disco Disco*, both works by al-Dighidi. The first in particular provided no reconciliation whatsoever between the character's sexuality and other elements of her personality. Even more telling is that these characters were associated with rape-revenge plots.

The female avenger must not be considered just a by-product of or reaction to male possessive violence but may on the contrary signal an aggressive rejection of its very existence. Yet, the dressed up female killer, the ultimate incorporation of the femme fatale, may at the same time embody sick sexuality. In *Night Talk* we encounter a similar comment on sexuality. In distancing Nadia from her employer, who lives on the sex business, we are reminded of the virgin–whore dichotomy, but at the same time the 'whore' is clearly pictured as one possible response to male domination. Sex, as exemplified in this case as a means of gaining social and political control, demands, if not moral, at least social justifications.

These partly contradictory, partly complementary positions expressed in the filmmaker's works were doubtless the reason for the divided views on her that reproached her above all for not having any restraints in representing sexuality. However, these ambiguities may as well be read as the negotiations of a director, not only with the film industry but also with her largely male scriptwriters. This is why it would be another reductionism to relegate al-Dighidi to any ill-defined women's film categories, whether mainstream or vanguard. What her work is in fact about is the long-standing struggle of a woman with and against her sex in the context of her society's increasingly ferocious moralism.

CHAPTER 4

Female Stardom, Myth-production, and Morality

S tars, whether directors, such as Youssef Chahine or actors, to name only Omar Sharif, have always been all-too-natural by-products of Egypt's long commercial cinematic tradition. In fact an audience commonly recognizes a film by the names of the star performers and not by its director. Locating a tape in a video store is achieved by searching first of all for its leading actors. The names of stars, stories, and latest releases are circulated in numerous television programs and are the source of national pride. Moreover, Egyptian movie stars have become as much part of the country's public life as a feature of its contemporary urban space. Not only do magazines, newspapers, and postcards displayed by street vendors show their images, but so do huge painted or photographic posters that sit enthroned on the walls and rooftops of buildings, adding to the distinctive appearance of major cities. And as elsewhere, stars have tended to become part of daily life's private and public gossip, by representing "ordinary people whose joys and sorrows become extraordinary in the intensity stardom imparts to them" (Gledhill 1991, 213).

Thus it has been suggested that stars are likely to become symbolic agents of a people's imagined community and may operate as mediators of prevalent cultural discourses. In the light of this theory, the role adopted by female performers during the last two decades in the Egyptian cultural arena in relation to veiling and to Egyptian society's changing moral and ethical framework, seems unsurprising. It displays the ongoing discursive competition and interaction of different ideological stances such as Islamism and modernism. For, as Christine Gledhill has suggested, the star's image "is spun off from the persona and film roles, both condensing and dispersing desires, meanings, values and styles that are current in culture" (Gledhill 1991, 217).

Indeed, as a star's evaluation and the interpretation of his or her cinematic roles largely circles around several contradictory and binary concepts: conservative and enlightened, traditional and modern, native and imported, rich and poor, good and evil. The basic dichotomy in the normative system does not only saturate the actor's persona and cinematic text, but is reflected also on the structural level of the star system itself. This is clearly mirrored in the controversial status of female performers in general. For "it appeared that the form and context of entertainment and the sex of the performer were important criteria . . ." (van Nieuwkerk 1995, 13).

From the late 1980s until 1994, as many as twenty-one actresses and at least two actors had decided to retreat from show business for religious reasons (cf. Kamil 1994, 12 and back cover), a visible sign of the so-called morality that spread in Egyptian society. The most spectacular case was the singer and actress Shadia who had starred between 1949 and 1983 in some one hundred feature films. After donning the veil in 1987 she hardly appeared in public and refused to attend her honoring during the Cairo International Film Festival in 1995. Other formerly popular dropouts were Huda Sultan, Shams al-Barudi, Suhair Ramzi, Suhair al-Babli, and Madiha Kamil. Some of them, like Shams al-Barudi and singer Huda Sultan, had built up vamp personae with much sex appeal displayed in clothing and behavior. The secular press rushed to formulate explanations, such as that the apparently remorseful performers had accepted immense bribes from Muslim fundamentalist circles. The government-controlled political magazine *Ruz al-Yusuf* reported that the actress Ilham Shahin had refused one million U.S. dollars supposedly offered to her for that reason (Guda 1993, 12).

Indeed the late 1980s and early 1990s showed increasing signs of a 'new morality' on and off the screen, in dress, behavior, and in public opinion. An important catalyst for this development was the Egyptian cinema's dependence on the Gulf States as its major export market. Together with the petrodollars (which were also brought home by migrant Egyptian labor), prudishness moved into Egyptian movies. While Hussein Kamal's film, *My Father is Up the Tree/Abi fawq al-shagara* (1969) had been an attraction in its time because of its supposed one hundred kisses, during the 1980s and early 1990s hardly a kiss appeared on the screen. Female clothing became more moderate in what it revealed. At the same time the bodies of the actresses became more voluptuous and corpulent, as in the case of Suhair Ramzi, Layla 'Ilwi, and Ilham Shahin.

In the Egyptian media the new morality had surfaced in 1983 with an outraged debate sparked off by the prohibition of two mainstream productions of the same year, *Alley of Love/Darb al-hawa* by Husam al-Din Mustafa and *Khamsa Bab/Khamsa Bab* by Nadir Galal, starring two controversial but highly successful stars, 'Adil Imam and Nadia al-Gindi. Most journalists and officials spoke in favor of the verdict and demanded more respect for tradition and good morals. Since that time the press and the courts have started competing in censorship, initiating furious media campaigns as well as suing certain films and their makers (Farid 1995, 113). The most spectacular case was launched in 1994 by an Islamist lawyer against Youssef Chahine after the screening of *The Emigrant* (1994) which was accused of depicting one of the Qur'an's prophets, something that is prohibited by official censorship.

One of the forces that paved the way for this shift, was Sadat's ambivalent Islamization policy. In his attempts to diminish the influence of Nasserists and to suppress socialist ideology he at first silently approved Islamist tendencies and then tried even to contain them when planning to introduce the Islamic *shari'a* as a major source of legislation and by promulgating *al-'ayb* (shame) law in 1980, which served at the same time as a convenient means by which to censor critical ideas (Krämer 1986, 53). Also, it is assumed that the temporary emigration of 4.5 million Egyptian workers to the Gulf States in the early 1980s from the cities and the countryside, which followed the new regime's loosening of travel restrictions, contributed as well to the new ideology (Krämer 1986, 22). Confronted with religious and ideological conservatism in their host countries, the migrants came back not only with a large amount of hard currency but also with more conservative and pro-Islamist concepts.

The veiling phenomenon among actresses ceased relatively abruptly after 1994. One reason may be saturation, meaning that all those performers insecure enough to bow to religious pressure (or probably financial offers) had left, and those who remained felt confident enough not to quit. The heavy governmental crackdown on Islamists could also have been a decisive, if not stronger reason. According to Raymond Baker, the secular but only partially democratically legitimized regime of President Husni Mubarak, who succeeded Sadat in 1982, used the terrorist assaults undertaken by Islamist extremists, particularly in 1995, as a pretext to curtail the influence of the non-violent but socially active Islamic moderates via persecution, detention and censorship (Baker 1997, 125). The attack on the veiling of actresses by officially controlled media organs has to be perceived in that context. One of its major strategies was, if we believe Baker, to blur the distinction between the extremists and the rather intellectual and peaceful moderates (Baker 1997, 128).

The public attention given to the retreat of actresses stemmed from the strong symbolic and politically mobilizing potential of the veil. This political mobilization had been made visible during the first wave of new veiling introduced by the Islamist student movement in the late 1970s (Talhami 1996, 55). In addition, the mythical potential of stardom was able to transform veiling at that point into an advertisement for the New Islamist wave of the 1980s and its message to send women back into the home. In this respect, the veiling of performers was clearly distinct from the 'new veiling' that was embraced in the course of the 1980s by women of all social classes, who otherwise retained a modernist agenda in their way of life as Arlene McLeod showed in her book (1992).

Once veiled, most Egyptian actresses stopped working, thereby asserting a strict division between the performing arts and Muslim piety, the public and the private, women and labor. (Huda Sultan has become one of the few exceptions. She continued acting with an unobtrusive veil or *hijab*, and the same applies to new-generation star Hanan Turk.) This division was further underlined by the retreat of several male actors, such as Youssef Chahine's former cinematic alter ego Muhsin Muhi al-Din. Thus Egyptian fiction, televised or cinematic, has tended to present largely unveiled female characters, ignoring the strong presence of the veil in daily life and in public. This fact was to reinforce the schism between on-screen representations and off-screen conditions and to expose cinematic representation as clearly fictional (or even immoral) and opposed to people's real-life experiences. It seemed indeed as though the headline-grabbing veilings of famous actresses marked a victory of religion over entertainment. The whole profession was at stake. More importantly, the attempt to exclude certain women from the formation of collective fantasies became a tool for countering the secular myth production initiated by mass-mediated stardom.

Confronting Islamism

Recent religious teachings (disseminated, ironically, by the same prestigious mass media channels) have formulated a counter-discourse on audiovisual arts and fostered the negative view of performing women in particular. The most influential voice was that of the preacher Shaykh Mitwalli al-Sha'rawi, who assessed the role of actresses in the entertainment industry negatively, because they "incite sexual instincts." The equally popular Shaykh Muhammad al-Ghazali cited arts in the same breath as "atheism and prostitution" (Tadros 1994, 28–30). In the same vein goes a statement of Muhammad Qutb quoted by Muhammad Walid Gada' in his book *al-Mawqif min sinima islamiya* ('An Attitude Toward Muslim Cinema'): "Cinema in my view is the last art that could enter the realm of Islamic art, not because cinema as such is prohibited, but because its current trite, naked, degenerated outlook is very remote from the Islamic atmosphere, but it is able, as any other art, to become Islamic if it follows the principles of Islamic art" (Gadaʻ 1989, 71). Gadaʻ moves further to present women in particular as one of the major setbacks for the creation of Islamic cinema due to the very practical problem of how to present them in all realms of life, that is also at home and in private with a head cover (Gadaʻ 1989, 85).

Given this centrality of women to the religious debate, it is no wonder that Egypt's female stars were instrumental in the nationwide confirmation of the Islamists' point of view through the phenomenon of veiling in show business, which coincided with a wave of extremely violent Islamist attacks against tourists and Egyptian civilians that reached their peak during the years 1993 and 1994. The government reacted with tight security measures and massive sanctions, including human rights abuses. This went along with the veiling phenomenon being vehemently discussed in Egyptian print media and thereby becoming the source of severe controversies and counter-discourses.

Tellingly, the media apparatus, through television serials and a number of cinematic narratives and depictions, made its own use of sexual morals in rebutting the fundamentalist position, reflecting the regime's version of the crisis read solely as a security conflict—an adoption of the American "clash of civilizations" interpretation (cf. Baker 1995, 17). Other films appeared alongside the veiling phenomenon and presented ferocious, morally aberrant Islamist characters, their most spectacular example being *The Terrorist* by Nadir Galal (1994) starring 'Adil Imam, a political film that was released in Cairo and elsewhere under tight security measures. Imam (who had been blacklisted by the Islamists just like other performers) featured as a sexually and economically deprived young Islamist who agrees to carry out terrorist acts after the head of his group promises to solve his problems, first of all to find him a wife. However, after a dramatic twist, including a failed terrorist operation, he is taken into the home of a secular upper-class family, whose hospitable, moderate, and humane attitudes teach the terrorist a positive lesson.

The plot, as well as the characterization of the Islamists, attempts to denounce Islamism as a moral aberration that does not shrink from using any criminal method—to the effect that, as Raymond Baker put it, it seems that "at the heart of Egypt's ills stands the irrational terrorist, the enemy of culture and civilization, and not the failed policies and terrible desperation that produced him" (Baker 1995, 27). The major point of critique directed toward the Muslim extremists in *The Terrorist* is their sexual morality, depicted as covering women up on the one hand while enjoying polygamy excessively, marrying and divorcing women at will, in sum exposing an uncontrollable sexual desire that renders their whole religious credibility questionable. "Having squandered any opportunity in the character of the terrorist to explore the motivations and the mentality of those young people tragically drawn to the violent minorities, the film panders instead to adolescent fantasies of sex and violence" (Baker 1995, 25) embodied in some highly voyeuristic scenes, such as the camera following the buttocks of a nicely dressed woman walking in front of Imam, in his role as a terrorist, through the streets.

'Adil Imam (right) in *The Terrorist*, 1994. Cherchez la femme.

Other televised and cinematic fictional works adopted the same mode of denunciation. Woman director Inas al-Dighidi's film *Disco Disco* (1994) presented a morally strong single woman, a headmistress, who fights against ethical decay, criminality, and last but not least, Islamism. The petite, lady-like actress Nagla' Fathi featured in this heroic role. She shows not only responsibility toward her pupils but has also taken upon herself the burden of educating her younger brother who studies at her high school. He and other friends get introduced to drugs and are actively encouraged to use them by a local drug dealer. When the headmistress finds out she asks the authorities for help, but is denied any support, as the dealer is a respected and powerful entrepreneur. When no one takes positive action, she eventually confronts and kills the drug dealer.

Although incited by the absence of law and order to a violent reaction, the heroine of *Disco Disco* embodies the ideal of modern enlightened motherhood. Her courage and strength are related to her role as an educator and guardian of coming generations. She does not show an interest in romantic adventures: her relation to an admirer who wants to marry her comes secondary to her duties. Nonetheless she is shown as sexually vulnerable. The danger does not spring from the greedy drug dealer, though, but from a Muslim fundamentalist who forces his sister, one of the headmistress's female students, to take the veil and to stop attending school. When the (unveiled) headmistress confronts him for the girl's sake, he attempts to rape her. With this the film sets up a clear opposition between enlightened but virtuous modernism on the one hand and doubtful religious extremism on the other, and moreover between the two extremes of a selfless sense of community and avaricious materialist egotism. The character traits of the headmistress are decisive in setting up these differences. She is a serious, responsible character, who combines care for family members with committed work outside the home. The casting of Nagla' Fathi, who has no record of playing loose women or *femmes fatales*, and is married in real life to an acclaimed journalist, additionally underscores these characteristics.

What seems crucial to the film is that women and sexuality were used not only by fundamentalists in their attack on the performing arts, but also by the State and the secularists in their counter-attack. This is how women have been turned into the main subject of negotiation between both major ideological currents, and it does not imply that the latter hold a more liberal position. The core difference between the two positions lies primarily in the issue of veiling, while as some researchers have demonstrated, the new centrist (moderate) Islamists and the secular modernists agree on such disparate matters as the importance of conjugal love, female education, and women's outstanding contribution to the formation of the future citizen (though not always on female labor) (Abu-Lughod 1998, 251). What they share, moreover, is the same moral concept regarding women, notably the acceptance of the virgin–whore dichotomy, as will be shown later in the analysis of a New Realist film from the same period.

Reading Female Stars

Starting from Peter Brook's notion of myth and melodrama, Christine Gledhill counts among the star's functions that he or she "sets out to demonstrate within the transaction of everyday life the continuing operation of a Manichean battle between good and evil which infuses human actions with ethical consequences and therefore with significance" (Gledhill 1991, 209). Based on Edgar Morin's argument made in 1972 that film actors are the equivalent of twentieth-century gods in this secularized battle between good and evil, the star she perceives as a quasi-mythical figure who serves as a source of wishes and desire, a guideline of morals and ethics. In other words the aura of movie stars mirrors the modern individualist existence in a secularized post-sacral world that demands a new kind of mythology.

Yet this concept may not be fully at work in Egypt, given the uneven path of modernization that did not affect the whole population equally or to the same degree. From this perspective it seems uncertain to what extent stars attain such mythological power as described above, particularly if differentiating factors such as class, gender, and environment are taken into account, which do affect perception or the process of 'reading' films and their stars decisively. In fact, semiotics has provided a complex manner of comprehending this process. The "assumption here is that spectatorship is structured not just by the experience of going to the movies and being seduced by the spectacle on screen, but by the influence of a whole range of texts" (Mayne 1993, 64). Hence, the stars' appearance and perception should be understood as a contradictory process of writing and reading.

Star personae as well as the audience may constantly shift between 'the readerly' *(le lisible)* and 'the writerly' *(le scriptible)*, to use Roland Barthes' terms (c.f. Barthes 1974), which comes down to the essential query as to who produces the text(s) in question (Mayne 1993, 15). Although it is clear that a star is produced or 'written' by the industry and his/her consecutive film roles, along with other mass-mediated texts and images such as press reviews, he or she may also, as Richard Dyer noted, become an 'author' who subverts or contradicts the film text including common readings of his or her persona (Dyer 1979, 174). The same applies to the spectator who, being at the very place of reading, may as well resist, deflect, or subvert proposed texts.

The anthropologist Lila Abu-Lughod undertook one of the few empirical studies in Egypt that could help elucidate this point, in her analysis of the attitude of women from an Upper Egyptian village toward televised nightly serials and/or soap operas, their identification with characters and their acceptance of unconventional gender roles (Abu-Lughod 1997, 16). The results may not be entirely relevant to my argumentation as they are related to a rural television audience that may never have set a foot in a movie theater; yet Abu-Lughod's informants are an interesting group of spectators to consider, as their living conditions are thoroughly distinct from urban middle- or upper-class audiences. Furthermore they are subject to mass mediated messages without having sufficient opportunity to express and disseminate their own views and opinions through the same channels. The program of national public television often conveys the impression of being largely designed by and oriented toward the taste and ideas of the urban middle class, except for some marginal programs developed by regional channels.

Abu-Lughod states that modernist messages voiced by enlightened middle-class writers, for example regarding women's right to work, tended to be misunderstood or ignored by her informants as they could not be related to their experience, since Egyptian peasant women have to work very hard for their survival. Moreover, their life has been strongly defined and confined by their family and community and the need to keep up their good reputation. No wonder that the women she questioned tended, notwithstanding their occasional fascination and curiosity, to comment negatively on the clothing and behavior of female performers, judging it to be immoral and westernized (Abu-Lughod 1995, 58). This, despite the fact that some of those actresses enjoy high esteem in national television and the local press, and hold powerful positions in the film industry, as will be shown later, while radiating all the glamour of the local entertainment industry.

Yet individual characterization and evaluation does not count as much as the normative system in which the star operates. Recent feminist film theory has shed some light on the role of stars in the development of consumerism, fashion, design and cosmetics in correlation with cinema in the Western countries (Hollows 2000, 112–60). Such a link can certainly also be established in Egypt and the Arab world, where the element of overt resistance to 'Western' models has become more decisive since the mid-1970s, when the first wave of modern veiling began. Since than a considerable schism between the public dress code and the habits of the entertainment industry has been engendered. While more and more women dressed according to the new religious modesty filled the streets, Egypt's female stars continued to appear in bathing suits and miniskirts at least until the 1980s; something that makes it even more understandable why Abu-Lughod's poor rural informers, in spite of any fascination they felt, did not consider actresses part of their 'moral community' (Abu-Lughod 1995, 61).

Such an assessment indicates in the first instance a decisive ideological fissure in relation to this group, which is in fact shared by other segments of the population. A similar judgment, according to Karin van Nieuwkerk, is also facilitated by traditional concepts of shame and honor characteristic of the urban lower class, in which the negative view of female entertainers, contrary to that of males, finds itself reflected in the colloquial saying, *al-ragil ma yi'ibhush shi'*('in a man, nothing is shameful') and is rooted in a historical development that is partly linked with colonialism. In the nineteenth century, female musicians and dancers gradually became associated with cheap weddings and even with risqué entertainment. Dancers were particularly discredited after the British authorities set up licensed brothels. This caused prostitutes to shift to dancing in nightclubs (Franken 1998, 267). During the first decades of the twentieth century the reputation of female dancers, particularly belly dancers, improved temporarily, due to the dance's partial elevation to an almost highbrow art form. A new urban version developed, also referred to as oriental dance, drawing from Western ballet and other mass-mediated dances. Artistically interested star dancers, starting with Badi'a Masabni and some of her disciples like Samya Gamal and Tahiyya Carioca, refined the traditional dance to what we are familiar with in early Egyptian movies. However, as mentioned earlier, starting from the late 1960s, Egyptian modern oriental dance witnessed a certain degree of stagnation, if not decay, in quality as well as in public esteem, while more contemporary star dancers, such as Nagwa Fu'ad and Fifi 'Abdu among others, related on-screen belly dancing increasingly to sexual seduction.

The admittance of female performance and mimicry to Arab-Egyptian culture is, furthermore, relatively new. The popular 'lowbrow' *muhabbazun* performances, which used to present sketches at feasts and weddings from the late seventeenth century, were reported not to include any women. It may be suspected that the exposure of Muslim women in front of a mixed or a male-only audience was disliked for religious as well as cultural reasons. The earliest female performers of the region who appeared in the developing European-inspired classical Arab theater were therefore either Jewesses or Christian Syrians (Landau 1958, 74). The first Egyptian actress to set a foot on the stage of the Cairo Opera House, that is, a very 'highbrow' milieu, in 1894, was a Jewess called Layla (Landau 1958, 68). However, after the turn of the century Muslim women, just like others, joined the numerous

Tahiyya Carioca (center) in *The Hero*, 1950

troupes that started evolving at that time and some of them, most notably Fatima Rushdi in the late 1920s, even headed such troupes.

Professional training in the national Performing Arts Institute founded in the 1950s and the advent of television in 1961 helped to reevaluate acting as a profession. Since the 1960s a further step toward differentiation took place: "star performers have ceased working in the less prestigious popular performing arts circuit, after they reach the higher echelons of art" (van Nieuwkerk 1995, 13). The press, but in particular television, played an important role in elevating certain entertainers and performers to star status while it attained the power to exclude others as being common or even vulgar (van Nieuwkerk 1995, 62). Thus, notions of talent, professionalism, and acting capabilities became important to the evaluation process, which in turn oriented itself along the dichotomy of high and lowbrow culture. The film industry, as the predecessor of television, was the first to set up the idea of the 'higher echelons of art,' a discourse that has been taken up by press and television alike in their evaluation of cinematic products.

The Egyptian Star System

Unlike the United States, where the star system evolved gradually in the period 1906–1913 along with a special discourse of acting and almost independently of theater,[19] the formation and consolidation of the Egyptian film industry was highly dependent on the exploitation of already existing theater and music stars. Some of the earliest fiction films relied on the contribution of popular theater actors and their troupes. Examples are the short theater adaptations *Madame Loretta* (1919) by Leonard la Ricci starring Fawzi Gazayirli and *The American Aunt/al-Khala al-amrikaniya* (1920) by Bonvelli, which presented the comedian 'Ali al-Kassar for the first time on the screen.

From its beginnings the Egyptian film industry served not only the national market, but with its musical stars, among them 'Abd al-Wahab, Umm Kulthum, Farid al-Atrash, Asmahan, Layla Murad, and Huda Sultan, it was able to attract audiences all over the Arab world. With the industrialization of Egyptian cinema in the 1930s, stars became even more important. Subsequently they have remained essential to the promotion of cinematic products not only in Egypt but also in its neighboring countries.[20] In turn, until today, some of the most urgent structural production and distribution problems of the country's ailing film industry have been related to its star system and had become quite virulent during the 1980s and 1990s.

Since the 1980s the power of stars has been additionally fostered by the very system of film financing, as the majority of Egyptian producers stopped investing their own money in productions, but raised production loans from domestic and international distributors, thereby cutting their risks and profits alike, for these loans were equivalent to the selling of copyrights in advance, with the amount granted depending on the box office popularity of the leading player. This system resulted in a lack of investment in the film industry, while the narrow range of film budgets enforced recurrent topics and locales. At the same time the whole star system became highly inflexible, discouraging the introduction of new faces and relying on known but aging performers unconvincingly cast as young men and women. The latter were only gradually replaced at the turn of the millennium with a new generation of stars that included Hanan Turk, Mona Zaki, Muhammad Hinidi, Ahmad al-Saqqa, and Ahmad Hilmi, who now assume the same powerful position as their precursors.

And indeed, this replacement happened with the appearance of a wave of very successful 'new comedies and shopping-mall films,' largely dramas revolving around middle-class couples specifically designed for audiences of modern shopping mall movie theaters. The young faces in turn were able to shape and determine these particular types of film by refusing to star in other forms, particularly individual auteur films, as happened to director Daoud 'Abd El-Sayed whose screenplay *Messages from the Sea/Rasa'il al-bahr* was turned down by al-Saqqa and Hilmi in 2004/5 because its handicapped and melancholic main character caught in a mysterious erotic relationship seemed incompatible with their prevalent personae. The project remains unrealized to date.

It is noteworthy that the participation of one superstar suffices for a film in terms of production loan and advertisement, and that he or she usually prefers to be the only leading player. This in turn means that they become the main narratological bearers, a fact that has applied to women and men alike until the end of the 1990s (since then however it applies to male performers only). As a consequence some stars have attained tight control over film scripts and as a consequence the kind of characters presented. Nadia al-Gindi, for example, claimed in the late 1980s to have refused between sixty and seventy screenplays in the course of a year because of their alleged low quality (Darwish 1988).

In addition the distribution loan system and the need for box-office popularity have placed the Egyptian player in a kind of pyramidal structure loosely divided into three classes. Categorizations are of course relative, temporary, and flexible and do not necessarily coincide with a player's critical esteem. In some cases popularity and earnings may even be detrimental to the stars' reputation in terms of assumed acting capabilities and artistic quality, which in turn is linked to the kind of film genre a star is associated with and the directors he or she works with. The following outstanding classification of players who were active during the 1980s and 1990s is based on earnings and on the weight of the actor's role in the film narrative, or to borrow Hamid Naficy's term: the extent to which he or she becomes a "narratological bearer" (Naficy 1991, 32).

Roughly speaking, the lowest performer category comprised mostly comedians and variety artists who were often assigned to supporting roles. In a few exceptional cases, such as the body builder Shahhat Mabruk or the Karate specialist Yusuf Mansur, they could also play main parts, yet they acquired little prestige due to their low-budget films and the insignificant directors they worked with. Old actors and actresses who belonged to the second class could also be branded that way, such as Sana' Gamil, Amina Rizq, and Huda Sultan, who after long and partly glamorous careers ended up representing droll mothers and grandmothers. There were also several in-betweens, such as belly dancers Fifi 'Abdu, Lucy, and Nagwa Fu'ad or the comedians and variety artists Samir Ghanim and Samir Sabri, who, although charming, never really made their way to the upper echelons of acting.

Second-class players did not tend to represent odd and cranky person-alities. They attained leading roles largely in cooperation with another star but were not able to carry a film on their own. These actors were relatively productive and starred in up to four feature films a year apart from their the-ater and television serial performances, such as the blond and youthful Faruq al-Fishawi, who appeared in the 1990s as either a slick crook or an incor-ruptible lawyer; actress Ilham Shahin could be also placed in this category. She featured during the same period as either a victim of family and social circumstances or a tough businesswoman. Mostly she fell prey to corrupt husbands or criminal gangs. In terms of genre, character traits, and typology, the repertory of the second category was close to that of the top stars. The Mafioso, the police officer, the businessman, and the lawyer, whether good or evil, are some of the most prevalent professions male protagonists were associated with, whereas women, whether fallen angels or virtuous women in an impasse, were less defined in terms of prestigious professions.

While realist performers may be asked to represent a larger variety, third-class performers, just like farce comedians, were more likely to wear a 'mask,' that is, to be commonly typecast as a certain social type, with little psychological depth or prospect of development. Accordingly, many players of the first-class category tended to enjoy a relatively high artistic esteem in the eyes of the local critics due to their 'natural' acting on the one hand and because of their occasional participation in works that are more committed or realist oriented.

However, until the turn of the millennium the very top star positions have been occupied by the comedian 'Adil Imam and the femme fatale Nadia al-Gindi, at least in terms of payment and distribution loans, with Imam charging up to one million Egyptian pounds (approximately U.S.$200,000) for each production. Both stars have held this position for more than a decade, and both have had controversial artistic records, yet movie theaters were regularly reserved for their latest films on every Muslim holiday, whether 'Eid al-Adha or 'Eid al-Fitr. In January 2000, for example, *Hello America* by Nadir Galal starring Imam was released in thirty-three copies on the first day of the 'Eid al-Fitr holiday, and was still showing in some places in March. In terms of box-office success, it came fourth that year (al-Naggar 2002, 309).

Prostitute for a Good Reason

In Egyptian film criticism, general moral considerations have often been juxtaposed with the highbrow-lowbrow dichotomy. This schism runs commonly, in the eyes of the critics, through genres and directors, as we will see later, and along gender lines. Consequently the prestige of actors and actresses rises with their participation in committed realist films or other privileged works, such as Youssef Chahine's foreign coproductions. Moreover, an actor's or actress's 'moral' record, reflected in their on- and off-screen personae, complements their artistic evaluation. One telling example of this is former superstar Nadia al-Gindi, whose image was strongly linked to commercial cinema, and who became one of the most challenging cases for film critics to evaluate, with one headline calling her "The Woman Who Shook the Critics' Throne" (Amin 1995).

Already in the 1950s and 1960s, cinematic realism had been stylized into the valuable and politically correct opposite to Egyptian mainstream cinema, the 'dream factory.' The same applies to works of the subsequent realist wave, the so-called New Realism of the 1980s. They were characterized largely by their interest in social and political questions, a little melodramatic *mise-en-scène* and a quasi-authentic depiction of lower-class surroundings. Yet the genre remained just like earlier realism, due to a lack of financial alternatives, subordinated to the rules of the film industry, with plot structures and *mise-en-scène*, often converging with those of more popular genres.

More importantly, the use of stars remained obligatory for New Realism's politically committed directors, for financial reasons. Hence, some of their most outstanding films starred well-established names such as Farid Shawqi, Su'ad Husni, and 'Izzat al-'Alayli. Rising young stars of the time, such as Ahmad Zaki, Nur al-Sharif, Mahmud 'Abd al-'Aziz, Layla 'Ilwi, and to a certain extent Yusra, acquired their 'quality' artistic reputation under the same directors. The exceptions were Nabila 'Ubaid, 'Adil Imam, and Nadia al-Gindi. These enjoyed popularity at the box office but tended to be associated with triviality and low artistic standards. Thus, the most 'popular' superstars, al-Gindi and Imam, almost never worked with committed directors, or if they did, it was not necessarily a success—as when al-Gindi starred in Beshara's *Wild Desire/Raghba mutawahhisha* (1991) (unlike 'Adil Imam, whose appearance in Mohamed Khan's *The Champion/al-Harrif* (1984) was one of his few consistent dramatic film roles).

The most distinguished directors of this movement, Khairy Beshara, Mohamed Khan, 'Atef El-Tayeb, and Daoud 'Abd El-Sayed, drew their themes from the social and political conflicts that were sparked off by the *infitah* or Open Door policy launched by the Sadat government in the 1970s.[21] The three male performers who came to be most representative of the New Realist character were Nur al-Sharif, Ahmad Zaki, and Mahmud 'Abd al-'Aziz. These heroes in blue jeans, or young, disaffected, and defiant characters from the urban lower class started dominating the screen during the early 1980s. They either fought against the new materialism embodied by corrupt family members or businessmen, or, in the worst case, mutated into the henchmen of the new system, such as Nur al-Sharif in *Hatim Zahran's Times/Zaman Hatim Zahran* (1988) by Muhammad Naggar. Accordingly, it was oppressive social and political conditions that got these characters into difficulties, not love and romance.

In general the most central and plot-defining motif of the time was the threat to the individual, whether on the economic or ethical level. Actress Ilham Shahin, for example, starred in nineteen films between 1990 and 1996: one adventure film, nine family and social dramas (including two quasi-realist films), and nine gangster films. In all of them crime and danger were crucial themes. Typically, gender affiliation was of major importance to the kind of threats experienced by cinematic characters. As Lizbeth Malkmus stated, the titles of many dramatic Egyptian "films concerned with women. . . imply the illegal (using such words as morals, licit, proof, law, arrest) and many of those concerned with men imply the asocial (bully, smoke, hashish, beasts, bums)" (Malkmus 1991, 106). In other words, women appeared to be threatened on a moral and legal level, whereas men were confronted with social and economic dangers. Accordingly, female heroines woven into a dramatic narration were likely to be single women—unprotected in the traditional sense. Sometimes the danger was also projected onto the international political sphere, as in the case of Nadia al-Gindi.

Despite its socially committed and seemingly liberal orientation, New Realism did not necessarily untie the quasi-automatic association of women with morality. *A Hot Night/Layla sakhina* (1996) was one of the last works of the New Realist director 'Atef El-Tayeb. It stars Nur al-Sharif in a plot similar to their first film together, *The Bus Driver/Sawaq al-utubis* (1983), usually considered the starting point of New Realism. It features a taxi driver on a hot nocturnal pursuit through the city. His mother is in hospital awaiting urgent surgery, but money is lacking and he needs to collect it immediately. One of his customers, played by Libliba, turns out to be a prostitute who has just been robbed by her clients. She too is in search of money, as her landlord wants to throw her and her little sister out of their home the next day. The taxi driver feels pity for her and helps her find her runaway clients. On their way they pick up a black marketeer who sells foreign visas and work permits. After a gunfight, the couple is left holding an attaché case full of money. The driver decides to hand it in at the police station but is taken into custody himself. The prostitute proves more pragmatic. She has hidden the money and will, as is suggested in spite of the film's open end, hire a lawyer and take care of the driver's family.

The conflicts of this narrative do not rely on a powerful opponent but are divided among the representatives of different powerful social groups and institutions, such as hospitals, the police, and landlords. The latent anti-capitalist orientation is underpinned by various references to traditional moral codes intersecting with current concepts of gender roles. The prostitute is an absolutely positive heroine. Her moral aberration is placed in a social context, which causes sympathy instead of repulsion, for she finances the education of her younger sister who is not aware of her sister's profession. When the prostitute learns about the taxi driver's sick mother she offers to give him her last piece of jewelry. The driver too is chivalrous. He helps her to pursue her clients and even gets involved in a brawl for her sake.

Libliba and Nur al-Sharif in *A Hot Night*, 1996

These typical *awlad* and *banat al-balad* characteristics may be found in many different guises in numerous films with or without a realist orientation. *A Hot Night* refers to the whole package of values but gives human solidarity and loyalty absolute preference. The real culprits in the film are black marketeers, fraudsters, capitalists, and the state. Their undifferentiated representation shows that the objective is clearly to criticize the system as a whole. It relates social insecurity not only to general corruption but also more directly to state institutions. Crucial to the film, however, is its positive *bint al-balad* depiction of the prostitute. She is presented as more self-sacrificing and humane than representatives of more respectable professions. What adds to this reading is Libliba's performance. With a friendly face and round feminine features, she did not at that time have a history of playing fallen women or vamps. Moreover the narrative presents her as a victim of social circumstances. This mitigating view of an 'immoral profession' is not, however, positively linked with the idea of liberated or self-defined sexuality. In fact, sexuality is perceived in an abstract way as a means of social oppression. Hence, the film neither deconstructs common morality nor invalidates the virgin–whore dichotomy. It only shifts its ethical preferences or, more precisely, subordinates sexual ethics to social ethics.

There are also numerous non-realist film examples where, at least on the narrative level, oppressive materialism was considered worse than working in a profession of ill repute, particularly if it is out of need. In Sharif 'Arafa's cheerful musical *Silence!/Sama' huss* (1991) for example, superstar Layla 'Ilwi, plump, friendly, and coquettish, represents Halawa, a poor but determined *bint al-balad* who works as a belly dancer. Together with her husband, Humus, a second rate singer, she performs in lower-class weddings and saints' feasts (*mulids*) and finds herself pitted against a successful 'highbrow' singer in a dispute over a melody. An acclaimed 'highbrow' singer steals the melody of one of their common songs, transforms it into a patriotic song with which he appears on television and before high society. The story circles around Humus and Halawa's futile attempts to retrieve their melody. Halawa displays many aspects of a modest *bint al-balad* despite working as a belly dancer. What adds decisively to her respectability in the film is that she is married and protected by her husband.

The moral concept represented here in a seemingly unrealistic spectacle with all its mitigating factors seems quite powerful and is contrary to expectations rooted in reality. As Karin van Nieuwkerk stated in her study of female Egyptian entertainers, to practice belly dancing professionally is considered shameful ('ayb) by the urban lower classes, yet it is tolerated by the community in cases where it serves to support a needy family (van Nieuwkerk 1995, 181). Hence, the traditional critical position that corresponds to orthodox views qualifies them while arguing pragmatically for the necessity of survival. The same logic is often relied upon at the textual level, for indulging and excusing sinful cinematic characters; in other words, a woman may dance—for a good reason. Mitigation, however, does not invalidate but rather confirms the system and its moral binarism, on the cinematic textual level as well as on the level of daily film criticism.

The Virgin–Whore Dichotomy

Moral binarisms of popular cinema regarding women have often been translated into the virgin–whore dichotomy, visualized through fallen women, prostitutes, or belly dancers. The major box-office hit of the early 1970s, *Take Care of Zuzu* (1972) by Hasan al-Imam, featured the veteran film star Tahiyya Carioca as a retired belly dancer. One day she wakes up in a panic after a dreadful nightmare of her daughter Zuzu (Su'ad Husni) dancing in the sweaty atmosphere of a nightclub. The girl follows a customer into a dimly lit bedroom luridly furnished in red, and undresses at the sight of his banknotes. A strange fantasy indeed, imagined by a woman who is portrayed in the film as having herself worked as a lower-class belly dancer and entertainer. Within the film's plot this peculiar nightmare represents on the dramatic level a retarding moment, in which the romance between Zuzu and a young upper-class man seems to have been thwarted by a malicious plot.

Tahiyya Carioca herself was one of the major stars of the 1940s and 1950s who came to the screen through belly dancing but was soon considered one of the most distinguished actresses of her time. Because of her strong erotic presence but also her feistiness, she was often cast in lower-class roles, particularly as she gained weight and advanced in age. In 1972 when she performed as Zuzu's mother she had already acquired the fat motherly persona of her last years. Thus her panic in the film has quite an ironic connotation, in the context of her own glamorous career as a dancer.

As for Zuzu, she is depicted as a charming girl who has been brought up in a lower-class neighborhood, cherished by her mother and her band of wedding entertainers and enrolled, much to their pride, in the university. There she meets and attracts a handsome theater director (blond Husain Fahmi), the son of a prosperous and respected upper-class family. When his cousin, who has had her eye on him, learns about Zuzu's family, she hires the unsuspecting mother to entertain a private party. Zuzu is invited to the same party in the house of her admirer's parents and is shocked to find her mother performing, much to the amusement of the guests. Zuzu's anguish makes this the most melodramatic moment of the film. Taking off her jacket and tying a scarf around her hips, she asks her mother to step aside in order to perform instead of her. This symbolic action of the younger woman replacing the elder is not only charged with the emotional humiliation of the poor having to expose one's body in front of the rich, but also with social determinism, expressed in the enforced continuity between the two genera-tions. It is after this incident that Zuzu, convinced now of the futility of her own struggle for education and better social status, decides to drop her stud-ies and work as a belly dancer, a decision that engenders the mother's horrific dream.

Thus, the horror of Carioca's nightmare is also that of thwarted social ascent, condensed in the image of the girl's prostitution. This 'instant' transi-tion from virgin to whore functions within this specific drama 'only' as a retarding moment while in other instances it may be used to accelerate the drama, as we will see later in the case of Nafisa, the main protagonist of *Beginning and End/Bidaya wa nihaya* (1960) by Salah Abu Seif. For, contrary to Nafisa's symbolic punishment (suicide), Zuzu is saved by her lover after

Su'ad Husni, Husain Fahmi, and Tahiyya Carioca in *Take Care of Zuzu*, 1972

having become a prostitute. He gives her one of the most applauded slaps in Egyptian film history (audiences used to cheer and clap their hands at this moment), thus bringing her back to her senses—and to university.

Zuzu's luck is demonstrated by the fact that she escaped the fate of vice, unlike numerous other tragic and pitiable female characters, like the heroine of *Shafiqa the Copt* directed by the same Hasan al-Imam in 1963. Starring Hind Rustum, the film deployed a typical fatal entanglement of loss and female disintegration caused by duped love and thwarted motherhood. Set in the nineteenth century it featured dancer and entertainer Shafiqa, the mistress of As'ad Pasha. Because of her reputation she has been cast out of her family and obliged to leave her little son 'Aziz. Years pass and her unsuspecting son proposes to the pasha's daughter but is refused and humiliated. In an act of revenge Shafiqa exposes the pasha to his family. The pasha in response has her son jailed, while his daughter retreats into a nunnery. 'Aziz escapes from prison only to find his mother on her deathbed.

Shot in color and endowed with lavish settings, the 'sensual' aspect of 'vice' seems very much underlined by the *mise-en-scène*. Shafiqa was, moreover, performed by Hind Rustum, an actress resembling Jane Russell in sex appeal. Her character's immoral conduct is not excused by poverty, only rendered sympathetic by her longing for and subsequent solidarity with her son. The moment of exposure or revelation of truth in the plot forms a crucial turning point, just as in *Beginning and End* (1960) when Nafisa's brother learns about her profession. It is the moment when the fallen woman's secret is rendered public, when inside meets outside and the radical change of the heroine's fate is initiated. It is the moment of her death or in other words her symbolic punishment.

Another 1963 production, *Rabʻa al-ʻAdawiya* by Niazi Mustafa emphasized the opposition between vice and virtue by means of a decisive turning point including also an important temporal element to establish the moral dichotomy. Despite its being ostensibly the biography of Rabʻa al-ʻAdawiya, a medieval female *Sufi* saint who decided to retreat into the desert to live a spiritual life in celibacy, the film reflects the ideology and constraints of the 1960s. For Rabʻa's biography, as reported by Arab chronicles and investigated by a twentieth-century biographer (Smith 1928, 3–9), does not have much to say about her vice 'before' becoming a saint. What has been recorded is that her master released her when he woke up one night and saw the light of saintliness shining over her head. Thereafter Rabʻa retired into the desert and became a professional flute player.

In fact, female slaves at that time could not renounce the world so easily. This does not mean though that they were doomed to 'immorality,' as the the master's sexual right of the slave was exclusive. In fact, to force slaves into prostitution, for example, was prohibited by law (Ahmed 1992, 96). Disregarding the records, the cinematic adaptation portrayed Rabʻa (performed by Nabila ʻUbaid) *before* she retires from the world as an independent and somehow 'loose' woman who enjoys her life as an entertainer, singing and dancing at parties, something that strengthens the effect of her 'conversion' to the true path. This temporal schism between before and after underlines the moral binarism worked out through the heroine even more, and which is absent in the original narrative on the historical figure.

It may be suspected that the cinematic virgin–whore dichotomy with its narrative obligations is a quite modern enterprise. As I have argued elsewhere, the emphasis on conversion recalls the Protestant religious concept expressed in numerous Christian martyr stories presented by Hollywood cinema (Shafik 1998, 171). It may also be an indicator of the cultural and religious roots of the virgin–whore dichotomy being part of the Christian-bourgeois agenda. To be precise, I do not define it as exclusively Western or European, for North African theologians, most notably Saint Augustine of Hippo (d. 430), contributed as much to this binary gendered moral concept as did Christian thinkers from north of the Mediterranean. While sexuality was increasingly classified as diabolic, virginity became the sole means for a woman to escape the dreadful equation with seductive Eve (Rotter 1996, 87).

Nabila 'Ubaid and Farid Shawqi in *Rab'a al-'Adawiya*, 1963

The same dichotomy was perpetuated by the Victorian value system, which influenced Egyptian reformers at the turn of the century in their reassessment of femininity and woman's role. It differs tremendously from traditional Muslim perceptions, according to which woman is not the victim of her biological existence, "giving birth in pain," but powerful, able to unleash chaos or *fitna* (Mernissi 1987, 12–29). Muslim religious thinking and literary traditions cultivated this comparably misogynist but less binary discourse regarding female sexuality, as representing a source of unrest that could distract men from their social and religious duties. Control of female sexuality had to be achieved by means of control and surveillance of women, a view that developed in the course of time.

Regarding Arab-Muslim history Abdelwahab Bouhdiba distinguishes clearly between Qur'an and *sunna* as standing respectively for gender complementarity and dissociation: "The passage from the Qur'an to the *sunna fiqh* is a passage from a harmonious unity of the sexes to their duality" (Bouhdiba 1998, 123). This duality limps, however, as woman started to be "perceived as essentially, or exclusively, a sexual being, unlike 'the man,' who was only partly understood in terms of his sexuality" (Badran 1996, 5). Hence, traditional Muslim perception as expressed by Imam Ghazali in the end of the eleventh century AD saw culture as a product of sexual satisfaction, and not—as Fatima Mernissi points out in reviewing Sigmund Freud's theory—as the result of man's fight against sexuality (Mernissi 1987, 13).

Doubtless Egyptian cinema at times cultivated a diabolic image of sexuality, rather following the Christian agenda. For the virgin–whore dichotomy was fundamental to the kind of dramatic constructions described above. However, not all are as clear-cut as they seem. For even *Rab'a al-'Adawiya* has difficulties in accommodating the full dichotomy, as its protagonist could not be stylized into a victim of male desire. This applies even more to a number of films from the following two decades, that is, the 1980s and 1990s. They indicate an element of change apparent in cases when the drama fails to contain the tension of moral binarism without disruption. Usually this kind of disruption not only diminishes the credibility of the film but may also serve as a Trojan horse by inducing an imbalance to the dichotomy as such.

In *A Woman Bound to Fall* (1992) by Midhat al-Siba'i—a remake of *I Want to Live* (1958) by Robert Wise—the symbolic punishment does not come but keeps threatening the audience and the heroine for an endless series of scenes adding up to a long parallel action. On the one side, Shukri (Nur al-Sharif) a journalist and former fiancé of Ahlam (Yusra) searches for a witness to testify her innocence in a murder that she did not commit; on the other side she is slowly but surely preparing for execution. Only in the very last moment is she literally cut down from the noose.

Not unpredictably, the film starts in a brothel where the heroine Ahlam is shown in a recurrent and stereotypical scene in Egyptian film, arousing men by belly dancing. However, the whole set-up turns out to be fake, for a sudden police raid on the place reveals to the viewer that the male members of Ahlam's gang impersonate police officers in order to rob the terrified customers. Ahlam at first shows little moral scruple, but as the story develops she wants to return to normal bourgeois life, get married, and bear a child. From this moment on she is increasingly victimized. Her husband, a waiter in a nightclub, turns out to be a drug addict—she even gets raped in his presence; her former gang colleagues botch a robbery, kill two people, and accuse her of the murder. Even her former fiancé raises a ferocious press campaign against her, so that she is sentenced to death and has to give her child away.

Less concerned with virtue and virginity, this post-*infitah* film raises the question of morality and materialism. This linkage is made through a cinematic flashback in which Ahlam is seen in a dispute with Shukri, explaining why she is breaking off their engagement. His poverty, she claims, would kill their affection anyway. Thus, his campaign to cast her as a murderess is explained as rooted in his hurt pride. Yet after her death sentence he changes his mind and strives to save her. This unexpected turning point occurs with so little preparation that it seems like an open question mark. As the change cannot be properly accounted for by the action, the dialog makes Ahlam ask Shukri: "What has changed you?" But he does not reply, rendering his transformation even more odd. In fact, the problem here is that the male character is subjected to common melodramatic twists while the heroine's transformation herself is too gradual and complex to bow to easy black and white binarisms. For a clear-cut dichotomy depends on sharp borders, defined points of transition, a *before* absolutely different from the *after*. This is something that Ahlam's character simply cannot offer, because she is depicted as a subject who knew, shaped, and attained what she desired. Along with her ability to contain opposites and simultaneity it is this 'subjectivity' embodied by her 'materialist' demands that marks her also as a woman of the present, educated and ambitious.

This type of pragmatic post-*infitah* woman abounds, as for instance in *My Life, My Passion* by Magdi Ahmad 'Ali (1996). In contrast to *A Woman Bound to Fall* 'Ali's film may be well considered a committed 'realist' work, which revises the virgin–whore dichotomy from a 'progressive' perspective and deconstructs some of the modernist ideals such as romantic love and rejection of arranged marriage. The film presents three lower-middle-class women, educated but unable to attain to the dreams of marriage, stable income, and material wellbeing, because although employed, they do not earn enough to make ends meet. The only possible solution is utterly pragmatic in nature, namely to accept an arranged marriage. In this respect the film's title comes close to a parody. "My Life, my Passion" was the title of a Muhammad 'Abd al-Wahab song, reviving in this context the romantic love advocated and presented on the screen in his musicals, such as *The White Rose* (1933), *Long Live Love* (1938), or *A Bullet in the Heart/Rusasa fi-l-qalb* (1944). In complete opposition to the ideal set up in those films, the three contemporary heroines choose to marry despite the apparent absence of romance and love. Their choices are dictated by material necessities. What their female solidarity offers is a kind of conspiracy platform for the realization of their economic interests, as well as mutual emotional support.

The ironic notion that the 'Abd al-Wahab title creates does not derive only from the rejection of romance as a vessel for gender relations—so advocated in early Egyptian cinema—the irony is also that 'Ali's film discards the female muse, the pure unsullied virgin that conjures the artistic moment in the narrative or in the song, as we saw in 'Abd al-Wahab's master-narrative/song *The White Rose* for instance. The beloved or the object of desire initializes the words, the music, and the expression. No such thing occurs in *My Life, My Passion*: Sakina, interpreted by Ilham Shahin, is depicted as the most sincere and stubborn among the trio. Her wish to find a spouse seems impossible because she has lost her virginity to her first love and it seems unlikely that her new admirer will accept this fact. Her girlfriends insist on her undergoing hymen reconstruction surgery but she refuses in an attempt to live up to her own ideals of sincerity. The film closes, though, with her having bowed to social pressures so that her wedding does not signify the moment of fulfillment, the obligatory happy ending, but an instance of defeat and loss of self-respect. Thus, quite indirectly the character of Sakina manages to deconstruct the muse/virgin concept as a necessity for men in dealing with woman. At the same time, women's pragmatic response still bears the bitterness of surrender, for they are actually unable (in the course of this film at least) to replace the male concept with a less binary one.

This development has continued throughout the recent years, with an increasing number among the latest 'shopping-mall films' discussing issues of virginity and sexual morals in a quite outspoken and less traditional manner than in rape-seduction narratives since the 1940s. In contrast to *My Life, My Passion* most of them take place among the middle-classes, for example *Sleepless Nights/Sahar al-layali* (2003) by Hani Khalifa, *Downtown Girls/Banat wist al-balad* (2005) by Mohamed Khan, *Ouija* (2006) by Khalid Yusuf, and *Leisure Time/Awqat al-faragh* (2006) by Muhammad Mustafa. In all these films extramarital relations and the issue of male moral reservations versus real love are reconsidered. In *Downtown Girls*, for instance, the heroine confronts the young man who tries to seduce her in his flat with the embarrassing question: "When did you lose your virginity?"

It is apparent that in the 'committed' works of the 1990s, as well as in a number of shopping-mall films produced in the first decade of the new millennium dealing with the emotional problems of young middle-class couples,

Hind Sabri, Minna Shalabi, Khalid Abu al-Nagga, and Muhammad Nagati (left to right) in *Downtown Girls*, 2005

a certain tendency has surfaced that is less concerned, and less able, to establish a clear moral dichotomy in the face of women's sexuality. Clear-cut borders between virgin and whore are expressed either in the duality of characters or in decisive turning points in the life of the heroine, emphasizing the moral dichotomy. Now, notions that depart from that are increasingly making their way to the screen, culminating in the development of one specific star persona, that of actress Nadia al-Gindi, who appeared first in the mid-1970s.

Questionable Popularity

Al-Gindi's persona has always been controversial because of the repetitive plots, shallow character descriptions, and mediocre *mise-en-scène* of works she starred in. At first she used to feature in melodramatic thrillers, before shifting to plain action and espionage films. The latter, largely produced by her husband Muhammad Mukhtar, seem to have formed a particular way of compensating for the accusation of profanity, as she boasted about the high budgets of these films (up to five million Egyptian pounds—about US$1.3 million—in the 1990s, in comparison with an average film budget of one million Egyptian pounds) (*al-Ahram* 1999). In fact, the main arguments made against al-Gindi were plainly moral, evoking illicitness and decadence.

Often accused of relying primarily on sex appeal (Salih 1999), al-Gindi attempted to neutralize this view in dozens of apologetic statements saying: "I am not the star of seduction but the star of the masses," and "they wronged me by saying that I am making propaganda for drugs! They wronged me and said that I present films that disfigure the image of Egyptian society. They wronged me and said that I rely on excitation and seduction in order to sell my films" (Fahmi 1981). The causes of this image are complex and rooted equally in her on- and off-screen representations. At the age of fifteen, after winning a secondary film role as the prize in a beauty contest, Nadia al-Gindi married top star "'Imad Hamdi who was 34 years older, only to ask for divorce ten years later, in order to 'live her youth'" (Darwish 1979). During this period al-Gindi appeared as a supporting player in several films, then, in 1974 she attained a main part in Hasan al-Imam's melodrama *Bamba Kashshar*, reenacting the life of a famous dancer of the 1920s. She produced this particular film with her own private funding, because evidently no one else was prepared to offer her a leading role. Her popularity at the box office in this (otherwise extremely low quality) work paved her way to the top and her success was further cemented by the successful gangster-melodrama, *al-Batniya* (1980) by Husam al-Din Mustafa, in which she played a young mother duped by a drug dealer. One particular 'nonsense' line she repeated in this film several times to annoy her opponents, namely 'Say hello to the eggplants' *(salimli 'ala al-bitingan)* became a catch phrase in Egypt at the time. As a whole, al-Gindi's life story and fame seem to suggest an ambitious and unsentimental self-made woman who used her feminine weapons to lure and utilize a much older and more famous husband as a ladder to success, and who installed herself as a leading player without enjoying real popularity or critical esteem.

This image was further confirmed by the fact that the earlier victimized characters in al-Gindi's filmography were soon eclipsed by the persona of the ferocious femme fatale, the seductive avenger and the ruthless intriguer. During the 1980s her characters used to fight for their social ascent, as in *The Servant/al-Khadima* (1984) by Ashraf Fahmi. Here she played a servant who seduces the son of her old prosperous mistress, and makes him fall in love with and marry her. Supported by a secret lover she takes over her in-laws' company. At that moment she decides to get rid of her lover too, but gets killed first. What is most effective in underlining al-Gindi's character traits here is not just the plot but also her slim body, her tight dresses, her reduced facial expression, and her slightly raised eyebrow. Heavy make up adds to a strangely deadpan expression. In her films as well as in press photos she mostly wears tight, glittering clothes that emphasize her sex appeal.

Although al-Gindi seems to place herself very much on the dark side of the common virgin–whore dichotomy, her persona may be also understood as an attempt to accommodate femininity with power and spatial mobility. This could be read, following Jacinda Read's suggestion, as an attempt to negotiate and mainstream feminism (c.f. Read: 2000, 49). Al-Gindi's role in *The Samya Sha'rawi File* (1988) by Nadir Galal indeed negotiates questions of work and marriage, featuring as the clever but materially and sexually deprived white-collar worker Samya Sha'rawi. She is introduced as the widow of an army officer killed in the (1967) Six Day War. When she claims

Madiha Yusri and
Nadia al-Gindi in
The Servant, 1984

a pension, she learns that her husband had taken her as a second wife without her knowledge, thereby depriving her of the right to any financial support.

At this juncture she meets another officer (Faruq al-Fishawi) who promises help, then offers to take her as *his* second wife. Samya, fed up with her degrading and unrewarding job as a switchboard operator, agrees for the sake of the material and emotional benefits this offers. Despite being a second wife she is presented as enjoying the officer's erotic interest in her and his companionship. Another war breaks out (1973) and Samya's new husband is put in charge by a high-ranking friend of securing a huge sum of money meant for a secret military weapons deal. But he dies, and Samya (despite being shadowed by State Security to reveal the money's whereabouts) succeeds in securing the fortune for herself.

The course of the action shows the heroine as a courageous, intelligent, and moreover sexually experienced woman. Her attitude to marriage and love is merely pragmatic. She makes up for the legal and social advantages available to men, such as polygamy and access to institutional power and wealth, with her endurance, pragmatism, and feminine wiles. In addition, her character voices a profound anti-modernist skepticism. It shows the working woman in a very critical light due to low income and oppressive power relations at work (in one scene she is pictured in a heated argument with her boss because he does not want to grant her a vacation). Much in line with Arlene Macleod's findings that lower-middle-class women tend to show ambiguous feelings toward the benefits of work outside the home (Macleod 1992, 55), the heroine looks for marriage to improve her social position. Yet she does not quit. Instead, her second husband uses his power to secure her a better position, proving the *infitah* ideology that money and power count more than class and education.

Power struggle and sexuality are in fact the two major associative pillars on which al-Gindi's image rests. Many of al-Gindi's works allude overtly either to female sexuality, such as the stage play *Striptease/Striptiz* (1998) and the film *Wild Desire* (1991) or to power, such as *A Woman Above the Top/Imra'a fawq al-qimma* (1997), and *A Woman Shook the Egyptian*

Throne/Imra'a hazzat 'arsh Misr (1995). These titles illustrate why al-Gindi's persona is so easily associated with vulgarity. The same applies to her film narratives: in *The Spy Hikmat Fahmi* (1994) by Husam al-Din Mustafa she played the famous belly dancer Hikmat Fahmi. The latter had been one of the major sources of information for the Nazi secret service in Egypt during the Second World War. In the film, Fahmi becomes at one and the same time the mistress of a British general and the informant of her German lover. When her mission is uncovered she is captured and tortured by the British, but saved from execution at the last minute by the Free Officers.

In one of her subsequent films al-Gindi incorporated the more 'feminine' that is, emotional trait of motherhood into her persona. The espionage film *48 Hours in Israel* (1998) by Nadir Galal dealt with a woman searching for her younger brother captured by the Israeli Mossad before the October 1973 or Yom Kippur War. In the first part of the film the viewer gets 'sutured' through the editing into a sadistic notion of sexuality based primarily on abuse and domination that sets out to penalize femininity. The sequence starts with the heroine relaxing (in full make up and covered with

Nadia al-Gindi in *A Woman Shook the Egyptian Throne*, 1995

foam) in the bathtub in her hotel. A close-up of her uncovered arms and her face suggest a love scene to follow. However, she has no lover yet, but in the following sequence she is called to the lobby to meet the obviously sympathetic friend of her brother (Faruq al-Fishawi) to whom she feels emotionally attracted (but who later turns out to be a Mossad agent). Immediately after this scene she is captured by the Israelis and tortured. Among the abuses applied is the highly symbolic penetration of her fingers with a phallic object. Of course these shots are accompanied by her horrified screams. Here, exactly as in al-Gindi's other films, the submission to physical abuse and (alluded) sexual humiliation is matched by the heroine's moral strength and persistence, as she does not give in to her oppressors under any circumstances and finally succeeds in outwitting them by means of her intelligence. A similar trope is also reproduced in several of her other works, such as *The Samya Sha'rawi File*, where she likewise gets tortured by her male opponent.

Nadia al-Gindi in *The Samya Sha'rawi File*, 1988. Resistance despite torture.

This orientation may also be the reason for the actress's preference for action, namely espionage films and political thrillers, in which one of her trademarks is her refusal to be replaced by stuntmen in action scenes (*al-Ahram* 1999). This genre provides an excellent opportunity to counter physical threats (despite having a vulnerable female body) but also to become entangled in power games. Asked about her preference for the espionage theme, the actress commented: "These kind of movies address the national sentiment and raise the degree of affiliation. I consider this a patriotic task as it presents Egyptian heroism that any Egyptian may be proud of" (Dardir 1997). Thus, the kamikaze for the national cause who withstands seduction, terror, and physical torture recurs in all her espionage films, whether *Mission in Tel Aviv* (1992) or *A Woman Shook the Egyptian Throne*. The latter, set in prerevolutionary Egypt, shows the heroine collaborating with the Free Officers and contributing decisively to the fall of the last Egyptian king and the end of colonialism.

From Sexual Object to Sexual Subject?

Al-Gindi's recent press coverage does not criticize her openly, yet the interviews imply indirect reproaches through her apologetic statements. In spite of all the good (patriotic) reasons she gives for the looseness of her characters, she has difficulty in constructing a positive persona. Some of this is certainly due to the fact that her heroines are always read intertextually, in comparison. Furthermore, her apologies invalidate neither the moral system nor the virgin–whore dichotomy but rather serve to confirm them. Yet I would suggest that al-Gindi has used these dichotomies consciously by negating and negotiating both sides, with the aim of raising the question of female power.

Her character in *The Servant* (1984) for example represents a wicked opportunist and an irresistible femme fatale at the same time. Seduction and prostitution constitute the protagonist's major weapons in achieving her goals. However, her open allusions to sexuality and power are alien to the apologetic justification for female aberration offered by the traditional lower-class code.

Nadia al-Gindi in *Mission in Tel Aviv*, 1992. From femme fatale (above) to action heroine (opposite).

Al-Gindi's characters Hikmat Fahmi and the woman who 'shook the Egyptian throne' use their sexuality consciously in the political arena as a means of attaining influence over men and their dealings. They aim to participate in male power. But for a woman to be an agent of political and social conditions instead of their victim cannot be excused easily. It is exactly this aspiration to power, instrumentalizing femininity for combat instead of submission, that renders al-Gindi both ambiguous and trivial in the eyes of the critics. Moreover, her overt and joyous interest in sexuality as displayed in *The Samya Sha'rawi File* among other films, suffices to present her as morally questionable. She also has no reservations about displaying her feminine assets, as in *48 Hours in Israel* (1998), where, knowing she is observed by Israeli secret agents, she starts to undress in front of a lit window—and even after closing the curtains, continues undressing as a shadow—an assertion of seductiveness by the heroine who uses it to mislead her observers.

Nadia al-Gindi in *Mission in Tel Aviv,* 1992

Al-Gindi is certainly interested in creating a femme fatale image of herself. Ann Kaplan suggested, in analyzing Marlene Dietrich, that the femme
fatale figure should be read as 'erotic object (or narcissistic phallic replacement)' that transforms woman into a fetish in order to curtail her castrating
powers (Kaplan 1983, 59). Drawing on psychoanalysis Kaplan explains that
"men endeavor to find the penis in women. Feminist film critics have seen
this phenomenon (clinically known as fetishism) operating in the cinema;
the camera (unconsciously) fetishizes the female form, rending it phallus-
like so as to mitigate woman's threat" (Kaplan 1983, 31). Leaving aside the
fact that this particular aspect of Freudian theory has been subject to some
scrutiny, Gindi's appearance has some elements of the 'icy' destructive
vamp, yet her fetishistic 'phallic' qualities are not as clearly worked out as
in Marlene Dietrich's case. True, she freezes her facial expression and tends
to wear tight clothes, but at other times she underscores her more warm and
feminine aspects by wearing full skirts and patterned dresses. Even when

al-Gindi displays awareness of the desiring male gaze (Kaplan 1983, 51), she plays an active role in 'authoring' her own image and clearly strives for the position of subject, defying the objectified position of the femme fatale described by Kaplan. Thus, an important part of al-Gindi's disturbing appearance is her active participation in writing herself, not only as a sexual object, but also as a sexual subject.

The reason for this deviation, however it may be interpreted by more traditional, local concepts of female sexuality, just as it could be read as a sign of increased female empowerment, which would explain some of al-Gindi's box-office success. In fact the subject-object, active-passive, male-female dichotomy as inscribed in occidental gender perception is, as we have seen, not entirely compatible with the historical Arab–Muslim one. The traditional version ascribed to woman an immense devouring power because of her sexual *omnipotence*, as Moroccan sociologist Fatima Mernissi put it. Hence, female sexuality and sensuality were perceived as hardly controllable, requiring all the more male precaution and punishment. Contrary to that, the 'explicit' theory—to use Mernissi's terminology—that dominates the Arab world today has marginalized traditional theory. It believes man to be the active element, while woman remains passive. Yet this more recent conviction could not completely replace pre-colonial notions but rendered them largely 'implicit' (Mernissi 1987, 13). While some Egyptian intellectuals, most notably 'Abbas al-'Aqqad, struggled hard to reconcile both theories, Mernissi finds that Egyptian cinema has on the whole adhered to the 'explicit theory' that considers woman *al-jins al-na'im* or *al-jins al-latif* (the gentle sex) (Mernissi 1987, 14).

The resurgence of the 'implicit' theory of the sexually omnipotent woman, which comes to the fore in the cinematic persona of Nadia al-Gindi, could also be understood as a means to negotiate woman's position relative to man. For the notion of female sexual omnipotence combined with guile, a notion from traditional Arabic literature, has played a major role in her films. The plot of *The Samya Sha'rawi File* (1988) is essentially based on the heroine's ability to deceive. When her husband dies, leaving her with a suitcase full of money, she is pursued by a corrupt state security officer whom she is eventually able to dupe, keeping the fortune to herself. The film's last turning point is the most revealing in this respect. Samya and the officer hide the banknotes in a suitcase and head for the airport. On their way, Samya is thrown out of the car and her opponent takes off to Europe, where he is surprised to find his suitcase empty. In a cross-cut we see Samya at home enjoying her success.

In *48 Hours in Israel* (1998) by Nadir Galal, a similar *dénouement* emerges from the heroine's major trait. Playing against an Israeli secret agent David (Faruq al-Fishawi, al-Gindi's frequent on-screen erotic partner) she outwits him at the end. She agrees to hand over to David a microfilm containing top-secret information in exchange for the return of her brother, who has been kidnapped and taken to Israel. The neutral intermediaries, two Greek monks, turn out to be Egyptian secret agents who manage to overwhelm the Israelis and kill David. Al-Gindi's last coup comes also as revenge for the suffering she has been through; tortured and abused by an Israeli squad, she was also duped into a sexual relationship with David, her main opponent.

In fact, as often as the actress has evoked the virgin–whore dichotomy she has also astonishingly often denied the notion of guilt so fundamental to any binary moral structure. What is most telling in terms of an evaluation of sexuality is how in *48 Hours* the seduction scene is put—or better—not put into action. In a melodramatic context it would have been marked emotionally with a particular kind of music and specific gestures in order to underline it as a dramatic event for the heroine, foreboding unfavorable results. However, this seduction scene is not specifically marked by any melodramatic effects. Even later, there is no single emotional reference to this moral lapse, no trace of shame, humiliation, or guilt. The protagonist evidently does not care much about what would have been a drama or tragedy for a virtuous heroine.

On the contrary, plot and *mise-en-scène* contribute to eliminate the moral judgment so crucial to the virgin–whore dichotomy. The absence of a sense of moral failure or guilt is characteristic of the kind of wily seductress heroines al-Gindi has represented since the late 1980s. In fact, their affinity with the female guile and sexual omnipotence described in classical Arabic literature is striking, as is their insistence on sexual pleasure. In general, three major characteristics were attributed to woman in the (premodern) Arabic "anecdotal prose referred to by Western scholars as *adab*" (Malti-Douglas 1992, 6): eloquence, trickery, and uncontrollable sexuality. This resulted in the integration of woman (as trickster) into the pantheon of *adab* characters as a social type in her own right, along with the thief and the mad-man among others (Malti-Douglas 1992, 29–31), embodying first uncontrollable sexuality and second *kayd* or guile (Mernissi 1987, 15), with the latter often placed in the service of the first (Malti-Douglas 1992, 53). This female category has at times remained nameless and general, contrary to the specificity of male characters (Malti-Douglas 1992, 31). Al-Gindi's recent persona is a similar generalization of the category of woman, qual-ified only by the aspect of masquerade, and runs counter to the multiple femininities that started to emerge during the late 1980s and 1990s, as we saw in the work of Mohamed Khan, Inas al-Dighidi, and Magdi Ahmad 'Ali.

But what is still striking is her conscious association with a traditionally male-oriented genre, the action and the espionage film. This too sets her apart from film categories that prefer to emphasize notions of the 'gentle sex,' first and foremost the melodrama. Analyzing Nadia al-Gindi's persona, it becomes clear that moral categories in her evaluation are likely to com-plement or even eclipse 'artistic' ones. Hence, in more than one respect Egyptian stars may express, on the textual and contextual level, different and partly contradictory value scales, which stem from so-called traditional and/or religious ethics as well as current political ideologies, while inter-secting with class and gender. The notion of contradiction here is not only due to cultural peculiarities or to an uneven social development, but is also inherent in the star's capacity to embody contradictions, to be equally a myth and a commodity, to be both accessible on-screen and inaccessible off-screen, and to represent human agency open to identification, even while appearing in a mechanically reproduced medium (c.f. Mayne 1993, 126).

PART 3

Class

CHAPTER 5

Negotiating Class through Genre

C
lass has been an ever-present and ever-determinant factor in Egyptian cinema, yet it was one of the most neglected issues in studies of film in Egypt, for the question of class has not only shaped sequels of film narratives and thus been associated with certain genres, but has also played the role of a symbolic signifier regarding the appearance and status of film performers. Moreover it has left its traces on the process of film perception by audiences, as evident in the common division of movie theaters into 'classes.' What seems most striking, however, is that class has also contributed to film form through generic vocabulary developed for different audiences, from the early third-class *terzo (tirsu)* to the recent shopping-mall cinema.

One of the few studies that did pay attention to the extent to which the issue of class shapes Egyptian cinema was Jane Gaffney's study *The Egyptian Cinema: Industry and Art in a Changing Society*, published in 1987. Her major thesis was that Egyptian cinema abandoned its early elitist position, depicting pashas and upper-class environments, in favor of an entirely middle-class perspective embodied in the "dream of social mobility and self-improvement" (Gaffney 1987, 65) that she describes as being voiced and readjusted to changing socioeconomic and political realities ranging from the era of the *ancien régime*, through the post-coup-d'état period in 1952, until the presidency of Anwar al-Sadat. Following Arnold Hauser's theory regarding cinema she claims "that the psychology of the petit bourgeois is the mid-point where the people of the masses meet" (Gaffney 1987, 53). However, despite a highly consistent argumentation Gaffney does not take into account ideological contradictions and negotiations within every single film text that do prevent films from belonging exclusively to one 'class' perspective or, to put it differently, she does not perceive the actual virulence of class difference in prerevolutionary cinema and the significance of the spectator's own class position to his reading of cinematic products.

Gaffney's approach reflects the typical sociologist's misconception in dealing with film. By looking at cinema "as a mirror" (Gaffney 1987, 54)—a metaphor quite similar to the feminist 'image-of' approach—and by applying almost exclusively the technique of content analysis, it may generate a reductionist equation between representation and reality. Thus, our task will be to take up and qualify Gaffney's observations, to modify the understanding of early Egyptian cinema regarding class, to include more recent developments and, last but not least, to examine how the narrative of social ascent that draws a clear borderline between different social strata has been in parts complemented and/or replaced by signs of a rather diffuse inner bourgeois struggles and—more importantly—to discuss how class has informed film on a structural as well as on a textual level. Before doing so, however, it seems necessary to review the perception of recent class history in Egypt and its terminology.

Egyptian Class History

Extreme differences in social and political scientists' definitions of class exist; they range from regarding it as a monolithic body with defined characteristics or in contrast—which seems far more plausible—as a changing dynamic, contradictory, and temporary entity shaped by different factors, such as profession, income, education, place of residence, and relation to power (cf. 'Abd al-Mu'ti 2002, 42). For, contrary to early materialist assumptions, "it is no longer convincing to view and speak of a capitalist class as a potential or partially realized collective agent or agency" with common willed objectives (Vitalis 1995, 229).

Some recent exceptional attempts in film studies have likewise tried to apply non-essentialist concepts of class, proposing to comprehend social categories not as objective entities, but in accordance with Chantal Mouffe and Ernesto Laclau's terminology, as nodal points of antagonisms (Laclau 1990, 89 as quoted in Yau 1996, 144). In her analysis of Chinese mainland cinema, Esther Yau has demonstrated the usefulness of this approach applied to a country that was originally striving for a classless society, but where newly arisen social differences called for new categorizations. Thus, where the new postrevolutionary elite had eclipsed the traditional bourgeoisie, social hegemonies have been defined along other lines, similar to class differences in form but not necessarily in content (Yau 1996, 144).

Yet for the current study, despite the difficulties in defining class, there is still no alternative to the common categorization into middle, lower, and upper classes. However, it is important to bear in mind what Frederic Jameson called the "allegorical" character of the class concept (Jameson 1985, 719), in addition to the internal inconsistency of class, its temporary and shifting nature due to constant social change, as will shine through in the following account.

Mahmoud Hussein, who wrote one of the earlier profound examinations of modern Egyptian class developments, assigned to the bourgeoisie a pivotal role, whose highly congested process of formation he traced back to the appearance of large land ownership in the last quarter of the nineteenth century at a point when the private property concept eclipsed the former state centralized model, in which the state was the major landowner and peasants were tenants and/or labored as *corvée* (Hussein 1973, 18). This new elite remained until the early twentieth century an equivalent of the ruling class and was until the Second World War assisted and served by an upcoming, yet by and large still marginalized and fragmented middle class (Hussein

1973, 25). It was the Nasserist project of the 1950s and 1960s that brought about not only land reform but also the takeover of the ruling class by the newly formed state bourgeoisie, made up largely of military officers and technocrats of petit-bourgeois background, a social group that Hussein perceives as only socially but not culturally marginalized prior to the fall of the *ancien régime*. In contrast the rural and urban proletariat has lived very much "on the fringe of 'respectable' society" (Hussein 1973, 40). While in the countryside it made up 39 percent of the population in 1914, it doubled to 80 percent in 1958. At the same time the rural petite bourgeoisie dwindled from 53 percent to 15 percent (Hussein 1973, 48) a clear sign of an increased fissure, but also attributable to the exodus of the rural population into the cities, in particular the capital, which today holds almost one fourth of the total Egyptian population (Ghannam 2002, 26).

More recent studies, for example by Robert Springborg (1989) and 'Abd al-Basit 'Abd al-Mu'ti (2002), have qualified Hussein's model by underlining the contradictory and fragmented outlook of preindependence Egyptian bourgeoisie. Hussein already admitted the fact that the Egyptian bourgeoisie did not really form a consistent body and accused it of having failed in contributing to a real industrial revolution in its homeland. Yet opinions have been divided on the reasons. While some blamed feudalism and the late colonial project for having prevented the successful formation of a capitalist bourgeoisie (and intensive industrialization), others singled out the collision of interests among the Egyptian elite that was largely composed of capitalists who were also at the same time big landowners (Vitalis 1995, 223). In fact the ethnic, religious, and ideological heterogeneity of the pre-Nasserist traditional ruling class was due to the presence of strongly conservative and anti-liberal Turkish aristocrats on the one hand, and Muslim and Coptic landowners who were often reformist- and nationalist-oriented on the other, in addition to the largely modernist businessmen (Hussein 1973, 65).

Unitary categorization seems difficult for the post-1952 era also, as 'Abd al-Mu'ti has demonstrated. For the vertical and horizontal communalities

and the numerous cross-class interests of that period render the task to classify the middle class in particular extraordinarily difficult ('Abd al-Mu'ti
2002, 297), not least because this particular group is characterized by a
strongly varied degree of economic and cultural (including educational) capital. Its members may be engaged in a huge variety of dependent and
independent professions (academia, commerce, management, handicraft)
and creative activities on the one hand, and entangled in multiple production
and power relations on the other. In other words, one and the same 'class'
may simultaneously comprise elements as different as a factory foreman
who owns a small farm, a bureaucrat who runs a business, and a university
professor who has no property at all, but holds a seat in parliament.

In fact, the extent to which social classes and their 'interests' intersect
with other factors, such as gender, ethnicity, religion, and ideological orientation (less taken into consideration by 'Abd al-Mu'ti for instance), explains
and makes more plausible the fact that moral values and culture are pivotal
to social categorization as worked out by French sociologist Pierre Bourdieu. His perception of class has been strongly informed by Max Weber who
had added a new dimension to the Marxist model. According to Bourdieu,
classes distinguish themselves not only through their economic, but also
their cultural and educational capital, overtly displayed in behavior, preferences, views, and taste. Thus, "[d]istinction, or better 'class', the
transfigured, misrecognizable, legitimate form of social class, only exists
through the struggles for the exclusive appropriation of the distinctive signs
which make 'natural' distinction" (Bourdieu 1984, 250).

Bourdieu's concept has, however, despite its accuracy and capacity for
fine grading, been criticized for being too deterministic "as it makes no
place for individual or sub-cultural resistance to them or movement through
them" (James 2004, 192). Also, with some of his research data dating back
to the 1960s, he fails to include issues of transnationalism, hybridity, and
multiculturalism that have become increasingly important factors during the
last two decades against the backdrop of rising mobility, mass migration,
and globalization. Yet the idea of cultural capital as a second determinant in

the fight for class privileges, alongside property and the affiliated strategies of distinction, seems relevant in the context of film analysis, not least because of the strongly discursive aspect of the creation of on- and off-screen film messages.

This particular aspect, namely reception and spectatorship, has in the last two decades become the subject of major research in media and cultural studies. Trying to move away from mere content- and subject-oriented analysis in the 1980s, the Birmingham Centre for Contemporary Cultural Studies has come to stress the importance of class difference with respect to media reception. For that reason it refused the "exclusive concern with the psychoanalytical construction of the subject[22] as an essentialism that excluded any other determination that the social formation, in its historically specific forms, might exert and made any concept of ideological struggle impossible" (James 2004 196). Accordingly, to understand perception as an active process that depends on the position of the viewer (age, gender, race, religion, class, environment, and so on) is to admit not only the contradictory character of the text but also to imply the notion of resistance and change to text and reader alike.

Genre as a Means of Distinction
The dynamics of perception govern not only audience responses but also the way film critics evaluate certain developments in cinema. 'Ali Abu Shadi is an influential Egyptian film critic and former member of the New Cinema Society founded in 1969, which mobilized against commercial film in favor of a young and committed cinema. He has since become a high-ranking cultural functionary (head of censorship, director of the National Film Center, and director of the annual National Film Festival and the Ismailiya International Film Festival). In his chronology of Egyptian film genres he states that "The harshest criticism of genre cinema in general is that genres have usually affirmed the *status quo* and its existing values, and have resisted any innovation or change. More often than not, these values express dominant *mores* and ideology. They provide easy formulaic

answers to difficult questions in order to please their audiences. The exceptions are far and few in the history of cinema" (Abu Shadi 1996, 85).

It goes without saying that this definition cuts short the dynamism of film genres and underestimates their negotiative character. It perceives genres as playing simply an affirmative role for audiences without realizing their complex interplay with social and cultural struggle and negotiation. No wonder, then, that the evaluation of Egyptian film genres was part of the strategy of 'distinction' within film criticism, setting apart realism from the formerly most popular genre of all (and ironically the one most concerned with class difference), namely melodrama.

Indeed, since the 1960s, realism and melodrama have been perceived increasingly as mutually exclusive by Egyptian and foreign leftist film critics—a move that runs parallel to developments in the West (cf. Hallam and Marshment 2000, 98), which suppose that in Egypt the two genres represent divergent class interests, linking realism to lower-class and melodrama to upper-class interests, and dismissing the latter for its alleged exclusive preoccupation with upper-class surroundings (compare Gaffney's position). The juxtaposition of both genres to different historical eras, namely pre- and postrevolution (in other words, *ancien régime* on the one hand and nationalist progressive Nasserism on the other), doubtless reflects the simultaneous shift of power from the old landowning bourgeoisie to the new state bourgeoisie, and has been supported and entrenched by the ideological schism that by 1954 had set the old and the new political system apart.

In the 1970s and 1980s, both national and international criticism of the postcolonial era spoke enthusiastically in favor of Egyptian realism. The French critic Claude Michel Cluny, author of the comprehensive *Dictionnaire des noveaux cinémas arabes*, stated: ". . . sometimes Egyptian cinema succeeded in imprinting on realism . . . a rather strong and original authenticity thus transcending the old concepts of melodramatic dramaturgy, the bible of screenplay writers and producers" (Cluny 1984, 46). Melodrama was reduced in this context to commercialism, formulaic repetitiveness, and lack of authenticity. Egyptian critics had started advocating this view even more energetically in the 1970s, describing "pre-revolutionary" cinema as marked by misguided consciousness, marked by (among other things) its preference for splendid upper-class settings, those "feudal palaces" which were later, in more realist accounts, replaced by "the apartments of employees and the alleys of Cairo" (Farid 1973, 150).

Samir Farid, who was also interviewed by Cluny for his book, is one of the most influential contemporary Egyptian film critics. He was trained during the early days of the republic, and was a founding member of the New Cinema Society. In his early writing he worked hard to dismiss pre-revolutionary popular cinema in favor of realism. In his historical account of Egyptian cinema published in 1973 he divided the country's output into different periods, each dominated by a certain class and accordingly by a different ideology, a process that he pictured as moving from an upper-bourgeois and 'royalist' expression, clinging to theatrical genres such as melodrama, farce, and musical, toward a more national, petit-bourgeois realist output. He distinguished between six successive generations of film-makers: pioneers and royalists represent the first generation, members of what he calls the national bourgeoisie (namely native Egyptians) represent the second and third generations; the fourth generation appears with the revolution in 1952, and is succeeded by the transitional fifth generation, which, according to Farid, takes realism on to the 'post-realism' or 'infinite realism' of the sixth generation, graduates of the Higher Film Institute (Farid 1973, 149).

This account is of course very much a child of post-independence. It is based on a linear perception of history colored by an idealist belief in progress, that opposes pre-Nasserist popular cinema (defined here as pre-revolutionary) to national realist cinema. This binary view is also taken in the criticism voiced by non-Egyptian Arab representatives of New Arab Cinema, an example of which is Tunisian Férid Boughédir's Tunisian documentary *Camera Arabe*, shot in 1982, which blames the Egyptian film industry for being a dream factory that has hampered the development of a more serious Arab cinema.

In contrast, Abu Shadi's more recent account made in 1996 what Farid could not, or possibly did not wish to foresee in 1973, namely the persistence of melodramatic forms in Egyptian cinema up to the present day, for melodrama has survived and was produced on a very high scale, outnumbering straightforward realist works, even decades after the Nasser's revolution. Melodramatic narration and the associated mode of representation were introduced to Egyptian entertainment before, and along with, the advent of cinema. Yusuf Wahbi's theater troupe, for instance, which was founded in 1923, specialized in melodrama. Silent cinema adopted the genre on the spot. The first Egyptian full-length feature, *Layla*, released in 1927, presented a clearly melodramatic plot revolving around duped love.

Melodrama: A Controversial Genre

After the introduction of sound, melodrama was frequently combined with the musical film form, engendering some of the most distinguished box office hits of the Egyptian film industry and reaching out eventually into other genres, such as realism and action film, to name only *Layla/Layla* (1942) by Togo Mizrahi, Henri Barakat's *Eternal Song/Lahn al-khulud* (1952) and *The Call of the Curlew* (1959), *My Father is Up the Tree* (1963) by Hussein Kamal, Hasan al-Imam's *Shafiqa the Copt* (1963) and *Take Care of Zuzu* (1972), *al-Batniya* (1980) by Husam al-Din Mustafa, *Sons and Killers/Abna' wa qatala* (1987) by 'Atef El-Tayeb, *The Garage/al-Garaj* (1995) by 'Ala' Karim, *Smile for the Picture* (1998) by Sharif 'Arafa and, last but not least, *Tito* (2004) by Tariq al-'Iryan.

The plots of these films were usually based on love rendered impossible by insurmountable class differences, on seduction and rape, or on quasi-fateful events, such as diseases, and handicaps that transform the protagonists into pitiable victims. Individual happiness and love stood on one side, while 'tradition and family' rested on the other. If not by fate in general, the lovers would be confronted with an authoritarian father or a figure related to him as their major opponent. The latter would be a wicked person who helped impose the father's law, like the rich girl's crooked cousin or uncle in *The White Rose* (1933) by Muhammad Karim, the vicious cousin in the postrevolutionary *Mortal Revenge/Sira' fi-l-wadi* (1954) by Youssef Chahine, and the uncle in *The Call of the Curlew* (1959) by Henri Barakat. His task was to be the obstacle in the course of true love. And indeed, melodrama's adversaries were commonly linked to ideological binarisms. The most basic dichotomies are moral in nature, dividing the cinematic cosmos into good and evil, rich and poor, virgin and whore: a secularized form of the existential mythical drama, if we are to believe Christine Gledhill.

The reasons for melodrama's persistence in Egypt are varied, and include viewer needs and expectations, but are certainly also rooted in the very universal and, most importantly, class-related nature of this genre. Examining American melodrama, Anglophone film scholars noted that the dramatic discontinuity or arbitrariness of the action, expressed in sudden drops of expectation and emotional twists underlined by gestures and music, could be seen to reflect the arbitrary nature of class justice (Nowell-Smith 1985, 181; Mulvey 1989, 66), something that can certainly hold true for Egyptian melodramas as well. Geoffrey Nowell-Smith proposed considering the most typical melodramatic strategies, including music, as well as the use of symbolically charged objects and exaggerated gestures to indicate psychological states, as an utterance of "undischarged emotion which cannot be accommodated within the action, subordinated as it is to demands of family/lineage/inheritance" (Nowell-Smith 1985, 193). In the West it was this 'emotionality' (as opposed to a presumably realist objectivity) that caused the genre to be associated either with femininity or with the lower-class lifestyle: "Expressiveness comes to be seen as a feminine characteristic of drama, and in English criticism in particular, as a lower-class attribute" (Hallam and Marshment 2000, 19).

In other words, music, gestures, and objects may represent the location where the emotion is displaced to, an emotion created, according to analysts, by unfulfilled desire—desire that in the Egyptian case I would regard not only as sexual but clearly of social origin also. The sudden dramatic twists (underscored by orchestral music), the accidental resolutions often coinciding with 'utopian' reconciliations between rich and poor, were used to discredit melodrama as a product of the dream factory, the outcome of a 'false consciousness,' and this condemnation seduced 'revolutionary' cineastes and Third Cinema supporters into overlooking the factual histori-cal and thematic intersection of melodrama and realism.

For, comparing both genres, Christine Gledhill claims that "melodrama operates on the same terrain as realism—i.e., the secular world of bourgeois capitalism—but offers compensation for what realism displaces" (Gledhill 1991, 208), a compensation that is emotional in nature, of course. The basic 'secularist' orientation of melodrama in the Egyptian context certainly needs to be qualified, as the fatalism of the genre is not at all opposed to religiosity. This does not refute, however, inherent communalities, particularly on the historical axis. In the European context, if we believe Gledhill, the discursive split between realism and melodrama regarding class occurred at the end of the nineteenth century, with realism "epitomized in the work of the realist and naturalist writers and dramatists," who represented "a different class of social writers 'literati' rather than entertainers—on behalf of a different audience— the intelligentsia rather than a popular middle-class or working-class audience" (Gledhill as quoted in Hallam and Marshment 2000, 19).

It is during this period that melodrama, contrary to realism, acquired a working-class connotation in Europe. In Britain during the industrial revo-lution, melodrama and its aesthetic first evolved in "a terrain of the 'unspeakable'" for a non-literate audience composed of the new urban work-ing class (Mulvey 1989, 73). The schism between melodrama as a 'working-class' genre was also perpetuated on a structural level during the 1910s when, in both Europe and the U.S., conservatives tried to control cin-ema morally. The nickelodeons in particular were denounced as "dens of vice, breeding grounds of physical and moral degeneracy, their lower-class immigrant audiences overly susceptible to the 'immoral' and corrupting influence of melodrama" (Hallam and Marshment 2000, 22).

By 1912, realism was heavily advocated by Western critics who increas-ingly demanded "natural, sincere, unmelodramatic acting in popular film"

(Hallam and Marshment 2000, 21). This was quite in contrast to Egypt, where realism became linked to the idea of cultural authenticity and the 'truthful' representation of lower-class life conditions. Film historian Ahmad al-Hadari, who studied a large number of documents, articles, and debates since the introduction of film to Egypt, noted that the issue of authenticity was first discussed regarding Badr Lama's *A Kiss in the Desert* (1928). In an attempt to copy Rudolph Valentino's character in *The Sheikh* (U.S.A., 1921) Lama equipped his main character with a patterned waistcoat entirely untypical of Arab Bedouins, a fact that was faulted in the Egyptian press of the time.[23] An Egyptian magazine in 1928 dismissed the whole work as inauthentic, stating: "The only things that give you a sense that it is an Egyptian film are pictures of the Sphinx and the Pyramids; otherwise it does not relate to us at all" (as quoted in Saif 1996, 104).

Badr Lama in *A Kiss in the Desert*, 1928

It is not clear exactly when the representation of rural and urban lower classes, and an interest in social problems, became a powerful and indispensable criterion of cinematic realism. Al-Hadari suspects that this happened around 1939 when Niazi Mustafa's *The Doctor/al-Duktur* and Kamal Selim's *Determination* were released, both of which evolved around educated young men from modest social backgrounds. In fact, reading early press evaluations of the films of Salah Abu Seif, who was later considered one of Egypt's most important realist directors, like *Master Hassan/al-Usta Hassan* (1952), it seems that they were primarily concerned with technical quality and acting abilities. Only some critics, most notably the leftist Ahmad Kamil Mursi (cf. Yusuf 1992, 57) and al-Sa'id Sadiq, commented in addition upon the films' relation to reality. Reviewing Abu Seif's adaptation of *Thérèse Raquin* by Emile Zola, *Your Day is Coming/Lak yawm ya zalim* (1951) after its release, the latter wrote, "watching this film, you see a truthful picture of events in Egyptian society, you see alive characters whom you meet everywhere, and you find society's problems being treated" (as quoted in Yusuf 1992, 84).

The perception of realism as being capable of representing 'objective reality' has remained popular with Egyptian critics until recently, and realism is commonly presented as the opposite of melodrama. In Magda Wassef's *100 ans de cinéma*, film critic Kamal Ramzi admitted that melodrama implies "sympathy for the heroes' misery but does not lead this misery back to objective reasons," while realism, he thinks, "consists of seeing reality, comprehending it, discovering the objective reasons for a phenomenon, displaying the moments of its transformation on the individual and collective level, taking position for the forces that shape life" (Ramzi 1995, 144). Thus, realism was not one form of discourse on reality with its own set of conventions, like other genres (for a more profound discussion cf. Shafik 1998, 126), but was perceived as a means to represent reality in an 'objective' and presumably more adequate way.

In the face of the overwhelming impact of melodrama, and in trying to consolidate and establish a more privileged ideological position for realism, some pro-realist critics have created a quasi-melodramatic discourse of realism as marginalized genre, for example Erika Richter's East German publication of 1974 (also translated into Arabic). This position considers the achievements of the first wave of realist films even more remarkable because of their directors' ability to accomplish them despite the pressures of commercialism (Richter 1974, 181). For the "often blamed melodramatic principle forms in itself the basis of Cairo's reputation as the Hollywood of the Near East, which it acquired during the 1940s and which has remained attached to it until the present" (Richter 1974, 37). Egyptian realism, in contrast, she praises as the "contribution of a young nation state to world culture" and against the more popular melodramatic current whose popularity, she argues, was a result of the strong emotionality displayed in the local *One Thousand and One Nights* tradition (Richter 1974, 36 and back cover).

The advocacy of realism conceals, however, the fact that there exists a general problem in identifying cinematic realism, far more difficult than in the case of melodrama. On the one hand, 'realism' advanced into a major paradigm for popular Western cinema and, on the other, it lent its name to different alternative cinematic waves, such as the socialist realism of the Stalinist era, French 'poetic realism' during the 1930s, post-Second World War Italian neorealism, and British 'kitchen sink' New Wave, as well as different Third World realisms from countries including Mexico, India, and Egypt, and ending with so-called diasporic transnational 'social realism' as defined by Julia Hallam and Margaret Marshment.

That is why Raymond Williams, in writing about nineteenth-century literature, preferred to describe realism as the result of a certain ideological orientation rather than a fixed set of generic rules (Williams 1977, 63). Similarly, 'neo-formalist' film scholars like Kirsten Thompson and David Bordwell have coined the term 'realistic motivation' (Hallam and Marshment 2000, 15) as a marker of realism, which operates in correlation with a changing set of referentialities regarding what is understood as reality. Unlike that, popular mainstream realism is seen to be governed by formal verisimilitude, reflected in acting style and *mise-en-scène* that aims to achieve a "*real*-ization of fantastic environments, on making scenarios that are visually and aurally credible," which has recently been facilitated even more by computer technologies (Hallam and Marshment 2000, 64).

In an attempt not to set generic and formal realism into opposition, Hallam and Marshment have offered a useful classification schema that differentiates between three types of realisms: expositional, spectacular, and rhetorical. The first is characterized by an episodic narrative structure which focuses on the relation between character and environment; the second is largely found in biopics, historical spectacles, and the like, which may reproduce sociohistorical events; while the third proposes an argument about the conditions of the real, often through the heroic actions of an individual caught in a sociopolitical dilemma borrowing stylistic means from popular genres, such as melodrama (Hallam and Marshment 2000, 101). It is in fact this last form, that is, rhetorical realism that has been the most prevalent and most advocated throughout Egyptian film history.

Thus, the discursive schism sketched out earlier between realism and melodrama, is a difference in 'motivation,' not necessarily in form; however, it did strongly shape the predominant perceptions of the two genres in Egypt, reinforced by the spread of quasi-socialist ideas during royalist times, later fostered by the political leadership under Nasser. And in the post-Nasserist era too, the same schism was perpetuated, completely obliterating the mutual genesis of realism and melodrama and their common preoccupations. Thus, hardly anyone suspected that in fact colonialism and pre- and postrevolutionary ideological tensions may have been the real source of the setting apart of both genres, polarizing them into two seemingly different systems of representation. Melodrama, read through the eye of the realist paradigm, came to stand for inauthentic commercialism, while realism as a genre could be transformed into one of those "symbolic goods" (Bourdieu 1984, 66) to be used as an ideological marker for those who considered themselves enlightened, leftist–progressive and with a heart for the national cause.

Raped Class/Raped Nation: From Melodrama to Realism

In doing away with earlier ideological reservations, the historical analysis of Egyptian melodrama may offer an opportunity to understand some of the modalities that made it so popular among audiences of its time, that is, since the outset of Egyptian fiction film in the late 1920s. Early melodrama was as concerned with moral distinction as it was with social status, family, and generational and gender conflict. Negotiations and antagonisms along these lines were, however, very contradictory. Many works emphasized (for instance, by means of a threatened heterosexual love) the suffering of men and women alike, their common position as victims of society, even though women tended to be additionally handicapped by the moral system. Hence, rape and seduction narratives, which almost obligatorily centered on women, started spreading during the 1940s, a time that also heralded the end of British domination, characterized by strong national sentiments and attempts to Egyptianize the national economy.

According to Galal Sharqawi, in the 1942–43 season more than 50 percent of Egyptian films presented seduced or raped women (Sharqawi 1970, 109). A typical example of that phase, released in 1947, was *Fatima/Fatima* by Ahmad Badrakhan, starring the famous singer Umm Kulthum in the role of a young nurse who serves a rich pasha. Fathi (Anwar Wagdi), the pasha's brother, tries in vain to seduce her, until she agrees to marry him clandestinely *(zawaj 'urfi)* and to share with him her modest home set in a poor traditional neighborhood. Soon he decides to end the relationship, steals the marriage contract, and deserts Fatima who, now pregnant, has no way to prove that he is her child's father. Finally Fathi recognizes his error and returns to confess in front of all the neighbors the truth of their relationship.

In the year of *Fatima*'s release, the singer Layla Murad appeared in a similar story *Fate's Stroke/Darbit al-qadar* (1947) by Yusuf Wahbi. Having been seduced earlier, the heroine takes a job as the governess of the children of a rich man, whom she agrees to marry. Much to her agony, she then learns that his brother is her former seducer. When he tries to blackmail her, she solves the problem by confessing everything to her husband. In this film, as

Umm Kulthum and Anwar Wagdi in *Fatima*, 1947

in most cases, the disparity between upper and lower-class characters was crucial to plot construction and the theme of abuse. In this sense, the images of sexual exploitation, cross-class seduction, and rape were not just box-office sensationalism, but had a clear sociopolitical reference, not in a reflexive sense though, but rather as "the metaphorical interpretation of class conflict" (Elsaesser 1985, 168).

This metaphorical interpretation certainly added to the universality of the genre. For the utilization and popularity of this particular motif was by no means originally Egyptian. The Swedish film, *The Gardener/Trädgårdsmästaren* (1912) by Victor Sjöström, was one of the first in cinema to present a fallen woman, a poor girl who is raped by the father of her admirer, subsequently forced into prostitution, and who commits suicide at the end. A similar plot emerged also in non-European films, for example the Japanese film *Osaka Elegy/Naniwa Ereji* (1936) that interestingly did without explicit emotional strategies in its *mise-en-scène*, offering a more sober account of how its heroine was led astray, complying with the wish of an older affluent man to take her as his concubine. The appearance of the motif across cultures indicates a certain universality that in turn seems to confirm its basic discursive relation to class difference rather than local culture.

The seduction/rape motif was able to give expression not only to class difference but also colonial oppression, as we saw earlier. It is crucial to see the same motif resurface in realist as well as modernist films during the post-1952 period, though with a stronger emphasis on class difference. Indeed, quite a number of 'realist' films placed the rape-seduction motif among deprived rural women, for example Tawfiq Salih's *Diary of a Country Prosecutor/Yawmiyat na'ib fi-l-aryaf* (1969), and the less modernist, yet strongly social-oriented 'realist' film *The Sin/al-Haram* (1965) by Henri Barakat. The latter focused on a poor peasant woman who gets pregnant as a result of rape. Following the secret birth of the child she unintentionally suffocates the newborn and herself falls fatally ill, causing a lengthy investigation in the village that polarizes its inhabitants.

Egyptian realism of the 1950s and 1960s that crystallized primarily in the work of Salah Abu Seif, Tawfiq Salih, Youssef Chahine, and Henri Barakat remained marginal in practice and in numbers (Shafik 1998, 128). It failed, moreover, to detach itself from melodrama, to the extent that it seems justifiable to attach the adjective 'melodramatic' to it. Realist films in Egypt used popular stars and were, in contrast to Italian Neorealism, rarely shot on location. What earned its directors the respect of the critics was their concern with the underprivileged, focused largely on the urban lower class and occasionally on workers and peasantry. The impact of melodrama remained nonetheless, at the level of *mise-en-scène* as well as in plot construction, with seduction and female honor playing a pivotal role, but also in terms of a certain fatalism expressed in numerous tragic endings.

Beginning and End (1960) by Salah Abu Seif represents such a powerful merging of both genres, and nurtures quite typically the discourse of female victimization. Its story was adapted from a Naguib Mahfouz novel of the same title. Set in preindependence Egypt, it portrays a petit-bourgeois family composed of four siblings driven into poverty after the father's death.

The final blow to the family's decline is brought about by the only daughter's fate. Having failed to attract a good match because of her homeliness, Nafisa (Sana' Gamil) undertakes to support her mother and youngest brother by working as a seamstress. The young brother (Omar Sharif) has finally wins admission to the prestigious military academy. Meanwhile Nafisa has been seduced by the grocer's son. When he refuses to marry her, she takes to the street, becoming the main supporter of the family. One evening she gets arrested and her brother is asked to pick her up from the police station. In a state of shock, he obeys her wish and drives her to the riverside where she drowns herself, eventually followed by him. The nocturnal suicide of brother and sister, a sudden impressive turning point that marks the film's finale, is accompanied by sonorous orchestral music with a tilted camera and dramatic low-key lighting, and lingers on the facial expressions of Omar Sharif and Sana' Gamil.

Despite this striking list of melodramatic stylistic devices, in addition to the cross-class seduction theme, the film was still perceived as realist. That is doubtless due to its literary model—the realist orientation and 'motivation' of Naguib Mahfouz—plus the almost exclusively lower-class setting, and to the fact that it does not dwell too much on the moral dichotomies of melodrama, good and evil. The absence of a villain is as decisive as the reference to the more abstract power of poverty and social injustice, the real culprits. The emphasis on Nafisa's fate through the tragic end that terminates her brother's career and shatters all his dreams of respectability renders her story central to the film. Although one of her brothers had also acquired a questionable moral record, being hunted by the police for some criminal involvement, hers is worse in view of the traditional norm equating a girl's virtue with her family's honor.

However, Nafisa is not demonized; on the contrary, she is represented as the ultimate victim, similar to what we have already encountered in *A Hot Night*. First duped by the grocer's son, then humiliated, detested, and even driven to death by her most beloved brother for whose education she had prostituted herself—this is again the pitiable but expected fate of a heroine.

Her failure and shame are too great for life after them to be imaginable. Along the same lines is the failure of the Nafisa's brother to secure a better position in society. Such a despairing end seems remarkable for a film completed eight years after the abolition of the monarchy, but it probably sought to denounce the injustices and humiliations of the royalist and colonial past even more profoundly.

Rape-seduction plots remain also common to stories that were not set in the past, such as *The Call of the Curlew* (1959) by Henri Barakat, which takes a progressive turn, in contrast to *Beginning and End* and *The Sin*, criticizing Upper Egyptian crimes of honor. Adapted from a novella of the same title by Taha Husayn, *The Call of the Curlew* tells the story of two poor orphaned sisters from the countryside. The first, sent to work as a servant, is seduced and raped by her master, an affluent young engineer, and subsequently killed by her uncle in an attempt to clear the family's reputation. Her sister, performed by Fatin Hamama, finds refuge in a middle-class family where she is helped to acquire a certain education. Yet she does not find any peace of mind and is haunted by the idea of avenging her sister's death. She thus seeks employment by the same man and attempts to make him fall in love with her in order to be able to punish him. As time passes, ambiguous emotional ties start to link master and servant, oscillating between moral prohibition and deep desire. Eventually, they reach a dramatic climax: he dies in her arms, shot by a bullet intended for her.

The Call of the Curlew includes many of the recurrent motifs and constellations of melodrama, such as class difference, rape, the merciless father-figure, and punished desire. It also offers some of the irrational and emotional narrative twists so typical of the genre, for instance the surprising change of the engineer from notorious womanizer to devoted lover. Moreover, both the desire of the heroine and the viewer's expectations are violently thwarted by the killing of the engineer at the very moment when he and his beautiful servant are united in his first sincere embrace. Tragedy and looming moral danger (seduction) are conveyed not only by the plot construction but also by the set design, which creates a cold, dim impression.

Fatin Hamama and Ahmad Mazhar in *The Call of the Curlew*, 1959

In particular, the engineer's house is scarcely lit, equipped only with a few sharp-edged pieces of furniture. Its windows are shaped by small wooden frames that keep out the daylight and render the atmosphere gloomy and claustrophobic. Even exterior shots depict an unpopulated rural setting, dominated by sharply contrasted low-key lighting, isolating the human figures from their background, and heightening the sense of gloom that emanates from this doomed cross-class liaison.

Doubtless the film language in *The Call of the Curlew* achieves, along with its plot, typical melodramatic emotionality, yet what has turned it into a modernist-oriented text—apart from its literary source—is first, its denunciation of a 'premodern' habit, the crime of honor and therefore the killing of girls who by losing their virginity were considered to have dishonored their families, and second, its preoccupation with one of the pillars of modernist thinking, namely education. It is through her education that the heroine becomes more of a match for the engineer, and it is also one of the sources of the power with which she resists his seduction. Nonetheless, the motif of irreconcilable class difference that will be discussed later is still pivotal, due to the extreme poverty of the heroine's peasant family as opposed to the bourgeois prosperity and indulgent lifestyle of the engineer.

Who Represents the New Order?

Many films that envisioned an exceptional role for the university graduate cast him (for the character was usually male) in a positive, progressive light. In the fairly melodramatic plot of *The Land of Dreams/Ard al-ahlam* (1957) by Kamal El-Cheikh it is the young engineer, son of an ordinary peasant, who uncovers the dirty tricks of the feudal landowner and his cronies. In contrast, in the more development-oriented *The Lamp of Umm Hashim* and *Struggle of Heroes/Sira' al-abtal* (1962), it is the doctors who try to beat the vicious circle of ignorance and traditional power structure in the province, represented in the second case by the triple alliance of a local estate-owner, the village's head man, and the midwife. Less realist-motivated films mainstreamed the image of the graduate, too. The comic musical *Nights of Love/Layali al-hubb* (1955) by Hilmi Rafla starred singer 'Abd al-Halim Hafiz as the poor inventor of a non-inflammable fabric, who at the end of the film not only gets promoted but wins the heart of his company director's daughter.

If the graduate professional was the modern façade of the new order, workers and particularly peasants remained relegated to the prettily designed, yet folkloric backyard, rarely liberated from generic schematization and/or the nationalist or quasi-socialist rhetoric. Indeed, on the level of location, manners, language, and costume, the code of cinematic class affiliation has followed pretty consistent, uninterrupted, and schematized modes since the 1930s. While the palace or country estate of early times gave place to the elegant modern villa with garden and swimming pool, the cramped alleys of Cairo, with their modest, dilapidated houses and flats or the rooms on top of more modern multi-story buildings have remained a quite consistent feature. They boil down to two iconographic antipodes, corresponding to an overtly Westernized (in fashion and furniture, not necessarily in values) upper class on the one hand, and a more traditionally oriented lower class on the other. The inhabitants of the alleys have not been confined to workers, though, but have often included 'petit-bourgeois' characters, with education but without corresponding influence or property.

This process toward the inclusion of an although deficient depiction of lower-class environments did not go uncontested. As one of the former heads of censorship, Mustafa Darwish (in office from 1966 to 1968) wrote, official censorship as well as the press under the monarchy was hostile to the portrayal of Egyptian villages and the working class (Darwish 1989, 65). In general, the representation of the lower classes was not welcomed at that time. This is shown by a statement of Husain Sidqi, producer and leading player in *The Worker/al-'Amil* (1942) by Ahmad Kamil Mursi, a very rare treatment of its subject. He had starred in the earlier *Determination*, and said, "In it [*The Worker*] we were influenced not so much by *Determination* as much as [by] and interacting with our society's problems. It was the first film on the list of my productions that glorifies the struggle of workers and deals with their problems to the extent that it was banned when it was first screened in 1942, and it was a reason for speeding up the issuing of labor laws and the licensing to found workers' unions" (quoted in al-Tayyar 1980, 49).

If the fear of social unrest and working-class resistance was one reason for banning or at least having reservations about the representation of the lower class, then nationalist ideology was the other. One of the first cineastes to be accused of spreading a bad image of Egypt was 'Aziza Amir whose production *Layla* (1927) dealt with a peasant girl who is seduced, then driven out of her village, to be picked up by a rich man who ends up marrying her. Despite this utopist plot, Amir was blamed for "showing Egypt still caught in the Middle Ages while there are plenty of things to be proud of" (Darwish 1989, 65). This hostility was not completely abandoned after 1952. In particular, documentaries that dealt with the hardships of lower-class conditions were regularly accused of damaging Egypt's image abroad, to name only *Horse of Mud/Husan al-tin* (1971) by Ateyyat El Abnoudy and later the British *Marriage Egyptian Style* (1991), coauthored by the Egyptian anthropologist Reem Saad.

Doubtless, the Nasserist regime made it more acceptable to depict working class and rural conditions even though the censorship law regarding this particular point was not amended before 1976 (Darwish 1989, 67). A certain number of Egyptian realist films produced in the 1950s and 1960s dealt with poverty, ignorance, and oppression in the countryside, yet largely projected onto the past (cf. Shafik 1998, 128), most notably Youssef Chahine's epic *The Earth* (1970), which glorified a courageous old peasant's fight against exploitative landlords. This temporary interest in the fellahin has of course to be seen in the context of different land reforms, a phased one in 1952, and two others in 1961 and 1969, limiting the amount of land owned by single individuals. It may also have been prompted by the politically charged murder of a peasant leader in the village of Kamshish in 1966, following more than two decades of struggle between peasant leaders, the prerevolutionary power structure, and postrevolutionary authorities (Miqlid 1991, 250).

The same period saw simultaneously a strong folklorization of peasantry, intersecting with the allegorical feminization of Egypt as *umm al-dunya* (Mother of the World) on the one hand, which had started in the late nineteenth century, and as a *fallaha* (peasant woman) on the other. The latter found itself powerfully translated by the sculptor Mahmud Mukhtar into *Egypt's Awakening (Nahdat Misr)*, a monumental stone figure stylistically close to ancient Egyptian art, that displays a *fallaha* dressed in a long gown or *gallabiya* and a loose headscarf, holding the back of a rising sphinx (cf. Baron 2005, 67). The statue was erected in 1928 in a square in front of Cairo University, a sign of the peasantry's new role in the modernist postcolonial discourse. For the glorified image of the peasant, who by the 1920s had come to be "prized as the soul of Egypt," has acquired since the 1920s in cinema an idealist element that could be instrumentalized for nationalist ideology (Baron 2005, 68).

When Muhammad Karim made his staff wash not only peasant's cottages but also entire fields before shooting them for the literary adaptation *Zaynab* in 1930, he was later congratulated by the novel's author, Muhammad

Hasanain Haikal for rendering *Zaynab* into a source of joy in saying, "we want the entire Egyptian countryside to resemble the one in your film" (Karim's memoirs as quoted in Darwish 1989, 66). This is another reason why folkloric art was celebrated in the 'postrevolutionary' era. One of its representatives was the Rida Dance Group, which also issued two film musicals. It amalgamated different local dance forms, traditional belly dance as well as modern oriental dance, into a folkloric group dance element. This orientation could be seen less as a show of feeling for the 'real' rural population than as part of a developing communal national imagination, and even as a disguised expression of bourgeois culture, if we believe Pierre Bourdieu's idea that the "preference for 'folk' forms is fueled by a 'populist nostalgia,'" forming "a basic element in the relationship of the petite bourgeoisie to the working or peasant classes and their traditions" (Bourdieu 1984, 58).

Fatin Hamama as a deprived peasant woman in *The Sin*, 1965

Class Struggle or Reconciliation?

Jane Gaines made a quite surprising argument in stating Marxism's affinity with melodrama by pointing to its theory of 'melos' in *Capital*, that is, the notion of irreconcilability regarding class difference and struggle (Gaines 1996, 58–68). Moreover she considered its use of dramatis personae or 'personifications of the economic' to provide an additional linkage to the genre quite evident in a Marx quotation describing the contrast between bourgeois and worker: "The one smirks self-importantly and is intent on business; the other is timid and holds back, like someone who has brought his own hide to the market and now has nothing else to expect but—a tanning" (Gaines 1996, 59).

It is pretty clear that popular genres, with melodrama in the lead (followed by the action film as we will see later), have a disposition toward certain schematized and allegorical sets of class encounters and entanglements, such as peasantry versus feudal upper class, lower and upper bourgeoisie, urban lower class (not always explicitly working class) and upper bourgeoisie. They have been developed within the framework of specific plot constellations, usually scripted around exploitation and resistance. In Egyptian film these constellations have over the years moved slightly from patterns of overt sexual exploitation (melodrama) toward explicit economic exploitation (rhetorical realism and action film).

Yet, what in my view has helped melodrama in the Egyptian context to transcend itself into a kind of 'rhetorical' realism is the emergence of the idea of confrontation, or the rejection of consensus, and the motivation to expose social and political injustice allegorically. While the melodramatic structure positions its characters as passive victims who may or may not succeed because of (or despite) unfavorable conditions, more action-oriented films have chosen to stress the 'determination' to fight for one's cause. And this is exactly the formula that started to define the outlines of yet another popular genre spreading in Egyptian cinema, the action film, which did increasingly inform realism, particularly New Realism in the 1980s, and has meanwhile substituted melodramatic elements to a large extent.

Indeed it is with the 1950s that an inclination to bring about violent resolutions could be sensed more strongly. The increasing number of films that
ended in violent showdowns, one of the most prominent examples being
Youssef Chahine's *Mortal Revenge* (1954), run parallel to the general tendency to include more action elements, such as chases, shootings, brawls,
and an accelerated editing rhythm. However—as the analysis of action films
will show—this cannot necessarily be interpreted as a direct result of social
unrest or the like. Admittedly, in some postrevolutionary films these confrontations could assume a certain referentiality, picturing the allegorical
defeat of the old elite, like the rather picturesque final showdown of *Mortal
Revenge* in the ancient Karnak temple, where an evil aristocrat, representative of the old feudal order, menaces a young engineer of peasant stock and
eventually gets killed himself.

Not all struggle-oriented, 'realist' works fostered optimism. Some displayed a kind of pessimistic attitude toward social change (even though
transposed to the past). In *Beginning and End* (1960), *The Thug* (1957), *The
Earth* (1970)—all set during the monarchy—and in *The Rebels* (1968) by
Tawfiq Salih, the prospects of abolishing justice and social opportunism are
thwarted. It is worth noting that the pessimism of Egyptian realism must
itself be considered a revolutionary departure from the pre-1952 situation,
where it was prohibited by law, not only to depict the social situation as
hopeless, but to represent features of a political struggle at all (Shafik 1998,
34, 132).

This certainly forced a conciliatory tone upon the early 'realist' films
that might have been more outspoken, most notably Kamal Selim's *Determination* (1939). Often considered to mark the beginning of Egyptian
realism, this film did actually resolve its final conflict between the hero and
the alley's affluent butcher in a harmless comic brawl. According to Erika
Richter, Egyptian critics considered the film's "sore point" to be the "deus
ex machina" embodied by the pasha who in the end rescues the hero from
his economic ordeals, by the offer of a business partnership with his son. In
fact, the pragmatism displayed in *Determination* regarding the eventual

cooperation between prosperous aristocracy and the poor but educated middle class reflected Studio Misr's cautious attitude. As producer of the film, it refused to release the work under the title 'The Alley,' considering it too risky to advertise (Sharqawi 1970, 78).

It may be no accident that such a reconciliatory attitude comes much closer to more up-to-date reinterpretations of historical materialism, precisely Gramsci's notion of hegemony, which shifts away from the inevitability of a (dramatic) collision between the classes to the possibility of a pact or agreement between those in power and the less privileged, something that corresponds to the original Greek definition of the term as an authority that is based on consensus and not on coercion (Krell 2004, 296). Like no other film, *Determination* presented the possibility of a social symbiosis quite effectively—which has turned out to be closer to the realities of Egypt's post-royalist and post-independence development than the more confrontational 'revolutionary' narratives of irreconcilability.

Numerous post-1952 films followed the line of *Determination* in offering education as a solution to bridge and reconcile class differences, with *Mortal Revenge* again a notable example. The film's hero (Omar Sharif), the engineer son of a modest white-collar worker on a country estate, and the heroine (Fatin Hamama), daughter of the estate owner, grow up together and fall in love as adults only to discover the social obstacles that separate them. Only after a bloody shootout with the girl's cousin (Farid Shawqi) who wants her father's estate for himself, despises the peasants, and puts the life of the engineer's father at risk, are the lovers able to unite. What facilitates the reconciliation of disparate social positions here is doubtless the lover's university education, an allusion to the importance attached by Nasser's socialist government to free education at all levels.

A comparable explicit reconciliation of classes through education was presented, with an even stronger proregime connotation, in 'Izz al-Din zu-l-Fiqar's *Give My Heart Back/Rudda qalbi* (1957), one of the earliest Egyptian cinemascope films, still aired annually on July 23, the day of the

1952 revolution. The love story of the gardener's-son-turned-military-officer with beautiful Angie, the daughter of his father's employer, was meant to address the social changes engendered through the change of power in 1952, particularly nationalizations. In a highly arbitrary ending and after a lot of emotional ups and downs, the officer is finally brought to realize Angie's love when he is sent to the estate where he grew up, to implement a seques-tration order on his former beloved's belongings. Angie freely gives up all her jewelry—except for one tiny chain, which turns out to be a gift from him long ago.

Being part of the modernist agenda, education as a means of social ascent (or resistance) had in fact already been proposed during the 1930s and 1940s, in Niazi Mustafa's *The Doctor* (1939) as well as in early 'realist' films, *Determination* (1939) and *The Black Market/al-Suq al-sawda'* (1945) among others. After the coup, however, the government introduced free edu-cation and guaranteed state employment, both of which became instrumental in forming the new state bourgeoisie (state functionaries, including tech-nocrats and officers), offering an opportunity to fulfill social aspirations. And indeed, the nationalization of existing industry following 1952 along with the continuation of the substitute policy initiated by the preceding 'national' bourgeoisie (namely the attempts of Egyptians and *mutamassirun* to curb imports and increase local production) put the now ascending state functionaries in a favorable position to accumulate capital, redirect public investment, and gradually eclipse the former traditional elite, infiltrating them first, then rendering them dispensable (Hussein 1973, 186).

The new order, despite its outspoken socialist rhetoric and some overt political measures in that direction, doubtless also wore a petit-bourgeois face, as exemplified in its political leadership, embodied most prominently in Nasser's persona and social background. This explains also the ambiva-lence of popular cinema in dealing with the lower classes, as pointed out earlier, despite the temporary 'revolutionary' tendency to vilify upper-class and bourgeois characters. Indeed after 1952 the pasha and his allies were increasingly pictured as greedy, unscrupulous, despotic villains in stories set in the royal past—a vilification, however, that took place mostly on moral grounds and not because of any 'analytical' political concepts.

This is why Sami Salamuni, a filmmaker and critic of the 1970s and 1980s, criticized *Master Hassan* by Salah Abu Seif, one of the early realist films, which came out shortly before the coup in July 1952 and depicted a cross-class liaison, for its "naive" denunciation of the aristocracy, "merely attacking its torn morals embodied for him [the director] only in sexual shamelessness according to the understanding of popular classes of the morals of the upper bourgeoisie. Then, after the sexual victory of the working class (Master Hassan) against aristocracy (Zuzu Madi) Salah Abu Seif returns with his hero to the moral values of the popular quarter without any call for change of misery and backwardness" (Salamuni as quoted in al-Tayyar 1980, 51). Filmmakers like Salah Abu Seif, who was of petit-bourgeois origin himself, raised in the same poor neighborhood of Bulaq that he depicted in *Master Hassan*, was obviously more caught in his own class interests and reservations than preoccupied with any proper political analysis. This was just the kind of attitude to foster the production of cinematic villains.

Looking for a Villain

Popular Egyptian film introduced a number of contradicting juxtapositions of vice and virtue with class. Just as the cunning, opportunistic aristocrat and the wicked uncle who wants the beautiful heiress for himself were stock characters in many 'prerevolutionary' melodramatic plots, so the technocratic middle class (as in *The Call of the Curlew*) and even the lower social strata were at times given unfavorable roles after 1952. In the 1950s several quite popular works featured utterly vicious and irredeemable lower-class men, such as *Hamidu/Hamidu* (1953) by Niazi Mustafa starring Farid Shawqi as a criminal fisherman (in a story he authored himself), *The Beast/al-Wahsh* (1954) by Salah Abu Seif (in which a ruthless criminal, with the connivance of a big landowner, holds hostage a whole region in Upper Egypt until his gang is broken up by the police), and *Abu Hadid/Abu Hadid* (1958), again by Niazi Mustafa, set in a fishing community.

Farid Shawqi in *Hamidu*, 1953

Works to which the figure of the despot was constitutive tended to rely on 'Manichean battles,' presenting adversaries differentiated by their moral standing. At times, despotic viciousness was clearly divided along class lines with a strong, direct reference to the political order, starting with the quasi-historical spectacle *Lashin* (1938) by Fritz Kramp, one of the earliest Studio Misr productions completed during the reign of King Faruq. This film contrasted its youthful and beloved warrior-hero Lashin, who fought for the benefit of the impoverished masses, with a tyrant king. The latter's persona, however, was not tolerated by the censor and had to be altered in order for the film to be released (Abou Chadi 1995, 24). Another despotic king situated in Persia was presented in *Layla, the Bedouin* and caused the film's screening to be suspended for seven years, as its planned release coincided with Princess Fawziya's wedding to the Persian Shah.

After the coup the despot remained a recurrent and often allegorical figure, as in Salah Abu Seif's realist film *The Thug*, which pictured the struggle of market vendors against the 'King of the Market,' an unscrupulous racketeer. More outspoken Marxist works, such as *Struggle of Heroes* (1962) and *al-Sayid al-bulti/al-Sayid al-bulti* (1969) both by Tawfiq Salih, and *The Earth*, based on 'Abd al-Rahman al-Sharqawi's novel, focused on the battle of one heroic lower-class figure against the dominance of a group with shared interests, that is landowners or feudal landowners, village headmen, and military authorities.

The disastrous military defeat in 1967 brought about a clear tendency to discover vice and virtue in a wider range of social categories and to include a moment of exposure in which the rich are unveiled as lower-class *arrivistes*. One indicator of this development was the appearance of overtly political films (cf. Abu Shadi 1996) whose primary concern was the question 'Who is to blame?' — a question that assumed major importance after the Six Day War, which resulted in Israeli occupation of the rest of Palestine as well as Syrian and Egyptian territory and marked the decline of the Nasserist era.

Simultaneously, a number of films emerged that dealt with social struggle but were eager to divert the binary moral and social construction of earlier realist films toward a stronger focus on the failure of the system in general, or in other words, to give a more complex answer to the question of 'who is to blame,' by presenting it as a concerted action of several social actors. The character of the opportunist took on a heavyweight in those narratives, to think only of *Miramar* (1969) by Kamal El-Cheikh, where the crooked young Sarhan, a member of the ruling party, tries to dupe Zahra (the singer Shadia), a poor country girl, into a relationship.

Other works too, like Kamal El-Cheikh's *Adrift on the Nile* (1971), based like *Miramar* on the writings of Naguib Mahfouz, and later *The Culprits/al-Mudhnibun* (1976) by Sa'id Marzuq, focused on the moral corruption of those who opportunistically took jobs under the new government, but used them for their own benefit, forming an extended network of wrongdoers. Other films were centred on one just hero confronting ineradicable corruption, for example *The Bullet is Still in my Pocket/al-Rasasa la tazal fi jaybi* (1974), *Whom Shall We Shoot?/'Ala man nutliq al-rusas?* (1975), continued later by New Realist works, such as *The Bus Driver* (1983) and *Houseboat No. 70/al-'Awwama raqam 70* (1982).

Whom Shall We Shoot? (1975) by Kamal El-Cheikh was one of those narratives that started laying blame on the new technocrats who came to the fore with Nasserism, and must be seen against the backdrop of the housing crisis that was hotly discussed during this period. Sami is an engineer in a construction company. When one of its buildings collapses because of the use of inferior material, the owner of the company, Rushdi, is able to put the blame on innocent Sami, who is jailed and dies in prison. His friend Mustafa learns the truth and decides to take revenge. He hunts Rushdi down, losing his own life, but at the end Rushdi is identified as the real cuplrit and brought to justice.

The figure of a single powerful villain resurfaced in the 1980s in a real tidal wave of spectacularly scandalous 'dishwasher to millionaire' stories. *Attention, Ladies and Gentlemen/Intabihu ayuha al-sada* (1980) by Muhammad 'Abd al-'Aziz, *The Servant* (1984) by Ashraf Fahmi, and *The Doorkeeper Manages the Building* (1985) by Nadia Salim demonstrated how ruthless lower-class protagonists manage to sneak into and gradually come to dominate the life of bourgeois families. Clearly these films capitalized on social

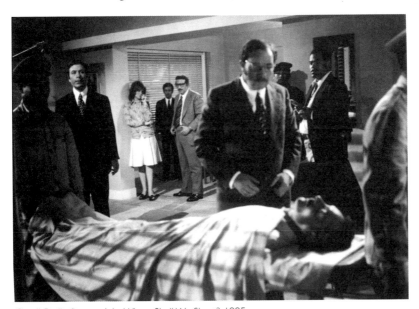

Gamil Ratib (bottom) in *Whom Shall We Shoot?*, 1995

contempt, bourgeois fears of being leveled out and/or imperiled by social descent, and the dismissive rhetoric of the 'middle class' confronted with a hitherto unknown social mobility. These narratives achieved a displacement of meaning regarding the centers of social (hegemonic) power, that is, the question 'who is to blame?' The ideologically contradictory character of these works is due to the fact that a lower-class character assumes a very powerful and despotic position within the drama that equates him with the elite. This was strongly generalized in the action-oriented films of the late 1970s and 1980s, whose denunciation of single despotic figures disguises a struggle within the bourgeoisie. The alliance of a lower-class criminal with the elite was already shown in early works like *The Beast*, but their social origin remained visible in dress and behavior, whereas that has drastically changed in the case of the *infitah*-imposter.

To be more precise, the nouveau riche or 'fat cat' became the most recurrent character during the 1980s, usually shown as a crook ascending from the margins of society to form part of the powerful economic elite. This recast cinematic class frontiers so familiar until the 1970s, and also introduced the motif of possible social descent. Interestingly, the New Realism of the 1980s and early 1990s took up the same motifs and dwelled on them, though in a less exploitative manner. *The People from the Top/Ahl al-qimma* (1981), *Hatim Zahran's Times* (1988), and *The Vagabonds/al-Sa'alik* (1985) for example featured shady characters from the margins making their way to the top by using illegal and immoral practices, such as theft, nepotism, and bribery, suggesting that the new *infitah*-class had managed to ascend from the bottom of society and push the respectable middle class to the margins.

Much credibility was attached to those films because of their realist character, not only on the formal but also on the narrative level, not least because they bluntly expressed the turmoil and threats the educated middle class experienced after the failure of the Nasserist model of state capitalism and the economic decline that characterized the early phase of the Open Door policy ('Abd al-Mu'ti 2002, 349). This motif of unprecedented upward class mobility, along with an allegorical depiction of the haunted academic, became pivotal to New Realism—and still resurfaces, as in the 2002 production *A Citizen, a Detective, and a Thief/Muwatin, mukhabir wa harami.*

The 'Fat Cats' Myth

The core group of New Realism, which became very popular with the critics for their social commitment (but not with producers), shared certain recurrent themes and formal characteristics, which helped to define them as 'realist,' such as shooting on location, sober acting, the reduced use of music, and socially committed themes with a strong focus on moral conflict. Ideologically this wave was clearly directed against the Open Door policy or *infitah* initiated by the Sadat administration in the course of the 1970s on the political and economic level, causing Egypt to leave the socialist orbit and approach the United States, a process that helped to consolidate a new national bourgeoisie but which gave people other than the military the opportunity to accumulate wealth through contracting and trading. Eventually it brought an Islamic segment to the fore, represented by Islamic investment companies that started to mushroom during the 1980s and permitted (much to the disapproval of many intellectuals) an unprecedented degree of wealth.

New Realist preoccupation with the 'underprivileged' did not necessarily include peasantry and workers but remained almost exclusively focused on the petit-bourgeois milieu. The predominantly middle-class perspective of New Realism may be sensed in the thematic orientation of the overwhelming majority of the twenty-six films between the 1980s and early 1990s that can be classified as New Realist in the above sense. Only six deal with the working class or with peasants. Half of those again (*Omar's Journey/Mishwar 'Umar* [1986] and *Missing/Kharaj wa lamm ya'ud* [1985] by Mohamed Khan, as well as *Houseboat No. 70* [1982] by Khairy Beshara) do not focus entirely on them, but present temporary friendly encounters between middle-class representatives and workers, peasants or other underprivileged people, dealing only incidentally with rural or working-class conditions. All in all, New Realism was rather interested in social problems related to the urban lower-middle class, such as the housing crisis, migrant workers, and political abuses.

One of the initiating works of New Realism was *Sleepless Eyes/'Uyun la-tanam* (1981) by Ra'fat al-Mihi featuring Farid Shawqi as the eldest brother dominating his three younger brothers and exploiting them in his car-repair workshop. On his marrying a poor but young and beautiful street vendor, the precarious equilibrium of his household starts to disintegrate. Two of the brothers find a way out by emigration, but the youngest (Ahmad Zaki) eventually kills the eldest in a rage. Crucial to this cinematic confrontation is the resort to violence, the bloody showdown, as a dramatically easy way to resolve the conflict for or against the hero. It is echoed in a number of other New Realist films, for example 'Atef El-Tayeb's *The Prison Cell/al-Takhshiba* (1984) and *The Execution Squad* (1989); in both films female avengers hunt down their oppressors, as well as *The Innocent/al-Bari'* (1986), which depicts the exploitation of a young rural Central Security soldier at the hands of his superiors.[24]

Ahmad Zaki and Madiha
Kamil opposing Farid Shawqi
in *Sleepless Eyes*, 1981

A similar resolution was also chosen for Daoud 'Abd El-Sayed's *The Vagabonds* (1985). The film focuses on the unexpected ascent of two friends, uneducated laborers (hereby alluding to a real-life success story, that of the supposedly illiterate Rashad 'Uthman who became an influential businessman and member of parliament). They are first shown living on the street and taking occasional jobs in Alexandria harbor. Eventually they find a way to start a drug-trafficking business that allows them to become two of the most prosperous businessmen in town. Later, one of them tries to court a professional woman from an impoverished bourgeois family. Through this subplot the film is able to emphasize the gap between the uneducated quasi-criminal nouveau riche and the 'respectable' middle class character who is unable to perform successfully in the new economic system engendered by the *infitah*.

The *Vagabonds*, based on a typical 'fat cats' plot, is meant to reveal the negative social effects of the *infitah* that halted Nasserist (and earlier nationalist) attempts to create an Egyptian substitute economy (where imports are

Mahmud 'Abd al-'Aziz and Nur al-Sharif in *The Vagabonds*, 1985

substituted by local production). The majority of films presenting that theme linked the nouveaux riches with criminal practices and dismissed them morally by exposing their materialism and lack of traditional sense of community. Quite in line with this logic, *The Vagabonds* closes in a tragic showdown: at the peak of their economic success the two former tramps, who have been closer than brothers, fall out over different business policies and eventually shoot each other, thus pointing out the moral that greed destroys friendship and solidarity.

Notwithstanding its realist discourse and the fact that *The Vagabonds* alluded to an exceptional real-life entrepreneur, this brand of cinematic narrative has to be considered on the whole mythical. For compared with reality, it highly exaggerates the span of lower-class mobility and falsifies the fronts of the social struggle by portraying the middle class caught between the new bourgeoisie and the urban lower class. In fact, in 1973, shantytown dwellers made up around 45 percent of Egyptian city's population (Ibrahim 1977b, 135). It is hard to imagine these "uneducated, hungry, unhealthy and needy persons, who have few opportunities for socioeconomic advancement" (Ibrahim 1977b, 136) as able to jump up the social ladder so quickly and turn en masse into the country's leading class.

Fact is rather what Malak Zaalouk has proposed: the new ruling class of that period "is a merger between fractions of the old traditional bourgeoisie, who where restricted under Nasser and once again revived with the Open Door economic policy, fractions of the bureaucratic bourgeoisie born with the state sector under Nasser and finally businessmen performing new activities and stepping in areas of investment with the least risk and highest profits, namely commercial agents" (Zaalouk 1989, 133). Fifty percent of commercial agents, who were thought most representative of the *infitah* economy, came from traditional trading and industrial bourgeois families; others had been technocrats, managers, senior civil servants (30 percent), liberal professions or academics (10 percent), military officers (6 percent), and large landowning families (2 percent). Only the tiniest part (2 percent) had been merchants or wholesale traders engaged in domestic trade alone, who usually lacked the educational standard of the others. Thus, only the last and smallest group fitted into the cinematically described 'lower-class' nouveau riche category. Even though the system evidently allowed a certain mobility, its recurrent cinematic representation could also have the effect of concealing the fact that the old bourgeoisie was by no means dethroned. Hence, realist filmmakers and writers were tempted to take an exceptional feature as generality in order to discredit the *infitah* phenomenon as a whole.

This becomes even clearer in the kind of moralism set up by a number of New Realist works. As we saw earlier, class bias was reflected in a strong moral binarism found in numerous typical *infitah*-critical works, to name only *The People from the Top* (1981), *The Bus Driver* (1983), and Mohamed Khan's *Return of a Citizen/'Awdat muwatin* (1986). In all those films the protagonists were confronted with the option to abandon their own kin for

Faruq al-Fishawi (center), Amina Rizq, and Mahmud al-Gindi in *The Flood*, 1985

the sake of social ascent and prosperity. In *The Bus Driver* the main character tries throughout the film to collect a certain amount of money in order to save the workshop of his sick father but is unable to obtain substantial help from any of his siblings. It turns out that one of them has been instrumental in indebting the workshop without the father's knowledge. In *The Flood/al-Tufan* (1985) directed by Bashir al-Dik, who was also one of the most prolific scriptwriters of New Realism, the plot evolves around siblings who conspire to murder their old mother in order to be able to tear down the house she is living in and sell the land at a profit. These narratives clearly depicted the struggle for accumulation of money and property as a sign of materialist pragmatism and moral decay, while modesty was related to 'traditional' quasi-religious ideals comprising community loyalty, generosity, honesty, and respect for one's parents. Interestingly the same argument, namely the reproach of a lack of culture, surfaced in the discussion on audiences.

Ironically, as Zaalouk discovered in her empirical study, the old elite also preferred to distinguish themselves strictly from successful 'newcomers' who started their activity in the mid-1960s or in the aftermath of 1967. "According to the self-selected elitist group, 'outsiders' lacked ethics, finesse and business experience" (Zaalouk 1989, 131). Thus the elite within the elite voiced exactly the same criticisms as those made in cinema against fat cats. What adds irony to this phenomenon is that the 'ethical' reservations put forward by the old elite against the rising businessmen are the same as those displayed in committed realist films. This is why we could claim that the 1980s filmmaker generation (largely from the urban middle or lower-middle class themselves), members of the less prosperous bourgeoisie equipped with the necessary cultural means of expression, that is, cultural capital, chose to denounce via (film) culture the more prosperous bourgeoisie for its excessive possession of economic means—and at the same time for its 'lack of culture.' This was also the logic that allowed and justified violent cinematic confrontations, if not the extinction of lower-class imposters, or, in other words, irreconcilability.

CHAPTER 6

Audiences and Class

E arliest cinema-going was at the outset a bourgeois habit in Egypt, as elsewhere in the Middle East and unlike Europe and the U.S. where the invention was soon proletarianized through lower-class distribution circuits such as the funfair and nickelodeon. Some of the more privileged foreign and national inhabitants of the two major cities Cairo and Alexandria must have been the first to attend the screenings that presented the new technical invention, first in the Tousson stock-exchange in Alexandria and then in the Hamam Schneider (Schneider Baths) in Cairo. In 1896, only a few months after their initial European screenings, the Lumière-*cinématographe* was used to project films to an exclusive audience in Egypt.

Yet the medium widened its scope steadily. In the following years, short screenings started to complement native theater performances and by 1912, cinemas were offering Western films with titles and inter-titles (written dialog inserted between scenes, as in silent movies) translated into Arabic, usually projected on a smaller, adjacent screen. At about the same time, local foreigners and native residents of Egypt started their own small-scale production. Both are a clear indicator that the less affluent and the less educated (that is, only Arabic-speaking) urban population started to be drawn to screenings composed largely of European fiction films that since the mid-1910s had started to adapt to the more sophisticated needs of Western middle classes in terms of morals and narration. This cinema seems to have appealed not only to the Middle Eastern elite but also to Egypt's urban petite bourgeoisie, which, although still socially and politically marginalized during the early decades of the twentieth century was culturally (and increasingly politically) rather active. It eventually reached a position that prepared its members to oppose British occupation, and by striving to obtain higher education for its offspring it was soon able to monopolize intellectual activity (Hussein 1973, 34–36), and who certainly also contributed to the creation of national cinema in Egypt.

Thus in the 1920s performers such as 'Aziza Amir and Amina Muhammad, who did not come from an illustrious social background, ventured to produce their own films, while the offspring of prosperous aristocrats' and traders' families, most notably Yusuf Wahbi and Togo Mizrahi, were among the first to set up small, provisional studios in 1928 and 1929. Furthermore the construction of modern well-equipped Studio Misr in 1933–34 allowed an increasing number of less elevated Egyptians to turn to filmmaking, as they received their professional training there, with directors like Salah Abu Seif and Kamal El-Cheikh as the most notable examples. Eventually, after the rise to power of the Free Officers in 1952 and the free education offered by the state-run Higher Film Institute since 1959, film could at least theoretically attract cineastes from all classes.

This however did not help to spread film in rural areas. Going to the movies in Egypt has remained an urban form of entertainment. With the opening of early *cinematographs* and, later in 1906, the Pathé movie theaters in Alexandria and Cairo, the number of theaters in Egypt grew constantly. However, as the absolute number of theaters always stayed disproportionately low in comparison to the country's population, Egyptian producers were strongly motivated to export their films. In 1954, when the number of cinemas reached its peak, they did not exceed 360 (al-Naggar, 2002, 311).[25] In the course of the 1960s, due to the introduction of television and the nationalization of around one third of all cinemas in 1963, the numbers decreased continuously—147 in 1992—as did the technical standard of theaters until the mid-1990s. Their distibution has remained uneven, with more than half of them concentrated in the two major Egyptian cities, Alexandria (twenty-one) and Cairo (fifty-nine) (al-Naggar 2002, 311). As no theaters exist in villages, regular access to films there started only after the introduction of television and VCR in the 1960s and 1970s.

Moreover, movie theaters reflect the pyramidal structure of society through their division into three categories. It is unclear when the threefold division into first, second, and third-class movie theaters was established. Yet it must have been quite early, probably during the first construction wave in the late 1910s, at a time when Alexandria with its strong cosmopolitan population including communities such as Greeks and Italians, was still the center of distribution and emerging production. An indiciation for this may be that the third class still keeps its colloquial name *al-tirsu* derived from the Italian *terzo* (third).

The third-class cinema differs in program and equipment from the first and second class. It does not present any new releases, but offers a program that usually comprises one Egyptian and one or two foreign films. It is repeated for several days; the (predominantly male) audience enters the theater at any time, often knows the films by heart, interacts vigorously with the action, and even comments on or reenacts it during the projection. An accurate depiction of the vivid atmosphere of those movie theaters can be seen in Yousry Nasrallah's 1993 feature film *Mercedes* (which also, incidentally, represents the cinema as a place for gay encounters). Today, third-class theaters are run primarily in the outskirts of towns, like the industrial Cairo satellite district of Helwan, or in the provinces, while in the major inner cities almost none exist any more (al-Naggar 2002, 303).

In the late 1970s the class system of movie theaters was further entrenched by the introduction of the VCR, and this was also instrumental in reinforcing gender segregation, for middle- and upper-middle class audiences, in particular women, increasingly began to watch films at home. This development was encouraged by the bad condition of the old first and second-class movie theaters, particularly in Cairo's and Alexandria's inner cities, as a result of the 1963 nationalizations. After two decades they had deteriorated to such an extent that suburban middle-class families started avoiding them, also because they presumably attracted a male, lower-class audience.

New releases are offered only by first and second class theaters. They distinguish themselves through ticket price, choice of program, furnishing, and technical standard of equipment and projection. The largest number of first-class theaters are found in Cairo and Alexandria, representing around 50 percent of all cinemas there. Starting in the early 1990s, their earlier decline was reversed: some state-run cinemas were leased or sold to private entrepreneurs and renovated, while the increasing numbers of modern first-class theaters equipped according to the latest standards, including Dolby stereo and digital sound, were built in Cairo's affluent suburbs. Some of these are located in the new shopping malls, which have sprung up all over town. A ticket costs up to LE25 (around U.S.$4), twice as much as in second-class theaters.

Social scientist Mona Abaza has demonstrated the extent to which the shopping mall developed the potential for creating a new, less hostile urban space in which women and youth can move more easily, assert their own presence in the public space, and partake in new lifestyles. However, even these spaces have been divided into 'popular' and 'chic' locations (Abaza 2001, 108), and may support social exclusiveness. Just like the new security-guarded gated communities that are spreading on Egyptian coasts and on the fringes of the metropolis' extended suburbs, some of the more imposing shopping malls are hardly accessible to the poor urban, even less the rural population, excluded not only by lack of financial means to access and enjoy these new locations, but also because their very presence and appearance, marked by different dress and manners, would be at best suspiciously watched, if not actually kept out by security.

Still, the shopping mall seems to have facilitated the appearance of a new, more gender-inclusive (but middle-class) 'youth' culture linked to the films shown in the mall, which are also attended by young middle-class girls and women who come and visit these places on their own—to the extent that Egyptian producers have started to develop specific 'shopping-mall films' designed for this particular audience. This has coincided with an increase of pop music concerts offering yet another opportunity for a non-segregated (but privileged) form of popular entertainment. This 'pop' culture has been spreading since the advent of satellite and cable television, and is also mediated by music channels and music videos, a development that can be sensed not only through the sudden shift from an older star generation to a new one, but also through the occasional appearance of some of those pop stars on screen. It has also contributed to a booming number of Egyptian movies that includes music videos, even if no professional singer has the lead.

Class Perceptions and Recent Popular Film

Doubtless the resurgence of the musical has been backed by the long tradition of film musicals in Egypt. This tradition recycled both traditional Egyptian and Western forms of music and dance, developing a novel and genuine form of these arts. It was moreover responsible for the country's first successful film exports during the 1930s (Shafik 1998, 103). What characterizes the musical but also most other popular film genres in Egypt is its constant mixing of various generic elements and the dominance of spectacle over narration. Spectacle crystallizes not only in musical numbers that may subvert any dramatic consistency (like the fragmentation achieved through farce and action), but also in the ritualized repetitiveness of style and motifs as well as in the inscribing of star personae into the film text.

This polarization of spectacle and narration is mirrored to some degree in the polarization of audience preferences on the one hand and critical esteem on the other, similar to the controversy surrounding realism and melodrama, for the lowbrow-highbrow art dichotomy that has often guided cinematic evaluations in Egypt is not necessarily in line with box office success. On the contrary, often box-office popularity subverts all normative criteria that critics have attempted to establish. Indeed accusations of triviality are recurrent in the debate on films. That these controversies are strongly informed by class can also be seen in the case of one of the most popular but also controversial recent spectacles, the major box-office hit of 2002, *al-Limbi/al-Limbi* by Wa'il Ihsan starring new generation comedian Muhammad Sa'd, which was caught in the crossfire of public evaluation.

As a matter of fact *al-Limbi* does not fit into the typical shopping-mall film scheme, if compared to Sandra Nash'at's *Thieves in KG2/Haramiya fi KG2* (2002), *Friends or Business/Ashab walla bizniz* (2002) by 'Ali Idris, and *Sleepless Nights* by Hani Khalifa, all centered around middle class suburban youth suffering from filial and/or emotional conflicts. In contrast, *al-Limbi* presents a lower-class underdog and his attempts to succeed economically and emotionally, thus relying on one of the most central plots of Egyptian cinema since the 1930s that capitalize on the dream of social mobility.

Front: Hanan Turk (second left), Mona Zaki (third left); Back: Ahmad Hilmi (second right) and Khalid Abu al-Nagga (right) in *Sleepless Nights,* 2003

Although the press watched the immense success of this film with puzzlement and consternation, accusing it of marking an unprecedented decline of the Egyptian film into a "cinema without reason" (Sa'd 2002). It was said to make absolutely no sense, dubbed in Arabic *hals* (nonsense) (cf. Akhbar al-Yawm 2002), denounced as being of very bad quality, presenting a constantly drugged main character, signifying "decadence and intellectual and moral depravity," a *sinima al-bangu* product (*bangu* means marijuana) ('Uthman 2002). The acknowledged critic and screenplay writer Rafiq al-Sabban issued an article under the title: "Cinematic lectures in triviality and silliness" (Sabban 2002). Even the film censor was called in because the film had made fun of an Umm Kulthum melody, and the press reported that the cineastes 'cursed' the film and wanted it to be banned from exportation for sullying Egypt's image (al-Hakim 2002).

This evident contradiction between the success of the film and its negative critiques was one of the questions that guided Dalia Nimr, a graduate student of the American University in Cairo, to investigate the interest of youth in cinema. In 2003 she conducted an empirical focus group enquiry comprising forty-six respondents, all female and regular moviegoers aged between 16 and 30, belonging to urban lower- and upper-middle classes. The results showed a clear difference in responsiveness to the film's meaning that correlated to the interviewees' social status but not to their age. While they all felt very much entertained by it and could "laugh from the bottom of their hearts," some of the upper middle class respondents considered the film funny but illogical, a mere compilation of humorous scenes. Some even thought it reflected a "negative model of Egyptian society" namely "a hooligan and street guy." These concerns were not voiced by those women considered lower-middle-class, something the researcher attributed to the fact that the film's hero belonged to the same social group as the respondents, who appreciated him for his achievement in developing from an unemployed loafer into a respectable father (Nimr 2003).

Nimr's examination follows the methodology of market research. Her insights give a certain indication of the class-specific nature of perception, but do not really pay tribute to the complicated nature of spectatorship that has troubled a number of film scholars. While some think that the issue of the "determinants, the 'why' of specific subject or spectatorial articulations" has not been sufficiently explained by cultural studies, discourse theory, or psychology (Pribram 2004, 163), others have attempted to give more down-to-earth but still not entirely new answers. Drawing upon Murray Smith's 1995 findings, Julia Hallam and Margaret Marshment for example proposed to distinguish between different spectatorial alignments without excluding 'difference.' Six distinct sorts of alignments, intellectual, moral, emotional, concern, interest, and aesthetic (Hallam and Marshment 2000, 134) seem in their eyes to explain the possibility of the viewer's partial emotional detachment and simultaneous maintaining of pleasure and/or interest. Even though the nature of the correlation between viewer alignment and class in Egypt are still little explored, the varied possibilities of viewer alignment give some indications for understanding the contradictory reaction to one and the same work that need to be combined with the dynamics of general social organization.

In any case, upon closer investigation the film text as such may offer some indications of a probable explanation for its controversial status. As stated earlier, *al-Limbi* deploys a quite common plot structure, a continuous chronological storyline, and clear-cut, albeit highly stereotypical characters. Its main protagonist, al-Limbi (Muhammad Sa'd) represents a young, very naive lower-class illiterate who has difficulties finding a job, a fact that obstructs his chances to marry his beloved Nusa (Hulla Shiha), a neighbor's daughter. Faransa ('Abla Kamil), al-Limbi's mother, forces him to help her earn money. She wants to move her little bicycle workshop to a Red Sea resort. When first they arrive they manage to earn a good many dollars—until they are stopped by the Tourist Police. Back home the plot thickens, as Nusa's father decides to marry her to a schoolteacher with a stable income and Nusa herself seems unwilling to wait any longer while al-Limbi makes futile attempts to earn a living. The turning point is brought about by al-Limbi's elderly friend Bach, who tells him that because of his father's generosity with other people at their weddings he may expect an immense amount of wedding gifts. With this Bach saves the day: al-Limbi decides to join literacy classes and is eventually able to win Nusa.

Looking at topic and plot structure, one feels reminded of numerous socially committed realist-oriented Egyptian films, from Kamal Selim's *Determination* in 1939 to Daoud 'Abd El-Sayed's *The Wedding Thief/Sariq al-farah* in 1995. But how then to account for the accusation of meaninglessness that has dominated the criticism of the film? This is certainly due to the fact that *mise-en-scène* and dialogs do not bear out its realist plot. They intentionally elude any 'politically' allegorical reading, a tradition that is, as I have shown elsewhere, very common in committed and realist cinema (Shafik 1998, 164). This applies to the protagonists' names for instance, such as the mother's name Faransa, meaning 'France.' Its choice turns out to be no more than a joke, for there is no identifiable reason why the mother has been given that name. The same applies to al-Limbi, whose name is derived from the British General Allenby, the much-hated military administrator of Port Said during the 1920s. Again the *informed* viewer looks in vain for a connection.

Also the film's style and numerous linguistic and comic gags as well as cheerful music clips fragment the film plot decisively, turning it into a typical farce comedy. Using a comedian to perform musical clips places it clearly in the tradition of earlier popular comedians, such as Nagib al-Rihani in the 1940s, as well as Isma'il Yasin and Shukuku in the 1950s, who introduced intoned speech in order to present musical numbers. The *mise-en-scène*—highly professional and well-crafted regarding photography, lighting, sets, and editing—leads constantly away from the 'social' subject of the film by using farce's typical device of stylization, expressed primarily in theatrical comic acting, particularly that of the main protagonist.

All in all, the latter unfolds a naive personality, strongly attached to his mother, who dominates, mothers, patronizes, protects, and exploits him at the same time. His infantile character is underlined even more by his staggering walk and a speech defect that makes him almost unintelligible. The dialog strongly supports al-Limbi's character trait by using fragmented syntax, as can be seen in a supposedly romantic scene, in which he feels obliged to recite poetry to his beloved:

al-bos, al-bos [kiss, kiss]

al-hudn, al-hudn [hug, hug]

mishta', mishta' [miss you, miss you]

al-shu', al-shu' [longing, longing]

widd ya widd [friendship, oh friendship]

wil ya wil [woe, oh woe]

halu ya halu [hello, oh hello]

min taraf akhuki al-Limbi [from your brother al-Limbi]

The songs performed in the film, shot in a typical music video style, with dancers and a lot of pretty girls, also have bland lyrics, mixed with some Dadaist 'non-sense' and performed in a stuttering rhythm. This applies in particular to the ABC song in which al-Limbi, assisted by his cheerful mother, tries to rehearse the alphabet while making many spelling mistakes because of his defective speech. This scene gives a hilarious demonstration of the character's infantilism and recalls the great joy of pre-school children in producing and listening to verbal nonsense.

In many parts the film rejects the production of rational meaning and focuses on the nonrational, preintellectual, prelinguistic state, inviting the viewer to participate in a temporary regression. According to Sigmund Freud this kind of regression into the fantastic repetition of an 'infantile scene' *(Infantilszene)* does not serve the ends of wish-fulfillment but may, just like laughter, assume a cathartic function, in representing "the effect of resistance, that opposes the advancing of a thought to consciousness on the normal way" [author's translation] (Freud 1961, 446). Supposing this applies to the special brand of 'regression' sketched out above, it could certainly represent one of the reasons for *al-Limbi*'s success and shows that, much as the film deals with social aspiration, it may be read as an emancipation story from the all-devouring mother or father, a topic that recurs in quite a number of 'shopping-mall

Muhammad Sa'd and 'Abla Kamil in *al-Limbi*, 2002

films,' such as *China's Magnificent Beans/Ful al-Sin al-'azim* (2004) and *Zaki Chan/Zaki Shan* (2005) by Wa'il Ihsan, among others.

In his analysis of generic developments and functionality in American fiction films (which can be applied, up to a point, to commercial film production elsewhere) Rick Altman states, "For ninety minutes, Hollywood offers generic pleasure as an alternative from cultural norms," that is "authorized opportunities for counter-cultural activity" (Altman 1999, 156). Generic pleasure is thought to be rooted in the transgression of cultural values, an augmenting transgression though, as it moves from breaches of etiquette to adultery, from brawls to murder, from slight creepiness to bloody carnage. Yet the idea of psychic transgression based on Freudian theory cannot be applied without qualification to the Egyptian audience, not least because it must be assumed that class affiliation is not without implications for individual psychic organization.

As Freud's (repudiated) disciple Wilhelm Reich has concluded in his 1933 study on the foundation of the Third Reich, religiosity, nationalism, and state loyalty were first and foremost propelled and exerted by members of the petite bourgeoisie, thus forming the major pillar of the fascist regime. He regarded this class's oppression of sexuality (as one of the major forces within the human psyche) as a precondition of the role it played in this context (Reich 2003, 55, 77). It may be assumed that patriarchal nuclear family organization with its oedipal structure has been instrumental in engendering this kind of psychic structure. In Egypt too the nuclear family has spread, particularly in the more urbanized and bourgeois environment, largely replacing the extended family (Abu-Lughod 1998, 12). An additional class-related factor is also the resistance to what Timothy Mitchell described as the colonizing "new disciplinary power" exerted through the military and the educational system (Mitchell 1991, 176) which certainly has played an additional role in the amount of suppression the individual has learned to perform. All of this may well be responsible for the varied degree of 'regressive' transgression refused or required by the spectator.

And at this point we may reformulate the question of where to locate the source of class-specific response to *al-Limbi*. In its particular case, lower-middle-class respondents, if we are to believe the focus group study cited earlier, enjoyed the transgressive pleasure quite unconditionally, whereas the more privileged spectators felt much more ambivalent about enjoying the transgression. Their criticism of its meaninglessness could also be interpreted as an attempt to control the irrational subconscious and the film's invitation to join a temporary state of regression.

Capitalizing on Triviality

Some of Egypt's most inspired committed filmmakers have tried to capitalize on the schism created by the lowbrow-highbrow dichotomy in order to get through to the box office without abandoning their own ideological agenda, an attempt not always rewarded with success. One of its most illuminating examples was *Tusks/Anyab* (1981). Coscripted by its director Muhammad Shebl, this musical and horror film parody was overtly inspired by *The Rocky Horror Picture Show* (1975). In a quite ambivalent way it attempted to exploit the appearance of Ahmad 'Adawiya, a very popular singer at that time who became best known in the early 1970s for his songs "Ya Lahw Bali" and "Iss Sah Iddah Imbu" using lower-class slang and baby-talk in combination with *sha'bi* (folk) music elements. *Tusks* was held in high esteem by film critics: "The film presents 'Adawiya for the first time in a very smart way. The director uses him on two levels: he is the Prince of Darkness, black, ugly, with tusks; and he is also the 'vulgar' singer—*al-mutrib al-mubtadhal*" (Bishlawi 1980). Ironically, the film flopped at the box office, precisely because—as I would argue—it used 'Adawiya in a negative role, reinforcing his ambivalent image.

Doubtless 'Adawiya was considered by some as synonymous with trivial art *(al-fann al-habit)*. However, as anthropologist Walter Armbrust put it, it was his "appeal to the masses—without any of the rhetoric of 'raising their cultural standards' that sets him apart from singers backed by the cultural establishment in print and on television" (Armbrust 1996, 184). The film in turn exploited 'Adawiya's lowbrow reputation by conferring upon him the negative role of the vampire as opposed to his sympathetic counterpart in the film, 'Ali al-Haggar, also a singer who has in contrast a classic highbrow musical repertoire. Hence, unlike its Western model, *Tusks* voiced the basic fears and biases of the Egyptian middle-class regarding their own social status instead of working to undermine bourgeois ideology.

In brief, the plot is framed by a character, doubling as narrator, and begins with a couple whose car breaks down on a country road in the middle of the night. As they search for help they end up in a palace inhabited by Dracula and his retinue who invite the visitors to attend a dinner party. While the girl feels herself attracted by Dracula's flirting, her fiancé is troubled by their strange surroundings. Meanwhile, the narrator reveals some of Dracula's general characteristics by linking him to the outside world. The prince of darkness features in a series of successive scenes in which he represents various corrupt and greedy characters who attempt to suck money from the helpless couple. Examples include the plumber who drives a Mercedes, the taxi driver, the butcher, the trader, and the schoolteacher, all of whom hoard commodities and demand excessive compensation from their middle-class customers for their services. Eventually, as in Murnau's film classic *Nosferatu* (1922), the couple manages to vanquish Dracula by opening the windows of the palace, thus letting in the sunlight that destroys the prince and his companions.

The plot contains several musical numbers that set up an opposition between 'Adawiya's popular music and the songs of the young bridegroom (al-Haggar). Whereas the former spices his colloquial lines with urban lower-class slang wrapped in relatively rough tunes, the latter has a much more polished performance style, in lyrics and melody. The contrast also has a visual component, which manifests itself in the physique of the two singers. Slim al-Haggar, with his light complexion complemented by the blondeness of his bride, contrasts sharply with the stout, dark-skinned, frizzy-haired 'Adawiya. 'Adawiya's looks are also mirrored in the negroid features of his first assistant, with whom he competes at the end for the girl's blood. Thus, the bourgeois couple are threatened not only with having their pockets emptied, but with being swamped by supposedly 'gross' lowbrow art and the ascendant aspirations of the lower classes. This makes for an interesting contrast with the original *The Rocky Horror Picture Show*, which seeks to mock bourgeois sexual morality and ideology.

It is not clear whether this unequivocal backing of the bourgeois perspective was the reason for the limited success of *Tusks,* or its rather clumsy *mise-en-scène*, yet it certainly did not possess the same transgressive potential as *al-Limbi*, nor the polished finesse of the highly satirical musical *A Citizen, a Detective, and a Thief* (2001) by Daoud 'Abd El-Sayed, which applied a promotional strategy similar to that of *Tusks* with much more success. In parody of a social success story, this film developed a new version of 'bourgeois horror' depicting a citizen's gradual decline from a Westernized bohemian into cultural and religious conservatism, becoming an acclaimed member of the new Islamic bourgeoisie.

As in *Tusks,* the question of class is depicted as a clash between highbrow culture and kitsch, a central motif of the film, on which its director (who also wrote the screenplay) elaborates on different levels, not so much evaluating as deconstructing it, by presenting the controversial popular *sha'bi* (folk) singer Sha'ban 'Abd al-Rihim in the role of the citizen's opponent, the thief. On the narrative level the film could be read as an allegory of class development in Egypt, with its focus on the cultured, rich, and handsome bachelor in the process of writing his first novel, who is overrun by a number of lower-class characters, the detective, the maid Hayat, and her boyfriend al-Margushi with whom he ends up as business partner. It is at that point that the intellectual rewrites his book according to the thief's ideas, to be published through the latter's publishing house. On the sexual level, too, things get increasingly mixed up, with the maid marrying the writer and the thief wedding the writer's former girlfriend. And later, their grown-up children fall in love and marry each other too.

On the temporal level the film condenses more than two decades—from the mid-1970s until the present—into its plot. By alluding indirectly to the leftist anti-Zionist student movement, suppressed during the first half of the 1970s, to which the citizen supposedly belonged, it also sets a clear quasi-political historical framework even though this particular reference in relation to the main protagonist turns out to be misleading. For the majority of the students at that time, despite being largely secularly oriented, were not members of the upper bourgeoisie but belonged to the middle and lower class, with a large proportion suffering heavy deprivation for the sake of their studies (cf. 'Abd Allah 1991, 134).

Yet in other terms, the film gives a quite stringent account of the formation of what it perceives as the new bourgeoisie, with the citizen/novelist as the centerpiece of the action. He seems to represent the creative individual, the educated, modern 'citizen' firmly installed in his highbrow cultural environment, at first victimized and then overrun in the course of the events by the tide of his lower-class acquaintances or in other words the 'masses,' who in collaboration with the state (embodied by the detective), take over first his house and then his mind. This depiction seems quite telling, if not contemptuous, putting the modern, educated, male individual in the spotlight and in opposition to the illiterate, conservative religious masses. Yet the

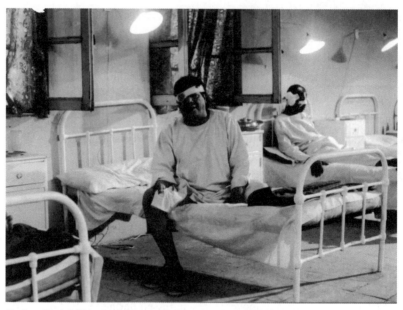

Sha'ban 'Abd al-Rihim in *A Citizen, a Detective, and a Thief,* 2001

film often distances itself on the stylistic level from its bourgeois hero, mocking his development and using at the same time the off-screen persona of the *sha'bi* (folk) singer 'Abd al-Rihim in the role of the thief to problematize the notion of lowbrow culture.

It is precisely the thief's character who first, defies 'high' culture and then redefines the taste and cultural orientation of the 'citizen' by criticizing, destroying and eventually reediting his literal output; a direct allusion to real conditions in Egypt, namely to religious censorship on literature, as practiced lately by the Islamic al-Azhar, in addition to 'social' censorship of cinema that developed gradually during the 1980s and continued throughout the 1990s. Thus, the film obviously tackles the previously mentioned new morality, or conservatism, that has seized Egyptian society since the 1980s and reversed many of those modernist developments made in the past, particularly in female dress codes as well as adaptation to 'Western' culture.

One of the film's major means to describe the radical social change is through its characters' dress, manners, language, and cultural interests. The 'citizen' is depicted as strongly westernized in dress and behavior. Not only is his villa furnished with precious antique furniture, but he also has uncomplicated extramarital relationships, loves European cuisine, wine, and Western classical music. He differs sharply from the other protagonists, such as the detective, who lives in a small cramped flat on a roof in an overcrowded lower-class neighborhood and dresses in the traditional *gallabiya,* and the maid Hayat and the thief, who live in even worse surroundings in the middle of a shantytown.

The course of the film shows how the three parties come together and end up wearing the same style of dress and living in the same kind of modern villa situated in one of the newly constructed affluent suburbs. They also come to share the same ideas and moral concepts. This is expressed by the citizen's gradual shift to cultural and religious conservatism, embodied by his growing beard toward the end of the film, indicating the birth of a new brand of conservative 'Islamic' bourgeoisie. Yet this development is shown as a fraud, for despite their respective marriages, the former thief is seen keeping up his relationship with the citizen's wife Hayat and the novelist is still courting his former girl friend, the thief's wife. This explains the two families' subsequent strong objections to their children intermarrying. Even though the film's finale does not fully explain these objections or link them in an overt way to the two couples' extramarital relationships, it implies that the parents are not quite sure about the paternity of their offspring, a state of affairs in overt contradiction to the moral standards promoted by writer and publisher.

This last narrative twist makes a strongly disparaging comment on the new bourgeoisie, as does the final scene, where everybody seems to settle into the new cheerful amalgam that is celebrated with a masquerade, a masked ball, accompanied by an 'Abd al-Rihim song:

On a nice occasion once I married a sheep off to a wolf.

Dear mouse don't jump! I'll marry you off to the cat,

You'll like the marriage and be all right,

No more roaming in the streets, no more sleeping on the sidewalks . . .

Tomorrow the mouse will carry mouse-kittens,
all mixed up, a different kind of kiddies,
so that love grows, no hatred anymore,
thanks to sympathy and promise-policies,
why not become just one
with all the difference gone?

The film does not just portray a highly ambivalent social compromise, it also sketches out, albeit ironically, the struggle between one powerful and one weaker party — without being too clear about who is mouse and who is cat — leading to an only ostensibly happy ending and the seemingly positive message that 'all difference is gone,' or in other words, that the bourgeois character has been deprived of, to cite Pierre Bourdieu's quotation of Proust, "the infinitely varied art of marking distances" (Bourdieu 1984, 66).

However, while on the narrative level the film depicts a bourgeois nightmare, of being swamped by the proletariat, it also distances itself from its privileged hero through its ironic and satirical style. On several occasions the plot is inter-cut with songs performed by the thief, which develop — particularly at the finale — a quite alienating effect, in the way they are juxtaposed to the film's outcome. The major source of dissociation is an anonymous commentator, a male non-diegetic voice-over that explains, at times quite flamboyantly, the events presented. For instance, when the detective beats up Hayat up for having stolen goods from the citizen's house after her sexual entanglement with him, she falsely claims to be pregnant in order to make him stop. At this the narrator's voice comments, "The citizen's battle was not over yet. By no means could he agree to leave any extension of himself in an environment so polluted by ignorance, poverty and corruption. How could he leave his son in Hayat's womb?" A short while later, the voice continues, "What had happened was an experience, from which the citizen learned a simple lesson: if a common language and shared values exist, the rules of the game will be known. But once you leave your familiar game and playing field, you will encounter unexpected risks."

Even more subtle irony is evoked by casting in the role of the thief the popular *sha'bi* singer Sha'ban 'Abd al-Rihim, who himself was the object of heavy public controversy for his alleged 'lowbrow' musical style. Because of the public discourse linked to his on- and off-screen persona he embodies hypocrisy and the double standard, one of the film's core motifs, not only in relation to moral values but also in relation to culture. This has also reflected on the film's evaluation. Doubtless director Daoud 'Abd El-Sayed has been respected as a committed intellectual artist who built up his name through his earlier New Realist works, a real *auteur*. This is why the film was generally perceived by the press as multi-layered, as it was intended. Yet some still mocked the director's casting of 'Abd al-Rihim. Filmmaker and former head of the National Film Center Hashim al-Nahhas wondered why the *sha'bi* singer was not used in a more ironic way, in order to distinguish the film from "the traditional manner of representing the song that Egyptian cinema has inherited since the era of Karim in his films with 'Abd al-Wahab until now" (al-Nahhas 2002).

In fact, the illiterate, coarse-looking former laundry-worker 'Abd al-Rihim had become the unexpected star of the season, despite his association with kitsch and low musical culture due in part to the social origins of his special brand of *sha'bi* music. It stems from the musical traditions of the urban lower classes and is performed at weddings, popular religious festivals, or even commercial events such as the opening of a new shop. Even if some of its performers succeed in having their songs distributed on tape, they are commonly denied access to television or satellite music channels except for specially designed 'folk' programs. When 'Abd al-Rihim made the top music charts it came as a surprise and ignited a fierce debate on cultural standards. He was criticized for his bad taste and his poor musical talent, in spite of achieving astonishing popularity among all classes with his comic-ironic lyrics. In particular, he made headlines with his provocative song, "I hate Israel," along with a television advertisement presenting the traditional local falafel as a new McDonald's specialty dish.

It is not clear how far 'Abd al-Rihim was the unwilling victim of the media, who derided him as the personification of bad taste—he usually wears very colorful patterned Hawaiian shirts which are considered unmanly or at least unsuitable for the city—and how far he actively encouraged this image through conscious self-presentation and his extraordinary sense of humor, as shown in an anecdote circulated among the film crews during the shooting of *A Citizen, a Detective, and a Thief.* Always wearing two large, expensive gold wristwatches, he was asked for the reason, only to reply that he wore one for himself and the other for anyone who wanted to ask him the time.

The anecdote conveys much of the ambiguity with which 'Abd al-Rihim offers up his persona to interpretation. The wearing of large flashy watches is associated with nouveaux riches; to carry two at once seems even more pretentious, yet the singer's own interpretation switches the meaning toward either generosity, which fits into the traditional *ibn al-balad* honor code of the lower classes, or parody, which seems even more likely in the light of the wording of some of 'Abd al-Rihim's songs (usually written by Islam Khalil, a modest teacher from rural al-Qanatir on the outskirts of Cairo).

Ironically, in some of those texts 'Abd al-Rihim reproduces the very reproaches leveled at him in public and in private for his low musical and artistic standards, and redirects them at other media stars. In his song "Fi Amsterdam" ('In Amsterdam') (tape title: *I Don't Succumb to Threats/Ma bathaddidsh*, 2000), for instance, he alludes to the film *Hamam in Amsterdam* that became the box-office hit of the season in 1999/2000. He dismissed the musical output of the main actor Muhammad Hinidi, who also performs a few musical numbers in the film, as trivial. The song begins with the words, "I'm off now to Holland, Amsterdam, leaving my team just like Ibrahim and Husam [Egyptian soccer players] . . . ." Then he adds several lines on a controversial issue which he thinks 'matters,' namely the pollution of the Nile river—before continuing his attack:

Folks, we should sing what matters!
Bilya al-Duksh registered a tape
some noise and some clapping

shouting, drums and jubilation
writing "mix-up" on its front.
Bilya al-Duksh was just a beggar,
listened to his own bathroom voice.
Now he sings, a man of art,
plans to shoot movies as a start.
Bilya al-Duksh, O gentlemen,
received the wooden disk award,
got also some certificates
from the festival in Munufiya [provincial town].
He spoke on television too
in a jacket multicolored,
said, "I made a new song
and called it 'Pestle.'"
What a pity, what a shame!
Arts have crashed like a plane,
singing spread in alleys, streets,
and at wedding feasts . . .

To blame others for a lack of art while himself using a highly limited range of melodies and rhythms clearly derived from 'wedding' music, seems to an outside observer to add to the irony of this particular song and the whole 'Abd al-Rihim phenomenon. And this is exactly the same strategy that director 'Abd El-Sayed applied, criticizing kitsch by generating it, thereby trying to deconstruct the preconditions of its emergence. Thus the filmmaker was able to exploit the singer's controversial mass-media persona in introducing him to film stardom, permitting him even more access to established mainstream culture, while at the same time denouncing that selfsame culture. In this also he departs decisively from the 1980s New Realist concept—so vividly presented in *Tusks*—of the bourgeoisie as the victim of social change, by making it complicit in the undermining of its own class.

Kings of the *Terzo*

As the case of Sha'ban 'Abd al-Rihim shows, not only individual films but also star personae became carefully constructed around their avowedly low-brow and lower-class status. This applies in particular to male actors who were able to excel in the action film, a genre that rarely found support among critics due to its alleged 'inauthenticity' and imitativeness on the one hand and its popularity among lower-class men on the other. The comedian 'Adil Imam, for twenty years the most popular and successful representative of the *terzo (tirsu)*, used to combine his action roles with comedy and/or social satire. While his display of physical force was loaded with ambivalence, his significance lay in the way he reenacted through generic means a certain type of class-defined masculinity, closely linked to the less privileged urban strata.

In fact, lower-class audiences seem to have played an increasing role for Egyptian film distributors since the end of the Second World War, particularly workers and craftsmen employed by the British forces, who earned enough to make going to the movies their main entertainment (Saif 1996, 110), which coincided with a boom in local film production. At the same time, directors are said to have been displaying considerable consciousness of 'third class' spectators, as al-Sharqawi stated in describing the tumultuous ending of Kamal Selim's film *Les Misérables/al-Bu'asa'* (1943) that just like his earlier *Determination* (1939), presented a happy ending brought about by a brawl (al-Sharqawi 1970, 84).

I was told in February 2006 by the manager of al-Hamra, one of the largest and oldest downtown Cairo video film stores, that since the 1980s it has been particularly a male lower-class audience that tends to buy and rent Egyptian action- (and sex-) oriented movies, such as films starring Farid Shawqi and Rushdi Abaza, stars of the late 1950s to 1970s. The latter appeared at times also as a gigolo, and featured in a number of films dominated by suspense and brawls, as well as sexual liaisons, such as *The Woman on the Road/Mar'a fi-l-tariq* (1958), a remake of the American *Duel in the Sun* (1946), and *The Road/al-Tariq* (1964).

The first signs of adventure and action (in other words the depiction of the male figure in a landscape, to use Laura Mulvey's feminist interpretation) in Egyptian film were introduced along with the Bedouin film, later dubbed the Oriental Western (al-Sharqawi as quoted in Saif 1996, 112). Yet, unlike the U.S. Western this genre had little to offer in terms of conquest and border fights but was interpreted melodramatically with films like Ibrahim Lama's *A Kiss in the Desert* (1928) and *Lady of the Desert* (1929) by Wedad Orfi, revolving around romance, crime, or deadly male competition. As a result, such works quite often presented women in main roles, constructing a number of stories around pretty Bedouin girls, such as *The Beautiful Bedouin/al-Badawiya al-hasna'* (1947) by Ibrahim Lama, and a series starring actress Koka and largely directed by her husband Niazi Mustafa. The production of this type of film ceased in the early 1950s; at the same time less folkloric genres such as the police film and the thriller appeared, along with a kind of local gangster sub-genre, the *futuwwa* or 'thug film.'

With this, Egyptian action films focused largely on a dual narrative concept that includes women also. Its strategy implies what has been common in a lot of Hollywood blockbusters, to take only *Titanic* (1997) as an example, namely "combining a story vehicle for male heroism and spectacular action with a heterosexual romance of cross-class conflict" (Hallam and Marshment 2000, 66), a combination that has recurred in Egyptian cinema quite similarly to this day in films such as *Tito* (2004). This I would describe as the double strategy of film industry: to keep its products family-friendly but also to bow to the audiences of the *tirsu*, that is, the urban and provincial lower class.

There is no doubt that the Egyptian action film flirted openly with an association with the lower classes, as can be seen among others in the thug cycle. Farid Shawqi, one of the earliest stars associated with this genre during the 1950s, was consciously displaying 'lower-class virility' along with an action-oriented persona. For this reason he dubbed himself 'King of the Terzo' *(malik al-tirsu)* in his 1978 autobiography issued by Iris Nazmi, in reference to his assumed popularity with audiences of third-class movie theaters, the urban lower class including workers and craftsmen (before he switched in the late 1970s to the elderly husband or paterfamilias.)

Shawqi modeled himself into the personification of lower-class virility for the first time through one of his early films, indeed his first self-production, *Master Hassan* by Salah Abu Seif (1952). In this film he featured as a worker from the lower-class neighborhood of Bulaq who gets ensnared by a beautiful *bourgeoise* from the affluent suburb of Zamalek, whose handicapped husband helplessly witnesses his wife's excesses. Shawqi had assumed the same persona, that of the strong, virile working man, in *Cairo Main Station* (1958) by Youssef Chahine who makes Hannuma, the beautiful soft drink seller fall for him instead of the handicapped Qinawi. By contrast, in Niazi Mustafa's *Hamidu* (1953) and *Sultan/Sultan* (1958) he represented lower-class criminals, the son of a fishing community in the first, and a servant in the second.

Farid Shawqi and Hind Rustum in *Cairo Main Station*, 1958

At the time Shawqi tried to compensate for his unsavory screen persona by presenting a liberal middle-class appearance off-screen and in the media (Armbrust 2000, 217). On-screen, his recurrent personifications of villains did not always have a clearcut or consistent class affiliation but displayed a cross-class criminality or viciousness. Shawqi more or less maintained his self-assumed kingdom of the *terzo* during the 1960s and 1970s. Even then he was not uncontested, for the slightly younger and more attractive Rushdi Abaza also featured in 'tough guy' roles; but his position was completely taken over by 'Adil Imam during the 1980s and 1990s. Simultaneously, the deterioration of former first-class theaters in downtown Cairo had gone so far that in the eyes of middle-class audiences they had become almost equivalent to the *terzo* in serving a chiefly male working-class clientele.

During the 1970s some new directors, most notably Samir Saif, were captivated by the action film genre and specialized in it. Saif's first film, *The Circle of Revenge/Da'irat al-intiqam* (1976), is a bleak story of a man who has been jailed for a crime he did not commit, and does not rest until he has hunted down those responsible for it. Just as in subsequent films by Saif, the tension arises primarily from the hero's quest. As spectacle, the action is modest, confined to a few gunshots, a chase through the aisle of a train and the successful escape of the hero on a vintage motorcycle. Then in 1981 Saif directed *The Suspect/al-Mashbuh* (1981) starring 'Adil Imam. That marked the beginning of a fruitful cooperation, and helped Imam to transform his persona from a subversive figure into a less ambiguous, potent hero, starring primarily in action films, often directed by Nadir Galal, which like no other films were completely immersed in a lower-class environment.

In *The Suspect*, a remake of the U.S. film *Once a Thief* (1965) by Ralph Nelson, Imam featured as a young thief who after marrying renounces his earlier shameful career. However, although he has finished his jail sentence, he is still persecuted by the police officer whose weapon he stole. But when the thief's son gets kidnapped by his father's former gang, the officer joins forces with him. In this narrative Imam is depicted as a victim of circumstances, initiated and later forced into a life of crime by an older brother. However, his redeeming feature is his *ibn al-balad* behavior, for he is shown as a faithful husband and devoted father, unashamedly lower-class in his inexpensive clothes and modest, poorly-furnished home (in contrast to his main adversary the bourgeois police officer), all of which he accepts for the sake of the promise he made to his wife.

Superstar 'Adil Imam's fame began originally on stage, in *School of the Rascals/Madrasat al-mushaghibin* (1972), where he played a troublesome student who mocks the modernist ideal of education; a later role showed him as a funny, yet still sarcastic lower-class desperado. His early films and persona reflected first and foremost a strong skepticism toward the notion of social mobility. The first 'Adil Imam film that could be classified as social comedy, *The Wallet is with Me/al-Mahfaza ma'aya* (1978), was followed by *Ragab on a Hot Tin/Ragab fawq safih sakhin* (1979), both by Muhammad 'Abd al-'Aziz, which became major box-office hits and installed Imam as the king of Egyptian comedy for more than twenty years.

Thus 'Adil Imam—and this may be one reason for his success—subverted the image of the bad *arriviste* of the 'who-is-to-blame' films of the 1960s and 1970s and remade it in the character of the sympathetic corruptible hero who falls prey to the system. In *The Wallet is with Me* (1978) he performed as 'Atwa, a drop-out who ends up as a pickpocket. In an attempt to start a new life he searches for a former classmate and friend Shukri, who has become head of a state-owned company, and asks him for work, to no avail. But fate intervenes when he accidentally picks up Shukri's wallet, whose contents prove his involvement in a high-ranking corruption scandal. Instead of reporting him to the police, 'Atwa decides to blackmail Shukri, who duly nominates him for a post in the company—only to turn him over to the police for his pickpocketing offences, as soon as he gets his papers back.

In an attempt to show the whole range of society's immoral survival strategies, from petty theft to high-level fraud, Imam frequently dismissed the whole system as corrupt and inefficient, as in *The Advocate/al-Afukatu*

(1984) by Ra'fat al-Mihi, and *Ramadan on the Volcano/Ramadan fawq al-burkan* (1985) by Ahmad al-Sab'awi, where he appeared as a duped fraudster, the engaging middle or lower-class crook who gets outwitted by even more powerful and professional gangsters. In *So that the Smoke Does Not Evaporate/Hatta la yatir al-dukhkhan* (1984) by Ahmad Yahia, a somewhat melodramatic film, Imam played a likeable opportunist who started as a poor student, without even the money to save his ailing mother from death, and has become a very prosperous businessman. Having sold his conscience, he eventually succumbs to a deadly disease, the result of his earlier lifestyle and involvement with drugs.

In the process of changing his original anti-heroic persona into a smart, tough lower-class guy, Imam gradually made the transition to action and gangster films: *The Suspect, The Festival/al-Mulid* (1989) by Samir Saif, *The Forgotten/al-Mansi* (1993) by Sharif 'Arafa, and the historical spectacle *Message to the Ruler/Risala ila al-wali* (1998) by Nadir Galal among the earliest. In *The Leopard and the Woman/al-Nimr wa-l-untha* (1987) he finally emerged as an unambiguous 'good' hero, in the role of an undercover

'Adil Imam in *The Leopard and the Woman*, 1987

policeman, and as a fictive national hero in *Shams al-Zanati* (1991) both directed by Samir Saif—a development much deplored by some critics. For now his persona began to direct blame at an external cause, the 'ruler,' in other words at one powerful figure, a return to the struggle-oriented plots of the 1950s and 1960s.

In Sharif 'Arafa's *The Forgotten* (1993), Imam represented a lonely railway signalman whose solitary sexual fantasies (a pin-up girl from his wall starts dancing) are suddenly interrupted by the beautiful Yusra, in flight from a rich businessman for whom she works as a secretary. Invited by her employer to a luxurious party in the countryside, she was about to be forced to prostitute herself to her boss's clients. Imam, a chivalrous and hospitable *ibn al-balad,* takes up her cause and defends the honor of this nighttime beauty against the muscular henchmen of the evil capitalist.

Despite his change of persona, Imam was able to maintain his leading position at the box office, while still criticized for his lower-class approach. In press reviews 'Adil Imam's esteem at first remained high because of his huge success with audiences, making him the best-paid actor and therefore also the most powerful star in Egypt since the early 1980s. Reservations regarding his triviality were made only occasionally or through indirect allusions, as in a critique by Hisham Lashin in 1981. After deploring "the schism between intellectuals and Imam" he defended the actor for presenting those things that have sunk to the bottom of society (Lashin 1981). Ra'uf Taufiq in turn complained that people saw in Imam only the man who earned thousands, and made him the scapegoat for all the negative aspects of Egyptian cinema and the "degeneration in general taste" (Taufiq 1984, 52).

Samir Farid was one of the few who dared to be ironical, comparing Imam's physical features with those of ET, and adding, "he will lose a lot of his audience when he appears with a full face, his hair cut for tens of pounds, wearing a Pierre Cardin pajama while he inhabits a hut on the roof top" (Farid 1983). The controversial debate regarding Imam's persona shines through his own counter-statements. In 1985 he defended *Khamsa Bab* as "a film with an aim and not trivial" (Fahmi 1984), though the work created such an uproar because of its alleged low standard that even the censorship was called in to ban it retrospectively. Ra'uf Taufiq described the star's position more bluntly when he quoted the actor as saying that he does not "read the criticisms of his films nor does he take interest in what has been written on him, because his real audience does not know how to read and write" (Taufiq 1984, 52). Hence, one of the insights offered by the previously analyzed film examples, and in particular Imam's star persona, is that the public discourse voicing accusations of triviality and nonsense implies a conservative and binarist view of art that distinguishes between sense and nonsense, social commitment and triviality, disregarding the potentials of film messages and doing away with psychological transgressiveness enjoyed by audiences.

Violence as Transgression?

Some of the main transgressions offered by the action film (the genre in which 'Adil Imam often starred) are its inclination to rapid movement, male muscularity, and physical violence, if not cruelty and carnage. On the international level, mounting screen violence and its increasingly graphic quality (cf. Hallam and Marshment 2000) has often been discussed and put in relation to real social problems. Censorship laws have been called in to protect the young, for fear that popular characters might function as role models and violence would be internalized. In Egypt, too, official regulations have banned the use of extreme cruelty and violence in film. As for the films themselves, in Egypt as elsewhere a mounting resort to violence, shootings, and brawls can be observed since the mid-century. In addition, particularly in the 1980s, New Realist films as well as a number of 'fat cat' narratives also followed the tendency to resolve conflicts through violence and bloody encounters, suggesting at first sight an increasing social antagonization in Egyptian society. The inclination to read those films as social and political allegories was also reflected in the fact that critics of the time drew a direct connection between some films and political events as Kamal Ramzi did in his 1987 study, for example linking *The Innocent* (1986) to the insurgence of the Central Security Forces a few months later.

True, some scholars propose that "the action scenario is not simply a narrative of empowerment, in which we identify with a heroic figure who triumphs over all obstacles, but is also a dramatization of the social limits of power" (Tasker 1993, 117). Thus, the number of violent showdowns in films critical of the *infitah* could be easily interpreted as resistance to that very policy and seemed to suggest signs of unrest or 'inflammation of the Egyptian street' *(ihtiqan)* to use the recurrent Arabic expression voiced also by Muhammad Hasanain Haikal (for example in an interview on Al-Jazeera on September 7, 2005 on the eve of Egypt's presidential elections) in the face of the country's difficult sociopolitical situation.

Doubtless any present-day 'inflammation' is but a new installment of a chain of events stretching back to Sadat's takeover in 1970 and the post-1967 turbulence, first given voice in consecutive student protests between 1968 and 1973, and in the subsequent mobilization of the Islamist student movement, the bread riots in 1979, the assassination of president Anwar al-Sadat in 1981, and numerous Islamist assaults on civilians including Copts and tourists, ending with the Luxor massacre in 1997. An additional factor that would speak for the migration of street violence to the screen is the general authoritarian character of Egyptian society and its political system.

However, this interpretation does not really seem plausible for several reasons, one of which is that much more democratic countries have produced an abundance of tremendously violent, and likewise 'realistic' films, which display much more ferocious, cruel, homophobic, and misogynist attitudes than Egyptian cinema ever did, to name only some classical American horror movies such as *Mother's Day* (1980) and *The Texas Chainsaw Massacre* (1974), or innumerable recent American war films that include horrifically graphic depictions of killings and mutilations. Moreover, the Egyptian 'street' was already 'inflamed' before the 1970s, starting with the revolution in 1919, the assassinations of Prime Minister Ahmad Mahir in 1945, and Nuqrashi Pasha in 1948, the proclamation of martial law in 1948, the Lavon Affair in 1954, and the wide-ranging crackdown during Nasser's reign on all forms of political opposition, to mention only a few events.

In the face of this continuing 'crisis,' I doubt that a direct relation between social unrest and violent action in cinema can be established (disregarding the occasional obvious referentiality to specific historical events and developments). Therefore we probably need to look for more global explanations related to the international mediascape instead, which may feed back into a local context. French philosophy in particular has offered explanations for violence in the media: Paul Virilio places the whole cinematic invention, its preoccupation with mobility, image 'shooting,' with its voyeuristic objectivation, submission (and destruction) of the world, into the context of modern high-technology warfare, that in turn resulted in a shattered human perception (Virilio 1989, 46). Similarly, Jean Baudrillard has described the media as a simulacrum, in which the constant ongoing stream of factual news imagery and fictional images melt into a complete undistinguishable "simulation" (Baudrillard 1983, 138–52). One of the setbacks of this view is that it presupposes a passive spectator who is unable to distinguish between fact and simulation, subject and object. Undoubtedly the concern with speed and motion is an important aspect of cinematic pleasure, if not its essence, since the time when the Lumière brothers' train first approached its audiences. For to speak in Richard Dyer's words, "The celebration of sensational movement that we respond to in some still unclear sense 'as if real', for many people is the movies" (Dyer 2002, 65).

On the other hand there are some even more spectator-oriented factors to consider. Apart from that sensational experience of movement there is the "reproduction of a masculine structure of feeling," which "is represented as experienced not within the body but in the body's contact with the world, its rush, its expansiveness, its physical stress and challenge" (Dyer 2002, 66) that is paired with a "delicious paradox." For action adventure movies "promote an active engagement with the world, going out into it, doing to the environment; yet the enjoyment of them means allowing them to come to you, take you over, do you," an experience of passivity that Dyer equates with sexual fellatio (Dyer 2002, 69).

Thus, the understanding of action points less in the direction of politics, more in that of the psychology of sexual difference in relation to the 'modern' urban technological environment. Moreover, the kind of sexualized orgiastic description made by Dyer underlines the cathartic nature of violent physical entanglements in action films and clarifies a certain common denominator between action film and melodrama that is summarized in their tendency to "sacrifice the chain of character-centered causality, foregrounding artistic motivation' to spectacular action scenes, simulated visions and the like, or in other words to subordinate narrative consistency to a 'disruptive force that creates gaps in the narrative" (Hallam and Marshment 2000, 70) that is related to the specific kinds of 'transgressions' the genre offers.

Authenticity, Underdevelopment, and Male Global Heroism

One of the longest-standing problems of Egyptian action has been precisely its difficulty in producing 'sensational movement.' Thus the genre used to center primarily on a modest display of physical force, crimes, or investigations. The editing, at first relatively slow, was successively accelerated until the late 1970s. With its most distinguished action performers during the 1950s and 1960s either tough or coarse but rarely handsome-looking, like Farid Shawqi, Mahmud al-Miligi, Rushdi Abaza, and in the 1970s and 1980s 'Adil Adham, Hasan Hamid, Mahmud Farag, and Salah Nazmi among others (Saif 1996, 64), the genre went through three different phases up to 1975: first, highly folkloric films, that is, the Bedouin film, the thug film, as well as Arab legends and adventures; a second wave started in 1952 with modern adventures—thrillers inspired by the film noir and the detective film, and feeding eventually into a third phase from 1963 to 1975 that was characterized by a strong deterioration in quality but not in quantity. Then, following 1975, with the advent of a new generation (among them Saif himself) a sort of revival could be witnessed along with a stronger mainstreaming of action film elements. In improving their *mise-en-scène*, using chases, changing scenes, varied fighting, and quick editing, directors like Saif tried to cope with and make up for technical deficiencies and low budgets. Nonetheless deficiency remained inscribed into the genre in the metaphorical as well as economic sense.

Egyptian action film was always considered a foster child of American film with a varied degree of 'Egyptianization.' Inauthenticity was one of the most recurrent reproaches made against the genre since *A Kiss in the Desert,* as Saif remarks, "the film critique did not pay sufficient attention to it, but their prevalent view is almost exclusively representing them as commercial films that do not carry artistic values worth of studying. In addition Egyptian action films were accused being a pale imitation of different American action film models, what makes them lack both elements, Egyptianity and authenticity" (Saif 1996, 30). However, Egyptianization, as Saif wants us to believe, was a precondition for the success of the genre among Egyptian audiences (cf. Saif 1996, 31, 118, 270). Indeed apart from the folkloric desert films, American film noir elements were the first to surface in Egyptian adaptations or 'inspirations,' such as Kamal El-Cheikh's thrillers. Yet the most compelling films were believed to be those able to convincingly buy into an Egyptian setting, such as *Hamidu* (1953) and *Sultan* (1958) by Niazi Mustafa, or *Struggle on the Nile/Sira' fi-l-Nil* (1959) by 'Atif Salim.

Interestingly this applies in particular to the 'thug film.' Their numbers have always been very limited, but represented nonetheless a recurrent phenomenon until the 1990s, with *The Husayniya Thugs/Futuwwat al-Husayniya* (1954) by Niazi Mustafa as one of its earliest examples (Salah Abu Seif's *The Thug* is one of the most acknowledged, yet less typical films). The thug cycle soon developed a recurrent schematic formula involving an urban lower class character who, thanks to his physical capabilities—including traditional stick fighting—is able to positively or negatively monopolize power in a traditional alley. This film type experienced a peak in production during the 1980s with *The Mountain Thug/Futuwwat al-gabal* (1982) by Nadir Galal, several films by Samir Saif, among them *Streets on Fire/Shawari' min nar* (1984) and *The Chased/al-Mutarrad* (1985), as well as *The Salakhana Thugs/Futuwwat al-Salakhana* (1989) by Nasir Husain.

The term *futuwwa* emanated originally during the Middle Ages signifying members of Islamic brotherhoods governed by chivalrous precepts. It acquired only later, in the colloquial Egyptian context, the connotation of thug, bully, or racketeer. On the screen it carries the latter meaning, but seems to have fused in its positive coding with the *ibn al-balad* character and the latter's high moral standing. The attractiveness of this sub-genre for the film industry was not only its connection to indigenous lower-class values but also its low-budget level of action due to the largely quasi-historical setting. The 'moral' standing of 'traditional culture' was made to compensate for the absence of technological sophistication.

In his study on the development of action film in Egypt, director Samir Saif argued that unlike melodrama, where the cross-class battle is metaphorically inscribed in class representatives themselves and less in their surroundings, this particular genre depends much more on the social environment as such, that being a decisive factor in engendering its heroes' cinematic conflict (that is, one man against the world) (Saif 1996, 74). This is also why the actual body of the (mostly male) hero and its problematic relation to the outside world is pivotal to this genre. This has implications for negotiations that take place regarding gender roles, class position, technological progress, and efficiency vis-à-vis the West.

The U.S. Western for instance, which is considered the forerunner of today's action film, is as old as the film industry, if we just think of Harry Porter's *The Great Train Robbery* (1908). In contrast, the more topical Hollywood action film was released from its marginality and funded with high budgets, but attained wider popularity only during the 1980s. Dismissed at times as "dumb movies for dumb people," the most contemporary U.S. examples have favored the visual display of violent action and the muscular (phallic) body over narrative and dialog (Tasker 1993, 5).

In her book *Hard Bodies* (1994), Susan Jeffords worked out convincingly the confluence of cinematic representations of the masculine 'hard body' and the official ideologies of the Reagan administration, that eclipsed the earlier post-Vietnam war period characterized by anxiety and indecision (coded as 'femininity') by imposing a new agenda of national restoration, individualism, and technological advancement ultimately expressed in the *Rambo* series (1982, 1985, 1988). Her "reading tellingly reveals shared presuppositions about just what a male (and the state) is and should be: i.e., sharply delineated, assertive, tough, and, when necessary, violent—in short, a 'hard body'" (Pazderic 1995).

However, the machismo of a "failed masculinity" as Yvonne Tasker chose to define Sylvester Stallone's 'Rambo' and other similar muscular Hollywood heroes (Tasker 1993, 121) that are characterized by expansiveness, physical stress, and an almost masochistic infliction of pain, are remote from Egyptian action films. In fact, unlike in the United States, as was the case with Arnold Schwarzenegger, for example, Egyptian body builders with mediocre acting talent like Shahhat Mabruk, who starred in several action films in the 1990s, could never leave his B-actor status, challenge less muscular popular actors like 'Adil Imam, and become a superstar himself. Thus in reversing Jeffords' argument, I would claim that the genre reflected the nation's general lack of national technological advancement in combination with the political appeasement of the post-Camp David Accords era, not just in a metaphorical sense; for the incapability of producing a perfect 'body machine' runs parallel to the fact that on the structural level the action film posed a profound economic problem for the relatively poor Egyptian film industry.

To be precise, low budgets and lack of know-how in special effects (including make up) kept the Egyptian action film technologically at a quite 'underdeveloped' stage. In particular, car chases tended to be either absent or short and deficient. The same applied to crashes, which usually involved little or no damage with a lot of inexpensive debris flying around in the collision. The difficulty of providing high-cost technology (also true for genres like the horror film, science fiction, and even the historical spectacle), reflected in an almost allegorical sense on the heroes of the genre, and in particular on superstar 'Adil Imam.

The latter's conscious construction of his own 'lower-class' cinematic persona did negotiate masculinity in relation to progress and technology, or to put it differently, through his lower-class defined masculinity, heavily based on the *ibn al-balad* honor code, Imam was able to offer a certain compensation for the lack of technological excitement. This implied also his probably unintentional representation of a deficient 'body machine,' at least throughout the 1980s and until the mid-1990s, expressed in the fact that he is neither handsome nor muscular, but had always insisted on getting involved in cinematic brawls which he usually won. The evident discrepancy between his unimpressive physique and the impressive force of his adversaries make these scenes hover on the fringe of comedy, despite the fact that they were usually not presented in an ironic or alienating way. In his late films, such as *The Forgotten* or *Message to the Ruler* the audience had to suspend its disbelief even more, graciously overlooking the obvious signs of age and weight problems and accepting the notion that the hero was young, strong, and muscular. As it was always Imam who backed the evidently much stronger attackers, you were simply not supposed to ask how this could happen. In fact, it was exactly this discrepancy

'Adil Imam and Yusra in
Message to the Ruler, 1998

between what was visible (that is, the de facto inefficient body machine) and what we were asked to believe that gave the genre its unconvincing image at that time.

Imam's insistence on combining comedy with action has certainly been due to his belief in the popularity of both genres, and did add to the above described 'deficiency,' like *The Leopard and the Woman* and the Seven Samurai-remake *Shams al-Zanati*. While the first compensated for the relative lack of technical facilities with a tight plot and constantly changing locations reflecting the breathless hunt of a police officer (Imam) for the leader of a drug gang, the second demonstrated the difficulty in accommodating the genre on a number of other levels. Although the story seemed highly spectacular, being set in the Second World War and featuring al-Zanati's fierce patriotic battle against a gang who took over a desert oasis, numerous comic elements and effects disqualify the 'seriousness' of the action. The choice of second-rate comedians for al-Zanati's men, their funny character traits, some comic situations, the inadequate historical set design—as well as inaccurate costumes—all indicate a profound deficiency and undermine the effect of the physical violence in the action scenes.

Doubtless a large number of Imam's films reflected the factual inability to accommodate the action movie properly. The futile attempt to display technical and male-defined potency, the mediocre special effects and ineffective 'musculinity' (that is, muscular masculinity; Tasker 1993, 132) tipped them into the realm of disguising, a masquerade. If muscular actors such as Sylvester Stallone and Arnold Schwarzenegger are seen to slip into a "parodic performance of masculinity" (Tasker 1993, 111) through overstatement, I read Imam's persona as a parodic insistence on an 'imagined' masculinity; a pointed inability to acquire successfully technology and physical efficiency.

To be more precise, he embodies, consciously or not, a deficiency that exposes his mimicry as fantasy recalling Frantz Fanon's analysis of the physical fantasies of the colonized subject: ". . . the dreams of the native are always of muscular prowess; his dreams are of action and aggression. I dream I am jumping, swimming, running, climbing" (Fanon 1985, 40). Imam's peculiar fantasies could of course be not only those of a formerly colonized individual, as was suggested in his highly allegorical *Message to the Ruler* (which starts with the British invasion of Egypt) but also the dreams of the lower-class underdog, whom he has so often chosen to embody, vis-à-vis the country's elite. Interestingly, those fantasies have lately been extended by Imam's successors to include the international arena.

It was primarily the stars of the new generation, first and foremost Ahmad al-Saqqa and comedian Muhammad Hinidi who represented young emigrants abroad, in films such as *Hamam in Amsterdam, Africano, Mafia, China's Magnificent Beans*, and *The War of Italy*. Not all went out to conquer Europe: Africa, Asia, and the Americas were also placed on the cinematic travel routes. Apart from their reliance on the 'glocal' nexus, this new wave of action films worked hard to resolve the decade-long film industry problem with action-film technology through importing the necessary know-how, or to be more precise, by shooting the difficult scenes abroad. The car chases and explosions in *Hamam in Amsterdam* and *Mafia* are a good example, as the films were shot in the Netherlands and South Africa respectively (with the cinematic pretense that the action takes place in Egypt in the case of *Mafia*). In addition, the director of these two films was one of the first in Egypt to resort to foreign expertise with respect to computer technology, using animation to improve his action scenes. The increase in 'efficiency' has also been reflected in the performer, culminating in the improved 'body machine' of Ahmad al-Saqqa, for instance. However, the efficient male body has not completely replaced the parodic representation of masculinity or male masquerade as embodied earlier in Imam. It found in fact a continuation in Hinidi's comic persona, as can be seen in one of his recent action films.

In his role as the cowardly offspring of a gangster and *futuwwa* family in *China's Magnificent Beans* (2004) by Sharif 'Arafa, the Hinidi character was unwillingly made to master Chinese martial arts, winning on the way the heart of an Asian beauty. The parodic nature of this film was enhanced by the plot and its main protagonist, who objects to becoming a gangster like the rest of his family members, being simply too scared to join in brawls or use

weapons. Nonetheless he is haunted all through the plot by criminal activities, even during his unintentional trip to China (predominantly shot in
Thailand), where he accidentally takes part in a cooking contest. There he not
only wins first prize with the national dish of Egypt (brown beans or *ful,* the
main element in the daily diet of the poor), but meets a beautiful young Chinese translator, whose father introduces him to martial arts. The importance
that the film crew has attached to the acquisition of this particular action-film
technology becomes evident in the epilogue, in which the credits are intercut
with shots from the making of the film, showing Hinidi being pulled high up
in the air on ropes for the Asian fighting scenes while helplessly crying out
the director's name, an image that may be also read as a humorous metaphor
of the male urban Egyptian underdog, unwillingly catapulted into the global
arena and attempting to cope with its multiple challenges.

Concluding Remarks

What *China's Magnificent Beans* and other 'globalizing' films, notably *An
Upper Egyptian at the American University*, *Hamam in Amsterdam*, and
Hello America have suggested is the symbolical juxtaposition of male lower-
middle-class representatives with Arab–Egyptian Muslim national identity,

Muhammad Hinidi in *China's Magnificent Beans*, 2004. Coming to terms with marital arts.

which sets up the *ibn al-balad* as the real ambassador, quintessence, or common denominator of the Egyptian nation. Moreover, it seems that, for Cairo's lower-middle-class men, the opportunity to ascend and imagine a positive future abroad brings about the necessity to symbolically reenact the encounter with the nation's own either marginalized or excluded Others: Nubians and Copts on the internal level, and Jews on the external level, or in other words, to reframe them within the 'glocal' nexus according to the common national narrative.

This kind of symbolic common social denominator has not remained unchallenged but has always been subject to various negotiations on the structural as well as on the textual level. True, the Egyptian film industry was subject to economic changes that moved it more into the ownership and dominance of its 'native' bourgeoisie; yet it always reflected different ideological class-related negotiations and strategies of distinction, for example, between lowbrow and highbrow culture, between new and old bourgeoisie, and between the needs of the *terzo* and the cultural and religious aspirations of the petite bourgeoisie. It has moreover given way to the formation of numerous on-screen battles and alliances, or to use 'Abd El-Sayed's metaphor in his film *A Citizen, a Detective, and a Thief*, it has allowed "mouse and cat to marry" as much as it gave an opportunity to confound the position of mouse and cat through cinematic myths. The dynamic inherent into this metaphor, signaling both struggle and reconciliation, has not just informed the structure of film plots but lies also at the heart of film's generic development, caught between melodramatic emotionality, cathartic resistance, and dreams of sexual and global empowerment.

This is how genres could become means of social and ideological distinction, as the evaluative struggle within national and international film critique attempted to break the hegemony of prerevolutionary melodrama and install postrevolutionary realism as the core of an authentic and more progressive film culture. Yet the alternating class perspectives and concerns have always expressed themselves through different generic frameworks. Just as the action film has negotiated concepts of lower-class masculinity and national identity since the 1970s, early melodrama did negotiate questions of modernity, gender roles, and the bourgeois family ideal including love-marriage. The idea of romantic love, for instance, as developed against the backdrop of allegorical cross-class rape and seduction narratives, helped to express and ventilate class injustice and hegemonial social reconciliation. With all this in mind, the theory that Egyptian cinema with its post-independence realism has simply abandoned its early upper-class perspective in favor of a predominantly middle-class perspective has clearly proven to be too reductionist, because it underestimates the 'dialogic' or multivocal quality of popular art and culture.

Hence, one important result is to comprehend the porosity of generic borders in popular cinema. They have allowed not only social ascent aspirations but also accusations of female opression in patriarchal society to be translated into the 'woman as victim' discourse, to traverse from popular pre-1952 melodrama into post-independence realism, and to commute back into the misery feminist works of the 1960s up to the 1980s. Even though these seemed to present modernist ideas and to promote women's education and public labor, they reflected moral reservations and ambiguities regarding women. Within this context the modernist view wanted to put young women in the service of the nation, although the modernist ideal of the mother as educator of nation was often cast negatively by equating mothers with ignorance and superstition—the nation's Dark Continent.

More empowering notions of femininity appeared toward the 1990s with female avenger and female bonding stories. Motherhood and friendship as venues for female bonding asserted a polysemic femininity that implied passivity and activity at the same time. They appeared not only in the 'realist' and committed films of male directors, but also in the mainstream commercial oeuvre of woman director Inas al-Dighidi. Simultaneously, the resurgence during the 1990s of the 'traditional' implicit theory of the sexually powerful woman through the star persona of Nadia al-Gindi for example (so challenging to misery feminism) has been accompanied by other negotiations as well. Conservative morality and modernist ideals including sexual virtue, love, marriage, and woman's employment were placed under pragmatic reconsideration in view of the ongoing social injustice.

Doubtless the major cinematic gender-related negotiations in popular Egyptian film have been dominated by the discourses of class, morality, and femininity crystallizing in some major omnipresent dichotomies, that is, virgin–whore, male activity–female passivity, rich–poor. Simultaneously, in quasi-feminist as well as in mainstream films, questions of morality—but more importantly, of power—were constantly at stake. Central to both was how to reconcile femininity with the idea of activity. Is woman a victim or a source of vice? Moreover, women's cinematic isolation on the level of editing and point-of-view shots, her subjection to the 'male gaze' seems to have paid tribute to the Christian-bourgeois idea of a passive female sexuality, but has been simultaneously qualified by the concept of a female seductive power. The Egyptian femme fatale is thus, like the female avenger, a product of the virgin–whore dichotomy, but by 'overstating' the seductive (yet not phallic) feminine, she has displayed an affinity to Arab-Muslim ideas of female sexual omnipotence.

Mostly bound to the virgin–whore dichotomy, women in film have tended to be represented as ethically and sexually vulnerable. As a consequence, they have been at the heart of any moral question voiced in and around cinematic texts. Moreover, along with sexual morals, women epitomize the ideological controversy between secular modernism and Islamism, a controversy that became particularly strong during the first half of the 1990s when several actresses started to veil themselves and renounce show business for religious reasons. As prevalent concepts of morality have played a crucial role in public evaluation, it has become clear that any mythical effect engendered by Egyptian stars is strongly dependent on their gender affiliation and which side of the moral dichotomy they embody on both the fictional and biographic levels. The morally controversial image of any female star has hampered her access to the moral community of at least some social groups, like the poor rural population.

Even though sexual immorality may be excused in secular modernist approaches and in accordance with traditional local views, it may not be excused merely for the sake of attaining sexual pleasure or power, as the case of superstar Nadia al-Gindi most strikingly illustrates. Hence, women's victimization, the suppression of sexuality, the display of social conscience, and a (qualified) modernist orientation, translated into the ideals of women's education and professionalization and displayed in 'realist' representation have formed some of the major prerequisites for a film or actor's elevation to highbrow status in the eyes of, first, the critics and, second, the public. In other words, being a prostitute for a good reason could not invalidate the quasi-automatic association of women with sexuality and their use to confirm a binary moral system. Yet despite any fetishizing, the case of Nadia al-Gindi showed that mainstream cinematic genres have been far more flexible than the critically acclaimed socially committed cinema or rhetorical realism in accommodating femininity with work and power, while at the same time expressing skepticism about the modernist project.

This eventually ran counter to immediate postrevolutionary attempts to put women in the service of the nation, a nation coded as female, to be defended by men from men. This gendered iconography found its epitome in the screen representation of the country's revolutionary pan-Arab leader Gamal 'Abdel Nasser, an ultimate expression of a unitary, univocal nation. Indeed, as the process of modern nation formation ran parallel to the introduction of the audiovisual media in the region, it is evident that Egyptian cinema has not only witnessed the evolution of Egyptian nationalism during the colonial and postcolonial eras, but has also contributed at times to the construction or 'imagination' of a modern national identity. In the course of this process it has tried to either eradicate the traces of its original de facto multiculturalism or reformulate it in terms of the 'national identity' ideology. Different strategies have been applied in this context to imagine a coherent Arab White Egyptian Muslim nation. The ethnic or religious Other, most notably Nubians, Copts, and Jews, has been excluded, belittled, demonized, or partially admitted within a framework of political correctness.

On the political level, the complete exodus of the Jewish population that followed the foundation of the state of Israel, the destruction of Old Nubia, and the gradual confessional (self-)isolation of Copts have accompanied the political and military challenges from outside and the attempts to consolidate the envisioned post-independence Arab Muslim nation. Thus, in spite of its verbal anti-sectarianism, Egyptian nationalism has reinforced the old multi-community or neo-*dhimma* state, a fact that has necessarily created discrepancies with the ideal of equal citizenship. Moreover, persisting social and political inequalities have led to a latent political mobilization of the different communities, tending in the Coptic case toward a religious counter-fundamentalism. Sectarian counter-nationalisms were meant to challenge the dominating unitary ideology, as the creation of an alternative Coptic film production showed. At the same time Muslim (and Christian) inclusive attempts and 'religious' heteroglossia have not always been welcomed.

This is not surprising, since deviant representations were at times perceived as separatism endangering national unity or undermining bourgeois religious morality. The fact that the expression of a sexual, religious, or ethnic Otherness still encounters taboos indicates clearly that there is a weak point in the existing perception of the Egyptian nation and in the notion of sexual identity. Official rhetoric and public discourse has been characterized by the denial of particularities on the religious and ethnic level and the insistence on binary difference regarding the sexes, something that will not change in the absence of a profound secularization and democratization of the whole of Egyptian society, which could enhance the representation of a diverse people living in a diverse world, both on and off the screen, or as I emphasized earlier, which reflects a non-essentialist concept of otherness that is able to multiply differences in order to move beyond any antagonizing process of 'Othering.' Yet, and this I hope to have made clear, popular Egyptian cinema has been as much a dynamic and exciting witness of these limitations as it has also been instrumental in negotiating and, at times, even transgressing them.

Notes

1. Greek names in this paragraph, including the author Khiryanudi (possibly Cherianudi) were checked by a Greek scholar but the originals may notwithstanding have been written differently.
2. Revolution is a misleading term, as the mass-supported protests against colonialism and the social system took place in 1919, while the overturning of the king in 1952 was rather a coup d'état undertaken by the Free Officers and was later labeled a 'revolution.'
3. Personal interview with Jacques Mizart, Paris, July 27, 2006.
4. Personal interview with Miriam Donato, Mizrahi's wife, Rome, November 18, 2001
5. According to Beinin, Hassoun had joined the Dror Marxist-Zionist youth organization as a teenager, but when Dror leaders in 1952 declared Marxism and Zionism incompatible he joined the largest illegal Egyptian Marxist organization and after his expulsion to France became an important figure in the preservation of Jewish-Egyptian cultural patrimony.
6. *Ful, qulqas,* and *mulukhiya* are national dishes.
7. Samir Murqus, personal interview July 9, 2006. The researcher himself thinks that the true figures range somewhere inbetween.
8. Cf. the notion of *Gegenöffentlichkeit* (counter-public) coined by Alexander Kluge in the context of his media studies.

9. *Ruz al-Yusuf*, July 21, 1997, 10

10. *Ruz al-Yusuf*, May 9, 1994, 78

11. Khairy Beshara, personal conversation, Cairo, August 1996

12. "Turkish-German Filmmaking: From Phobic Liminality to Transgressive Glocality?" Forthcoming. In *Muslims in Germany*, ed. 'Ala' al-Hamarneh.

13. Hamid confusingly describes Nubians as both Caucasians and members of the 'brown race.'

14. *al-Ahram al-masa'i* (most probably), January 24, 1992

15. For the notion of charisma see Willner, 1984; Lindholm, 1990.

16. http://www.variety.com/review/VE1117911463?categoryid=31&cs=1

17. For the colonialist and racialist origin of this subsequently psychoanalytical notion, read Mary Ann Doane (1991, 209–27).

18. Although this is not suggested by the Qur'an itself, if we believe Leila Ahmed.

19. The names of actors and actresses started to be revealed by Biograph, the major production-company of the time, only in 1913 (DeCordova 1990, 5).

20. For a more detailed summary of Egypt's star different star generations see Shafik 2001.

21. Muhammad Anwar al-Sadat became president in 1970 and was killed by Muslim extremists in 1981. During his presidency he changed the country's former Arab-Socialist orientation by initiating the Open Door policy and the peace process with Israel. These policies were a by-product of the shift of the country's political alliance from the then Soviet Union to the United States.

22. The psychoanalytical constuction of the subject was propagated by an important section of film theory at that time.

23. Ahmad al-Hadari, personal conversation, 30 January 2006

24. See Baker 1995 for an insightful critique of this idealist, backward-looking work.

25. Other sources speak of only 350 cinemas in the same year (Mahfouz 1995, 126). The number 'Ali Abu Shadi stated, 454, may, by contrast, be exaggerated (Abou Chadi 1995, 28).

Bibliography

Abaza, Mona. 2001. "Shopping malls, Consumer Culture and the Reshaping of Public Space in Egypt." *Theory, Culture and Society* 18 (5): 97–122.

'Abd Allah, Ahmad. 1991. *al-Talaba wa-l-siyasa fi Misr*. Cairo: Sina li-l-Nashr.

'Abd al-Fattah, Nabil. 2003. *Siyasat al-adyan. Sira'at wa darurat al-islah*. Cairo: Maktabat al-usra.

'Abd al-Fattah, Wa'il. 2003. 'Adil Imam yantasir fi al-tajruba al-danimarkiya: aqni'at al-nijm al-'abir l-il-tabaqat. *Sinima*, no. 21 (December): 46–51.

'Abd al-Gawad, 'Isam. 1995. "al-Shurta tusadir aflam al-anbiya'." *Ruz al-Yusuf*, December 25.

'Abd al-Mu'ti, 'Abd al-Basit. 2002. *al-Tabaqat al-ijtima'iya wa mustaqbal Misr*, Cairo: Merit.

'Abd al-Rahman, Magdi. 2002. *Ra'idat al-sinima fi Misr*. Alexandria: Bibliotheca Alexandrina.

Abou Chadi, Ali. 1995. "Chronologie 1896–1994." In *Égypte: 100 ans de cinéma*, ed. Magda Wassef, 18–39. Paris: Institut du Monde Arabe.

Abu-Lughod, Lila. 1995. "Movie Stars and Islamic Moralism in Egypt." *Social Text* 42 (1): 53–67 (repr. in: Roger Lancaster and Micaela di Leonardo, ed. 1997. *The Gender/Sexuality Reader*. New York: Routledge, 502–12).

———. 1997. "The Interpretation of Culture(s) After Television." *Representations* 59, 109–34 (repr. in: Ortner, Sherry. 1999. *The Fate of "Culture": Geertz and Beyond*, 110–35. Los Angeles: University of California Press).

———. 1998. *Remaking Women: Feminism and Modernity in the Middle East*. Cairo: The American University in Cairo Press.

Abu al-Magd, Mirvat. 2001. "'Arsh al-simima la tahkumuh imra'a." *Ruz al-Yusuf*, July 14–20, 74–76.

Abu Shadi, Ali. 1996. "Genres in Egyptian Cinema." In *Screens of Life. Critical Film Writing from the Arab World*, ed. Alia Arasoughly. Word Heritage Press: Quebec, 84–129.

―――. 1998. *al-Sinima wa-l-siyasa*. Cario: Dar Sharqiyat l-il-Nashr wa-l-Tawzi'.

'Afifi, Zaynab. 1990. "al-Rumansiya . . . bida'a rakida fi suq al-sinima." *al-Gumhuriya*, June 26, 1990.

Ahmed, Leila. 1992. *Women and Gender in Islam*. New Haven: Yale University Press.

Al-Ahram. 1999. "Nadia al-Gindi tussir 'ala ada' al-al'ab al-khatar." July 7.

Akhbar al-Yawm. 2002. "al-Limbi ma lahhu al-Limbi." September 22.

'Ali, 'Afaf. 1985. "Inas al-Dighidi . . . wa-l-film 'afwan ayuha al-qanun.'" *Sabah al-khayr*, October 17, 46–47.

Altman, Rick. 1998. "Reusable Packaging. Generic Products and the Recycling Process." In *Refiguring American Film Genres*, ed. Nick Brown, 1–41. Berkeley: University of California Press.

―――. 1999. *Film/Genre*. London: British Film Institute.

Amin, Nura. 1995. "Imra'a hazzat 'arsh al-naqd." *al-Ahali*, October 8.

Anderson, Benedict. 1991. *Imagined Communities*. London: Verso.

Armbrust, Walter. 1996. *Mass Culture and Modernism in Egypt*. Cambridge: Cambridge University Press.

―――. 1998. "Terrorism and Kabab: A Capraesque View of Modern Egypt." In *Images of Enchantment*, ed. Sherifa Zuhur, 283–99. Cairo: The American University in Cairo Press.

―――. 2000. "Farid Shauqi: Tough Guy, Family Man, Cinema Star." In *Imagined Masculinities*, eds. Mai Ghassoub and Emma Sinclair-Webb, 199–226. London: Saqi Books.

El-Assyouti, Mohamed. 2004. "A Permissive Tyranny." *Al-Ahram Weekly*, 17–23 June.

Ayad, Christophe. 1995. "Le star système: de la splendeur au voile." In *Egypte: 100 ans de cinema*, ed. Magda Wassef, 134–41. Paris: Institut du Monde Arabe.

'Ayad, Fatima. 1990. "al-Mukhrija Inas al-Dighidi. Lastu mutakhassisa fi aflam al-mar'a." *al-Wafd*, February 25.

Aziza, Mohamed. 1978. *L'image et l'islam*. Paris: Éditions Albin Michel.

Badran, Margot. 1996. *Feminists, Islam, and Nation*. Cairo: The American University in Cairo Press.

Bahgat, Ahmad Ra'fat. 2005. *al-Yahud wa-l-sinima fi Misr*. Cairo: Sharikat al-Qasr li-l-Tiba'a wa-l-Da'aya wa-l-I'lan.

Baker, Raymond. 1978. *Egypt's Uncertain Revolution under Nasser and Sadat*. Cambridge, MA: Harvard University Press.

_____. 1995. "Combative Cultural Politics: Film Art and Political Spaces in Egypt." *Alif*, no. 15: 6–38.

Baker, Raymond William. 1997. "Invidious Comparisons: Realism, Postmodern Globalism, and Centrist Islamic Movements in Egypt." In *Political Islam*, ed. John L. Esposito, 115–33. Cairo: The American University in Cairo Press.

al-Bandari, Mona, Mahmud Qasim, Ya'qub Wahbi, eds. 1994. *Mawsu'at al-aflam al-'arabiya*. Cairo: Bayt al-Ma'rifa.

al-Banna, Ragab. 1997. "al-Kharijun 'ala al-kanisa." *al-Ahram*, August 10.

Banton, Michael. 1998. *Racial Theories*. Cambridge: Cambridge University Press.

Baron, Beth. 2005. *Egypt as a Woman. Nationalism, Gender, and Politics*. Cairo: The American University in Cairo Press.

Barthes, Roland. 1974. *S/Z*. New York: Hill and Wang.

Baudrillard, Jean. 1983. *Simulations*. New York: Semiotext(e).

Beinin, Joel. 1998. *The Dispersion of Egyptian Jewry: Culture, Politics and the Formation of a Modern Diaspora*. Berkeley: University of California Press.

Bergmann, Kristina. 1993. *Filmkultur und Filmindustrie in Ägypten*. Darmstadt: Wissenschaftliche Buchgesellschaft.

Bhabha, Homi. 1990. "DissemiNation." In *Nation and Narration*, ed. Homi Bhabha, 291–322. London: Routledge.

Bishlawi, Khayriyya. 1980. "Hal yara Drakyula daw' al-nahar?" *al-Masa'*, December 15.

al-Bishri, Tariq. 1988. *al-Muslimun wa-l-aqbat fi itar al-jama'a al-wataniya*. Cairo: Dar al-Shuruq.

Boddy, Janice. 1989. *Wombs and Alien Spirits*. Madison: University of Wisconsin Press.

Bouhdiba, Abdelwahab. 1998. *Sexuality in Islam*. London: Saqi Books.

Bourdieu, Pierre. 1984. *Distinction. A Social Critique of the Judgment of Taste*. Cambridge: Harvard University Press.

Britton, Andrew. 1991. "Stars and Genre." In *Stardom. Industry of Desire*, ed. Christine Gledhill, 198–206. London: Routledge.

Brooks, Peter. 1976. *The Melodramatic Imagination: Balzac, Henry James and the Mode of Excess*. New Haven: Yale University Press.

Buonaventura, Wendy. 1994. *Serpent of the Nile. Women and Dance in the Arab World*. New York: Interlink Books.

Carroll, Noel. 1990. *The Philosophy of Horror*. London: Routledge.

Cluny, Claude Michel. 1984. "al-Sinima al-maghribiya." In *al-Sinima al-'arabiya wa-l-ifriqiya*, ed. Muhammad al-Qalyubi, 44–52. Beirut: Dar al-Hadatha.

Connolly, William E. 2002. *Identity/Difference*. Minneapolis: University of Minnesota Press.

Cooper, Mark M. 1982. *The Transformation of Egypt*. London: Croom Helm.

Croft, Stephen. 2000. "Concepts of National Cinema." In *World Cinema: Critical Approaches*, eds. John Hill, Pamela Church Gibson, Richard Dyer, E. Ann Kaplan and Paul Willemen, 1–11. Oxford: Oxford University Press.

Cultural Development Fund. 1994. *Panorama of Egyptian Cinema 1992*. Cairo: Cultural Development Fund.

Danielson, Virginia. 1996. "Layla Murad." *MESA Bulletin* 30 (1): 143–45.

Dardir, Intisar. 1997. "Nadia al-Gindi . . . wa i'tirafat khassa." *Akhbar al-Nujum*, November 8.

Darwich, Mustafa. 1989. "Censure et espace." In *Le Caire et le cinéma égyptien des années 80*, eds. Jean-Charles Depaule, Marie-Claude Bénard, Ayman Salem. Cairo: le Centre d'Études et de Documentation Économiques, Juridiques et Sociales.

Darwish, 'Adel. 1999. "Nasser. The Myth and the Magic." *The Middle East*, no. 287 (February): 5–47.

Darwish, Salah. 1979. "Nadia al-Gindi tulliqat min 'Imad Hamdi." *al-Gumhuriya*, March 8.

———. 1988. "Mu'zam al-sinaryuhat qass wa lazq." *al-Gumhuriya*, May 19.

deCordova, Richard. 1990. *Picture Personalities*. Urbana: University of Illinois Press.

Doane, Mary Ann. 1991. *Femmes Fatales. Feminism, Film Theory and Pschyoanalysis*. London: Routledge.

Dyer, Richard. 1979. *Stars*. London: British Film Institute.

———. 2002. *Only Entertainment*. London: Routledge.

de Jong, F. 1984. "Die mystischen Bruderschaften im Volksislam." In *Islam in der Gegenwart*, eds. Werner Ende and Udo Steinbach, 487–504. Munich: C.H. Beck.

Elbendary, Amina. 2003. "Love Lost in Shubra." *al-Ahram Weekly*, July 31–August 6.

Elsaesser, Thomas. 1985. "Tales of Sound and Fury. Observations on Family Melodrama." In *Movies and Methods*, vol. 2, ed. Bill Nichols, 165–89. Berkeley: University of California Press.

Fahim, Hussein M. 1983. *Egyptian Nubians, Resettlement and Years of Coping*. Salt Lake City: University of Utah Press.

Fahmi, Tharwat. 1981. "Nadia al-Gindi tarudd 'ala al-ittihamat." *Akhir Sa'a*, May 13.

Fanon, Franz. 1985. *The Wretched of the Earth*. Harmondsworth: Penguin.

Farid, Samir. 1983. "'Adil Imam min kumbars ila najm al-nujum." *al-Gumhuriya*, September 6.

———. 1973. "Nahw manhaj li-kitaba 'ilmiya li-tarikhuna al-sinima'i." *al-Tali'a* 3 (March), 149–57.

———. 1984. "Surat al-mar'a fi-l-sinima al-'arabiya." *al-Hayat al-sinima'iya* 21 (Spring): 4–15.

———. 1985. *Surat al-mar'a fi-l-sinima al-'arabiya*. Cairo: al-Lajna al-Iqtisadiya wa-l-Ijtima'iya li-Gharb Asya.

———. 1995. "La censure, mode d'emploi." In *Égypte: 100 ans de cinéma*, ed. Magda Wassef, 102–17. Paris: Institut du Monde Arabe.

———. 1987. "al-Fidyu." *Sinima* 84–86.

Fernea, Robert. 1994. "Thirty years of Resettlement: The Nubians in Egypt." In *Population, Displacement, and Resettlement*, ed. Seteney Shami, 156–58. New York: Center for Migration Studies.

Fluehr-Lobban, Carolyn. 2004. "A Critical Anthropological Review of Race in the Nile Valley." In *Race and Identity in the Nile Valley*, eds. Carolyn Fluehr-Lobban and Kharyssa Rhodes, 133–57. Trenton: The Red Sea Press.

Franken, Marjorie. 1998. "Farida Fahmi and the Dancer's Image in Egyptian Film." In *Images of Enchantment*, ed. Sherifa Zuhur, 265–81. Cairo: The American University in Cairo Press.

Freud, Sigmund. 1961. *Die Traumdeutung*. Frankfurt a. M.: Fischer-Verlag.

Gada', Muhammad Walid. 1989. *al-Mawqif min sinima islamiya*. Cairo: Dar al-Wafa'.

Gaffney, Jane. 1987. "The Egyptian Cinema: Industry and Art in a Changing Society." *Arab Studies Quarterly* 9 (1): 53–75.

Gaines, Jane. 1996. "The Melos in Marxist Theory." In *The Hidden Foundation. Cinema and the Question of Class*, eds. David James and Rick Berg, 56–71. Minneapolis: University of Minnesota Press.

Geiser, Peter. 1980. *Cairo's Nubian Families*. Cairo: The American University in Cairo Press.

Ghannam, Farha. 2002. *Remaking the Modern. Space, Relocation and the Politics of Identity in a Global Cairo*. Berkeley: University of California Press.

Gibra'il, Nagib. 2005. "Haqiqat ikhtifa' al-masihiyat." *al-'Arabi*, no. 990.

Gledhill, Christine. 1991. "Signs of Melodrama." In *Stardom. Industry of Desire*, ed. C. Gledhill, 207–29. London: Routledge.

Gordon, Joel. 2002. *Revolutionary Melodrama. Popular Film and Civic Identity in Nasser's Egypt*. Chicago: Middle East Documentation Center.

Grace, Hanna. 1997. "al-Sinima al-qibtiya." In *Nashrat al-dawra al-thaniya min barnamij dirasat wa watha'iq al-dawra* (festival brochure) December 9, 1997, 1–10. Cairo: Mihrajan al-Qahira al-Sinima'i al-Dawli.

———. 2003. "al-Mu'assasa al-diniya al-masihiya wa-l-siyasiya." *al-Dimuqratiya* 12:81–92.

Grossberg, Lawrence. 1996. "Identity and Cultural Studies: Is That All There Is?" In *Questions of Identity*, eds. Stuart Hall and Paul du Gay, 87–107. London: Sage Publications.

Guda, Suhair. 1993. "al-Hijab bi-milyun dular." *Ruz al-Yusuf*, October 11.

al-Hadari, Ahmad. 1989. *Tarikh al-sinima fi Misr*. Cairo: Matbu'at Nadi al-Sinima bi-l-Qahira.

Hadidi, Mona. 1977. "Dirasa tahliliya li-surat al-mar'a al-misriya fi-l-film al-misri." Doctoral thesis. Cairo University.

Hadj-Moussa, Ratiba. 1994. *Le corps, l'histoire, le territoire. Les rapports de genre dans le cinéma algérien.* Paris: Éditions Publisud.

Haikal, Muhammad Hasanain. 1994. *Aqbat misr laysu aqalliya.* Cairo: al-Markaz al-Qibti li-l Dirasat al-Ijtima'iya.

al-Hakim, Ayman. 2002. "al-Sinima'iyun yal'anun al-Limbi wa yutalibun 'adam tasdirih." *al-Qahira*, August 13.

Halevi, Ilan. 1987. *A History of the Jews Ancient and Modern.* London: Zed Books.

Hall, Stuart. 1980. "Coding and Encoding in the Television Discourse." In *Culture, Media, Language*, eds. Stuart Hall, Dorothy Hobson, Andrew Lowe, Paul Willis, 128–38. London: Hutchinson.

———. 1981. "Notes on Deconstructing 'The Popular'." In *People's History and Socialist Theory*, ed. R. Samuel, 227–40. London: Routledge.

———. 1993. "Culture, Community, Nation." *Cultural Studies* 7 (3): 349–63.

———. 1997. "The Spectacle of the 'Other.'" In *Representation. Cultural Representations and Signifying Practices*, ed. Stuart Hall, 225–79. London: Sage Publications.

Hallam, Julia and Marshment, Margaret. 2000. *Realism and Popular Cinema.* Manchester: Manchester University Press.

Hamid, as-Sayyid. 1994. *an-Nuba al-jadida.* Cairo: Ein for Human and Social Studies

Hammuda, 'Adil. 1994. "La li-'unsuriyat al-umma" *Ruz al-Yusuf*, May 2.

Hani, Muhammad and Usama Salama. 2000. "I'lan bara'at awan al-ward min al-isa'a il-al-aqbat." *Ruz al-Yusuf*, December 23–29, 69–75.

Hassanain, Magdi. 1994. "al-Qibti 'ala al-shasha al-bayda'." *al-Ahali*, May 11.

Hassoun, Jacques. 1987. "The Traditional Jewry of the Hara." *The Jews of Egypt. A Mediterranean Society in Modern Times*, ed. Shimon Shamir, 33–67. London: Westview Press.

Hassouna, Moustafa El-Said. 1990. *Leadership Efficacy and Weberian Charisma. The Case of Gamal Abdel Nasser 1952–1970.* Microform thesis. Kent: University of Kent.

Hillauer, Rebecca. 2005. *Encyclopedia of Arab Women Filmmakers.* Cairo: The American University in Cairo Press.

Hobsbawm, Eric. 1992. *Nations and Nationalism since 1780.* Cambridge: Cambridge University Press.

Hollows, Joanne. 2000. *Feminism, Femininity and Popular Culture.* Manchester: Manchester University Press.

Hussein, Mahmoud. 1973. *Class Conflict in Egypt 1945–1970.* London: Monthly Review Press.

Huwaydi, Fahmi. 1997. "Linasma' sawt al-kanisa." *al-Ahram*, July 15.

Ibrahim, Saad Eddin. 1977a. "Egypt's Islamic Militants." In *Arab Society. Social Science Perspectives*, eds. Nicholas Hopkins and Saad Eddin Ibrahim, 494–507. Cairo: The American University in Cairo Press.

———. 1977b. "Urbanization in the Arab World." In *Arab Society. Social Science Perspectives*, eds. Nicholas Hopkins and Saad Eddin Ibrahim, 123–47. Cairo: The American University in Cairo Press.

Ihab, Ashraf. 1993. "al-Mukhrija Inas al-Dighidi." *al-Fann*, August 9, 23–25.

Irigaray, Luce. 1990. "Macht des Diskurses. Unterordnung des Weiblichen." In *Aisthesis. Wahrnehmung heute oder Perspektiven einer anderen Ästhetik*, eds. Karl-Heinz Barck, Paul Gente, Heidi Paris, 123–40. Leipzig: Reclam Leipzig.

James, David. 2004. "Is There Class in this Text? The Repression of Class in Film and Cultural Studies." In *A Companion to Film Theory*, eds. Toby Miller and Robert Stam, 182–201. Malden: Blackwell Publishing.

Jameson, Frederic. 1985. "Dog Day Afternoon as a Political Film." In *Movies and Methods II*, ed. Bill Nichols, 713–33.

———. 1986. "Third World Literature in the Era of Multinational Capitalism." *Social Text* 15 (Fall): 65–88.

al-Jazeera. 2005. "Ahl al-nuba." Program for television on *Wijhat Nazar*. September.

Jeffords, Susan. 1994. *Hard Bodies: Hollywood Masculinity in the Reagan Era*. New Brunswick: Rugers University Press.

Johnston, Claire. 1988. "Dorothy Arzner: Critical Strategies." In *Feminism and Film Theory*, ed. Constance Penley, 36–45. London: Routledge.

el-Kalioubi, Mohamed Kamel. 1995. "Mohamed Bayoumi: Le pionnier méconnu." In *Egypte, 100 ans de cinéma*, ed. Magda Wassef, 42–51. Paris: Institut du Monde Arabe.

Kamil, Majdi. 1994. *Fannanat wara' al-hijab*. Cairo: Markaz al-Raya li-l-Nashr wa-l-I'lam.

Kaplan, E. Ann. 1983. *Women and Film. Both Sides of the Camera*. New York: Methuen.

Kerkegi, Max. 1967. "Les nubiens au Caire." In *Nubie*, ed. Otto Meinardus. Cairo: Cahiers d'Histoire Egyptienne, 211–17.

Khiryanudi, Jani Mila. 2003. *al-Yunaniyun fi-l-sinima al-misriya*. Alexandria: Bibliotheca Alexandrina.

Khoury, 'Adel Theodore. 1994. *Christen unterm Halbmond. Religiöse Minderheiten unter der Herrschaft des Islams*. Freiburg i. Br.: Herder Verlag.

Köhler, Wolfgang. 1994. "Verunglimpft, oft auch verfolgt. Sind die Kopten eine Minderheit?" *Frankfurter Allgemeine Zeitung*, August 23.

Krämer, Gudrun. 1982. *Minderheit, Millet, Nation? Die Juden in Ägypten 1914–1952. Studien zum Minderheitenproblem im Islam* 7. Wiesbaden: Verlag Otto Harrassowitz.

———. 1986. *Ägypten unter Mubarak: Identität und nationales Interesse*. Baden-Baden: Nomos Verlagsgesellschaft.

Krell, Gert. 2004. *Weltbilder und Weltordnung. Einführung in die Theorie der Internationalen Beziehungen*. Baden-Baden: Nomos Verlagsgesellschaft

Laclau, Ernesto. 1990. *New Reflections on the Revolution of our Time*. London: Verso.

Landau, Jacob. 1958. *Studies in the Arab Theater and Cinema*. Philadelphia: University of Pennsylvania Press.

Lashin, Hisham. 1981. "al-Khusuma bayn 'Adil Imam wa-l-muthaqqafin." *al-Ahrar*, November 11.

Laskier, Michael M. 1992. *The Jews of Egypt 1920–1970*. New York: New York University Press.

Lewis, Bernard. 1992. *Race and Slavery in the Middle East*. Oxford: Oxford University Press.

Lindholm, Charles. 1990. *Charisma*. Cambridge: Basil Blackwell Inc.

Littmann, Enno. 1950. "Arabische Geisterbeschwörungen aus Ägypten." *Sammlung orientalischer Arbeiten* 19. Leipzig: Verlag Otto Harrassowitz.

Lüders, Michael. 1988. *Gesellschaftliche Realität im ägyptischen Kinofilm. Von Nasser zu Sadat (1952–1981)*. Frankfurt: Peter Lang Verlag.

Macleod, Arlene Elowe. 1992. *Accommodating Protest. Working Women, the New Veiling, and Change in Cairo*. Cairo: The American University in Cairo Press.

Magdi, Safiyya. 1986. "Surat al-mar'a fi-l-sinima al-misriya." In *al-Insan al-misri 'alla al-shasha*, ed. Hashim al-Nahhas, 35–58. Cairo: al-Hay'a al-Misriya al-'Amma li-l-Kitab.

Magdi, Tawhid. 1997. "Layla Murad safira li-Isra'il. Kayfa rafidat Layla Murad an takun safira fawq al-'ada li-Isra'il." *Ruz al-Yusuf*, no. 3606, July 21, 41–52.

Mahfouz, Medhat. 1995. "Les salles de projection dans l'industrie cinématographique." In *Égypte: 100 ans de cinéma*, ed. Magda Wassef, 124–33. Paris: Institut du Monde Arabe.

Malkmus, Lizbeth and Armes, Roy. 1991. *Arab and African Filmmaking*. London: Zed Books.

Malti-Douglas, Fedwa. 1992. *Woman's Body, Woman's Word*. Cairo: The American University in Cairo Press.

Mayne, Judith. 1993. *Cinema and Spectatorship*. London: Routledge.

Menicucci, Garay. 1998. "Unlocking the Arab Celluloid Closet. Homosexuality in Egyptian Film." *MERIP*, no. 206 (Spring). <http://www.merip.org/mer/mer206/egyfilm.htm>

Mernissi, Fatima. 1987. *Geschlecht Ideologie Islam*. Munich: Frauenbuchverlag.

Miqlid, Shahinda. 1991. "Mulahadhat hawl tajrubat Kamshish. al-Tatawwur al-ijtima'i wa-l-siyasi li-l-qarya." In *al-Mas'alla al-fallahiya wa-l-zira'iya fi Misr*, Markaz al-Buhuth al-'Arabiya, 245–52. Cairo: Markaz al-Buhuth al-'Arabiya.

Mitchell, Timothy. 1991. *Colonising Egypt*. Berkeley: University of California Press.

Moghadam, Valentine. 1993a. *Gender and National Identity. Women and Politics in Muslim Societies*. London: Zed Books.

_____. 1993b. *Modernizing Women. Gender and Social Change in the Middle East.* Cairo: The American University in Cairo Press.

Morgan, Maggie. 1998. "The Self and the Nation. Four Egyptian Autobiographies." Unpublished MA thesis (manuscript). Cairo: The American University in Cairo.

Morin, Edgar. 1972. *Les stars.* Paris: Seuil.

Mulvey, Laura. 1989. *Visual and other Pleasures.* Bloomington: Indiana University Press.

al-Muqadasi, Gene. 2000. "Sinima nisa'iya? Aflam Inas al-Dighidi wa Nadia Hamza." *al-Bahithat* 6:365–86.

Murqus, Samir. 1995. "Musharakat al-shabab al-qibtiyun fi-l-haya al-siyasiya." *Awraq dirasiya,* no. 4.

_____. 2004. "La islah bidun muwatana." *al-Dimuqratiya* 13 (January): 115–18.

_____. 2005. *al-Akhar. . . al-hiwar . . . al-muwatana.* Cairo: Maktabat al-shuruq al-dawliya.

Mursi, Salah. 1995. *Layla Murad.* Cairo: Dar al-Hilal.

Naficy, Hamid. 1991. "The Averted Gaze in Iranian Postrevolutionary Cinema." *Public Culture* 2:29–40.

_____. 2003. "Phobic Spaces and Liminal Panics: Independent Transnational Film Genre." In *Multiculturalism, Postcoloniality, and Transnational Media,* eds. Ella Shohat, Robert Stam, 203–26. New Brunswick, NJ: Rutgers University Press,

al-Naggar, Ahmad al-Sayyid, ed. 2002. "Sina'at al-sinima fi Misr." In *al-Itijahat al-iqtisadiya al-istratijiya 2001,* ed., Ahmad al-Sayyid al-Naggar, 301–33. Cairo: al-Ahram Center for Political and Strategic Studies.

al-Nahhas, Hisham. 2002. "Fi'ran Dawud 'Abd al-Sayyid al-miqatqata." *al-Qahira,* February 2.

Nichols, Bill, ed. 1985. *Movies and Methods,* vol. 2. Berkeley: University of California Press.

_____. 2001. *Introduction to Documentary.* Bloomington: Indiana University Press.

Nimr, Dalia. 2003. *Youth's Perspectives on the Egyptian Cinema,* unpublished paper conducted in Fall 2003 at the American University in Cairo, JRMC 504 (Research Methods in Mass Communication).

Nowell-Smith, Geoffrey. 1985. "Minelli and Melodrama." In *Movies and Methods II,* ed. Bill Nichols, 190–94. Berkeley: University of California Press.

Pazderic, Nickola. 1995. "Hard Bodies." *Postmodern Culture* 6(1)
<http://infomotions.com/serials/pmc/pmc-v6n1-pazderic-hard.txt>

Penley, Constance. 1988. "Introduction: The Lady Doesn't Vanish: Feminism and Film Theory." In *Feminism and Film Theory,* ed. Constance Penley, 1–24. London: Routledge.

Pribram, Deidre. 2004. "Subjectivity and Spectatorship." In *A Companion to Film Theory,* Toby Miller and Robert Stam, 146–64. Malden: Blackwell Publishing.

Qasim, Mahmud. 1997. *Surat al-adyan fi-l-sinima al-misriya.* Cairo: al-Markaz al-Qawmi li-l-Sinima.

_____. 1998. *al-Mar'a fi l sinima.* Cairo: Dar al-Aymann.

Ramzi, Kamal. 1987. "Arba' qadaya jadida fi-l-sinima al-misriya. al-'Unf, al-infitah, marakiz al-quwwa, al-thawra al-mudada 1975–1985." Unpublished study for the 5th Damascus Film Festival.

———. 1995. "Le réalisme." In *Égypte: 100 ans de cinéma*, ed. Magda Wassef, 144–59. Paris: Institut du Monde Arabe.

El-Rashidi, Yasmine. 2004. "They Don't Love this Movie." *Al-Ahram Weekly*, 15–21 July.

Read, Jacinda. 2000. *The New Avengers. Feminism, Femininity and the Rape-Revenge Cycle*. Manchester: Manchester University Press.

Reich, Wilhelm. 2003. *Die Massenpsychologie des Faschismus*. Köln: Kiepenheuer & Witsch.

Richter, Erika. 1974. *Realistischer Film in Ägypten*. (East-)Berlin: Henschelverlag Kunst und Gesellschaft.

Rotter, Ekkehart & Gernot. 1996. *Venus, Maria, Fatima*. Zurich: Artemis & Winkler Verlag.

al-Sabban, Rafiq. 1992. *Tribute to Layla Mourad*. Cairo: 16th Cairo International Film Festival.

———. 2002. "Durus sinima'iya fi-l-tafaha wal-balaha." *al-Qahira*, July 30.

Sa'd, Mahmud. 2002. "Sinima bila 'aql." *al-Kawakib*, July 16.

Sa'id, Ihsan. 2003. *Surat al-mar'a al-misriya fi sinima al-tis'iniyat*. Alexandria: Bibliotheca Alexandrina.

Saif, Samir. 1996. *Aflam al-haraka fi-l-sinima al-misriya 1952–1975*. Cairo: al-Markaz al-Qawmi li-l-Sinima.

Salih, Muhammad. 1999. "Nijmat al-jamahir." *al-Ahram*, April 23.

Schneider, Steven. 2000. "Monsters as (Uncanny) Metaphors: Freud, Lakoff, and the Representation of Monstrosity in Cinematic Horror." In *Horror Film Reader*, eds. Alain Silver and James Ursini. New York: Limelight Editions.

Shafik, Viola. 1988. "Realität und Film im Ägypten der 80er Jahre." MA thesis. Hamburg University.

———. 1998. *Arab Cinema. History and Cultural Identity*. Cairo: The American University in Cairo Press.

———. 1999. "Women, National Liberation, and Melodrama in Arab Countries." *al-Raida* 17 (2/3): 12–18.

———. 2001. "Egyptian Cinema." In *Encyclopeadia of Middle Eastern Cinema*, ed. Oliver Leaman, 23–129. London: Routledge.

———. 2001. "Prostitute for a Good Reason. Stars and Morality in Egyptian Cinema" *Women's Studies International Forum* 24 (6): 711–25.

Shaheen, Jack. 2001. *Reel Bad Arabs. How Hollywood Vilifies a People*. New York: Olive Branch Press.

Shakry, Omnia. 1998. "Schooled Mothers, Structured Play." In *Remaking Women: Feminism and Modernity in the Middle East,* ed. Lila Abu-Lughod, 126–70.

al-Sharqawi, Galal. 1970, *Risala fi tarikh al-sinima al-'arabiya*. Cairo: al-Hay'a al-Misriya al-'Ama li-l-Kitab.

Shohat, Ella. 1995. "Post-Third Worldist Culture." In *Gender, Nation and Diaspora in Middle Eastern Film/Video*, ed. Jonathan Friedlander. Los Angeles: UCLA.

Shohat, Ella and Stam, Robert. 1994. *Unthinking Eurocentrism. Multiculturalism and the Media*. London: Routledge.

Shusha, Muhammad al-Sayyid. 1978. "Ruwwad wa ra'idat al-sinima al-misriya." Cairo: n.p.

Smith, Margaret. 1928. *Rabi'a the Mystic and Her Fellow-Saints in Islam.* Cambridge: Cambridge University Press.

Smith, Murray. 1995. *Engaging Characters. Fiction, Emotion and the Cinema*. Oxford: Clarendon Press

Springborg, Robert. 1989. *Mubarak's Egypt. Fragmentation of the Political Order*. Boulder: Westview Press

Stacey, Jackie. 1992. "Desperately Seeking Difference." In *Screen: The Sexual Subject*, ed. Mandy Merck, 244–57. London: Routledge.

Tadros, Marlyn. 1992. *al-Aqbat bayn al-usuliya wa-l-tahdith*. Cairo: al-Dar al-'Arabiya.

———. 1994. *Women: The Perspective of Fundamentalist Discourse and its Influence on Egyptian Artistic Creativity and Cultural Life*. Cairo: Legal Research Center for Human Rights.

Talhami, Ghada Hashem. 1996. *The Mobilization of Muslim Women in Egypt*. Gainesville: University of Florida Press.

Tasker, Yvonne. 1993. *Spectacular Bodies. Gender Genre and the Action Cinema*. London: Routledge.

Taufiq, Ra'uf. 1984. "Hal yastahiqq 'Adil Imam hadha al-'ajr?" *Sabah al-Khayr*, February 2.

al-Tayyar, Rida. 1980. *al-Madina fi-l-sinima al-'arabiya*. Beirut: al-Mu'assasa al-'Arabiya li-l-Dirasat wa-l-Nashr.

Thabet, Madkour. 2001. "Industrie du film égyptien." In *Cinéma & Monde musulman, Cultures & interdits*, ed. Wafik Raouf. *Euroorient* 10: 26–53.

Traube, Elisabeth. 1992. *Dreaming Identities. Class, Gender, and Generation in 1980s Hollywood Movies*. Oxford: Westview Press.

Troutt-Powell, Eve Marie. 1995. *The Colonized Colonizer*. Cambridge: Harvard University.

'Uthman, Amal. 2002. "Sinima al-bangu." In *Akhbar al-yawm*, July 27, 2002.

van Nieuwkerk, Karin. 1995. *A Trade like Any Other. Female Singers and Dancers in Egypt*. Austin: Texas University Press.

Virilio, Paul. 1989. *Krieg und Kino. Logistik der Wahrnehmung*. Frankfurt: Fischer Verlag.

Vitalis, Robert. 1995. *When Capitalists Collide. Business Conflict and the End of Empire in Egypt*. Berkeley: University of California Press.

Wielandt, Rotraud. 1980. *Das Bild der Europäer in der modernen arabischen Erzähl- und Theaterliteratur.* Beirut: Orient-Institut.

Williams, Raymond. 1977. "A Lecture on Realism." *Screen* (Spring): 61–74.

Willner, Ann Ruth. 1983. *The Spellbinders: Charismatic Political Leadership.* New Haven: Yale University Press.

Wood, Robin. 1985. "An Introduction to the American Horror Film." In *Movies and Methods II,* ed. Bill Nichols, 195–220.

Yau, Esther. 1996. "Compromised Liberation." In *The Hidden Foundation. Cinema and the Question of Class*, eds. David E. James and Rick Berg, 138–71. Minneapolis: University of Minnesota Press.

Yusuf, Abu Saif. 1987. *al-Aqbat wa-l-qawmiya al-'arabiya.* Beirut: n.p.

Yusuf, Ahmad, ed. 1992. *Salah Abu Sayf wa-l-nuqqad.* Cairo: Abullu li-l-Nashr.

Zaalouk, Malak. 1989. *Power, Class and Foreign Capital in Egypt. The Rise of the New Bourgeoisie.* London: Zed Books.

Index of Names

Page numbers in *italics* indicate illustrations.

Index of Film Titles

Page numbers in *italics* indicate illustrations.

Photographic Credits

All photographs in this book were provided courtesy of Muhammad Bakr, except:

30 *Mistreated by Affluence*, El-Leithy Film; 52 *St. Dimyana*, courtesy Samir Saif; 77 *Africano*, courtesy Al-Arabia Cinema Production & Distribution; 95 *The Night Baghdad Fell*, courtesy Al-Arabia Cinema Production & Distribution; 97 *Layla, the Bedouin*, courtesy Institut du Monde Arabe; 216 *A Hot Night*, courtesy Institut du Monde Arabe; 227 *Downtown Girls*, courtesy Mohamed Khan; 252 *A Kiss in the Desert*, courtesy Institut du Monde Arabe; 271 *Hamidu*, courtesy al-Subki Video Film; 286 *Sleepless Nights*, courtesy Al-Arabia Cinema Production & Distribution; 296 *A Citizen, a Detective, and a Thief*, courtesy Diogenes Film; 316 *Message to the Ruler*, courtesy Aflam Misr al-'Arabiya.